Personnel in Context

Third edition

David Farnham is principal lecturer in industrial relations at Portsmouth Polytechnic. In addition to teaching, industrial and consultancy experience in the personnel area, he has written widely in a range of academic and professional journals. He is co-author of *Public Administration in the United Kingdom* (with Malcolm McVicar) and *Understanding Industrial Relations* (with John Pimlott), now in its fourth edition, published by Cassell in 1982 and 1990 respectively. He is also author of *The Corporate Environment*, Institute of Personnel Management, 1990.

PERSONNEL
in Context

Third edition

David Farnham

Institute of Personnel Management

First published 1984
Updated version 1986
Reprinted 1987
Reprinted 1988 (twice)
Reprinted 1989
Third edition 1990
Reprinted 1992

Note: wherever appropriate the convention has been followed whereby he and him are used to cover she and her.

Phototypeset by Wessex Typesetters, Frome and printed in Grea Britain by Short Run Press, Exeter

British Library Cataloguing in Publication Data
Farnham, David
Personnel in context—3rd ed
1. Great Britain. Personnel management
I. Title   II. Institute of Personnel Management
658.300941

ISBN 0–85292–451–8

Contents

List of figures

List of tables

Preface to first edition

There are a number of personnel management texts in Britain such as Thomason (1981), Torrington and Chapman (1983) and Torrington and Hall (1987), with Niven (1967) and Marks (1978) providing histories of personnel management from its origins to the mid 1970s. Apart from Crichton (1968), there is no recent study focusing on the wider organizational and environmental contexts in which personnel decisions are made and implemented. This book aims to fill the gap in the literature. It is written mainly for students studying for the professional examinations of the Institute of Personnel Management (IPM). It should also be useful to those studying personnel management and related subjects on other degree and diploma courses.

The book has three aims. First, it provides an introduction to modern personnel work in Britain. Secondly, it examines the background and contexts within which personnel management policies and activities take place within organizations. Thirdly, it outlines the implications of these contexts for the personnel management function. In this way, students are introduced to the nature and scope of modern personnel management and to the various contexts within which personnel practices take place.

As well as having to be technically competent, those training for the personnel function require knowledge and understanding of the academic studies underlying personnel management. This enables them to be well informed, to have a capacity for sound judgment and to be able to view organizations and their environments with a reasonable degree of detachment. The emphasis in this book, therefore, is an academic one. The role of personnel management in organizations is analysed, discussed and critically assessed, taking account of the wider contexts within which it operates. It is not a handbook of personnel management practices. It is a comprehensive study not only examining and summarizing much of the literature and research in the field, but also demonstrating the complex environment of personnel as a management function. Students are also introduced to subject matter and material which they will examine more fully as their studies proceed.

A standard definition of personnel management is provided by the IPM (IPM, 1980). It describes personnel management as 'that part of management concerned with people at work and with their relationships within an enterprise'. The aim of personnel management, says the IPM, is to bring together and develop into an effective organization those men and women working in an enterprise 'and, having regard to the well being of the individual and of working groups, to enable them to make their best contribution to its success'. Personnel management is part of every manager's job but is the particular concern of personnel specialists. In larger enterprises at least, the personnel management function is usually carried out by both line managers and personnel specialists. There are, first, the personnel activities and tasks which are part of every manager's job and of all managerial work. Secondly, there are the specialist activities and tasks of personnel staff working in personnel departments.

The contexts of personnel management are those socioeconomic and technological influences affecting managerial and employee behaviour within organizations. Some are internal contexts such as the corporate objectives, organizational structures and managerial power bases of enterprises. Others are external including their political, economic, social and legal contexts. Personnel management is strongly influenced by both the internal and external contexts within which personnel activities take place. Personnel and line managers are generally able to influence the internal contexts of personnel management but they are not able to control the external contexts.

The diagram opposite provides a useful framework for studying personnel in context. Part I of the book looks at the background and internal contexts of personnel management. In Chapter 1, the cultural and historical contexts of personnel management are examined and its social and institutional settings are outlined. Chapter 2 turns to personnel management's organizational context. The issues discussed include: different types of organization; the relationship between objective setting and policy making; and the ways in which enterprises are structured in order to achieve their purposes. Chapter 3 places personnel management in its managerial context by examining the nature of managerial work, the managerial process and the main managerial functions within organizations.

A framework for studying personnel in context

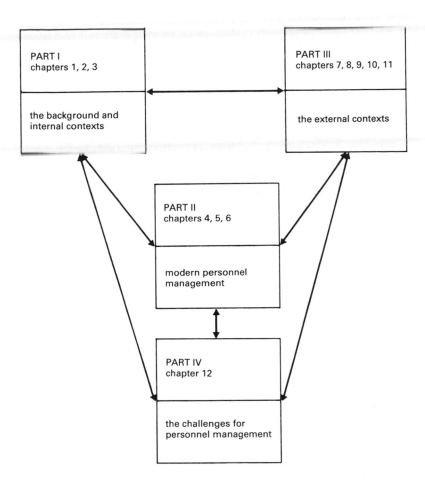

Part II examines modern personnel management. In Chapter 4, the issues and perspectives underlying the nature and scope of the personnel function are discussed, focusing particularly on the respective roles of line managers and personnel specialists. Chapter

5 looks at personnel work and personnel policy. It examines the activities and tasks involved in specialist personnel work, the ways in which personnel departments can be organized and the importance of personnel policy in organizational decision making. Chapter 6 considers personnel specialists as an occupational group and to what extent personnel management might be considered a profession.

Part III turns to the external contexts of the personnel function. The political context is defined and discussed in Chapter 7, with particular emphasis on liberal democracy and the implications of political pluralism for personnel management. Chapter 8 examines the economic context within which personnel management takes place and stresses the importance of economic policy and the state of the labour market in determining the organizational climate within which personnel policies and practices operate. In Chapter 9, the social context of personnel management is explored. Amongst other things, this looks at demographic trends, social class and women in employment. There are two chapters on the legal contexts of personnel management. Chapter 10 considers the individual aspects of labour law and the institutions for enforcing the statutory employment rights and union membership rights of individuals at work. Chapter 11 focuses on the collective aspects of labour law such as the statutory rights of trade unions and the law on trade disputes.

Part IV concludes the book. It examines the various challenges to personnel management in the 1980s. It is argued in Chapter 12 that the personnel function is facing three main pressures after two decades of steady expansion and growth. These are economic recession, technological change and social uncertainty. In response to these influences, three developments are taking place within personnel management. First, the activities and the distribution of tasks within personnel work are shifting. Secondly, personnel specialists are having to adapt personnel policy and practices fundamentally in response to new and demanding contexts acting on enterprises. Thirdly, there are increasing claims on the personnel function to be both efficient and effective according to organizational and managerial criteria.

This book could not have been completed without the help and cooperation of a number of people. I would particularly like to thank my colleague and friend Linda McCormack for reading my first draft and then commenting on it and discussing it extensively with me. My library colleagues Jim Basker, Terry Hanson and Ian Mayfield provided invaluable services in identifying, obtaining and checking various sources for me; Jim Basker also provided the index. Alastair Evans, John Pimlott, Rob Thomas, Derek Torrington and Erich Suter kindly commented on particular parts of the book and Ron Hodrien, Polytechnic Information Officer, and Sylvia Horton generously agreed to read the final proofs. My thanks are also due to: Sally Harper and her staff at the IPM for their professionalism and speed in publishing this text; Frances Farnham for typing and retyping various stages of the manuscript; Anne Yell and Marion Weaver for typing the references and footnotes; and Charlie Chase for his technical help. Finally, I thank Felicity Farnham for her unqualified support and encouragement in enabling me to write and finish this book within the time limits prescribed. Any remaining errors of fact, judgment or omission are, of course, mine alone.

Portsmouth Polytechnic
1 June 1984

David Farnham

Preface to third edition

In comprehensively updating the empirical data of the earlier edition, I have not altered the basic structure of the book. I have, however, totally rewritten the final chapter, focusing on developments in human resources management and recent changes in the personnel function during the 1980s. I wish to acknowledge that an earlier draft of the ideas embodied in Chapter 12 first appeared as an article in the spring 1989 issue of the *Sundridge Park Management Review*.

1 June 1990   David Farnham

Part I

The background and internal contexts

1
The cultural and historical contexts

Modern personnel management in Britain has not developed in a social and economic vacuum. As a managerial function, it is as much a product of complex cultural and historical forces as is its employee counterpart, contemporary trade unionism. These cultural and historical contexts have helped shape the personnel management function within both private and public enterprises. The emergence and growth of personnel management have been affected by the changing politicoeconomic contexts in which personnel policy and practices take place. It is these background contexts which are examined first.

Industrialization

England was the first country to industrialize. It was the first country to break through from an agrarian, handicraft, preindustrial society to one dominated by industry and machine production. This process of industrialization, known as the 'industrial revolution', began in the eighteenth century, though it grew out of a number of trends already discernible in English society for some hundreds of years. It then spread to other parts of Britain, to Europe and overseas, transforming in 'two lifetimes the life of Western man, the nature of his society, and his relationship to the other peoples of the world'.[1] According to Landes (1969), at the core of the industrial revolution was a series of technological changes. One was the substitution of mechanical devices for human skills such as in spinning and weaving. Another was the use of steam power which replaced animal and human strength in making and producing things. A third was a marked improvement in the extraction and working of raw materials, 'especially in what are now known as the metallurgical and chemical industries'.[2]

Accompanying these technological changes were new forms of industrial organization. Productive units grew in size, for example, so that large mills and factories gradually replaced small workshops and homes where manufacturing had previously been done by small groups of outworkers. The factory system which developed also resulted in new types of work organization and working relationships which became depersonalized and socially stratified. On the one side, there was the 'master' whose task it was to supply his enterprise's financial capital (either by borrowing or from reinvested profits) in order to market his products, hire servants and direct their work activities. On the other side there were the wage labourers or the hired 'hands'. These two groups had little in common with each other apart from their economic relationship, the 'wage nexus' which bound them together, and the functional one by which the master supervised and disciplined his subordinate workers.

The transformation of British society from a preindustrial to an industrial one did not take place overnight. In its initial stages at least, the industrial revolution was typified by the emergence and establishment of coal, iron and cotton as Britain's staple industries. By 1850, for example, Britain produced about 50 per cent of the world's iron, 50 per cent of its cotton cloth and some two thirds of its coal, even though over 20 per cent of its labour force continued to work on the land.[3] Once started, however, industrialization was both an accumulative and a continuous process. New industries emerged whilst old ones declined. Thus electricity, gas and oil gradually supplanted coal as major sources of energy; plastics, man made fibres, car assembly, chemicals and electrical engineering slowly became Britain's new staple industries; and the internal combustion engine and mass communications steadily replaced the railways and the letter post as the prime means of transportation and communication. These industries too have changed over time so that today information technology and robotics continue to challenge the industrial and business *status quo*.

The economy steadily expanded throughout the nineteenth and into the twentieth century irregularly and cyclically. Thus peaks in economic and business activity were followed by troughs in industrial output and falls in market demand. Periods of trade expansion and growth were followed by economic recession and stagnation. Relatively high levels of employment of labour and capital were succeeded both by unemployment of people and other resources and by bankruptcies of businesses and firms. The industrialization process in Britain, therefore, has been a continuous, an accumulative and a fluctuating one. It has not yet ended and our stock of advanced technological knowledge has slowly grown over the past 200 years, especially since the end of the second world war, so that technologically 'industrial society is the most advanced that the world has ever known'.[4]

Industrial capitalism

For Aron (1961), an industrial society 'is one in which large scale industry is the characteristic form of production'.[5] Large scale industry and the enterprises comprising it have a number of common features. First, they use highly developed scientific and technological knowledge in the productive process, such as in steel manufacturing, chemical processing and oil refining, as well as in hospitals, banking and transport. Secondly, modern industrial organizations have extensive technical and social divisions of labour. Typically, for example, they employ a wide range of personnel with varied technical skills. These include: technicians and technologists; professional and scientific workers; managers and administrators; craft and maintenance workers; clerical and secretarial staff; the highly skilled and less skilled; and so on.

A third feature of modern large scale enterprises is the vast capital resources[6] required to run them. As existing capital is used and depreciates, it has to be renewed if such enterprises are to remain economically viable. Fourthly, in the interests of economic efficiency and organizational success, industrial enterprises, whether of the manufacturing or the service type, and whether privately or publicly owned, are hierarchies of power governed and administered by internal bureaucracies. These policy making and bureaucratic structures headed by senior managers are necessary, since those controlling industrial organizations are expected to adopt rigorous economic and financial criteria in the use of the material and labour resources employed within them. If they did not do so 'there would be enormous losses of wealth and energy'.[7]

Compared with the preindustrial world, work in modern industrial enterprises is separated from home and family life and is 'paid for'. Also, there is often an instrumental or calculative attitude to paid work by those in low status jobs which are often seen as being alienating and meaningless by those doing them. On the other hand, there is also an emphasis on professionalism and self advancement among those with more interesting and higher status roles within such organizations.[8] In their case, organizational success and job commitment are linked with career opportunities for themselves. These complementary and contrasting attitudes towards industrial work in its various forms have important implications for those who manage industrial enterprises and for how work is structured and organized within them. They also influence the ways in which those who act on behalf of employers recruit, reward, train and motivate their subordinate employees.

Empirical studies of the industrial world have led some students of industrial society, such as Kerr and his associates (1973), to conclude that 'each industrialized society is . . . like every other industrialized society'.[9] In their pioneering work on the problems of labour and management in economic growth, their central thesis is that there is an inherent logic of the industrialization process. In their view, this eventually leads all societies, growing from different starting points and following a variety of routes, towards a common industrial culture or 'mode'. They call this 'pluralistic industrialism'. For them, this is a society without class divisions and where, as the power of science and technology to provide rational solutions to societal problems expands, there are no conflicts about the fundamental directions which society should take.

Under pluralistic industrialism, the management process within industrial enterprises is professionalized and workers tend to become moderate and conservative in their outlook. Kerr and his colleagues also argue that the central problem of industrial relations within pluralistic industrialism is not capital versus labour but 'the structuring of the labour force – how it gets recruited, developed and maintained'.[10] They further suggest that pluralistic industrialism produces tripartite systems of industrial relations, representing employer, employee and governmental interests. Their task is to determine and administer the 'web of rules' governing industrial relations. In this way, they argue, each 'system is subject more to evolutionary change than to revolutionary revision'.[11]

This 'convergence' thesis of industrialism and related ones such as those of Bell (1974) and Touraine (1971)[12] have been criticized by both Marxist and non-Marxist writers. Brown and Harrison (1978) point out, for example, that a basic feature of convergence theories is their stress on technological change as an independent factor leading 'to modifications of the social institutions central to the process of providing economic benefits to society'.[13] Further, whilst using systems theory[14] to describe the socioeconomic features of preindustrial and industrial societies, writers such as Kerr and his colleagues treat technology as an input from outside the industrial system to which the latter must adapt. Yet there is no reason to suppose that technology should be treated as an independent variable. Indeed, as Brown and Harrison stress, technology is 'very much a social product, and ought not to be relegated lightly to the role of an external influence to which society adapts'.[15]

Convergence theorists also view science and technology as neutral, value free, world wide systems of knowledge which, when applied to societal problems, bring about the end of ideological conflict and of fundamental political debate within them. Critics such as Brown and Harrison argue, however, that many of the developments associated with technological advance, such as those in weapon manufacture and defence systems for example, can only be interpreted as part of the process of ideological control within both democratic and totalitarian industrial societies. In their view:

> far from technology and particularly knowledge technology marking the 'end of ideology', there is a very important sense in which the claims for value freedom associated with the new decision-making methods are a mystification which serves to disguise the extent to which the new technology is the servant of old masters.[16]

By this view industrial societies, like preindustrial ones, are neither technologically determined nor value free. Their economic and technological infrastructures are highly integrated but the 'relationship between the technicoeconomic structure and political control is perhaps the major source of difference between them'.[17] Industrialism in other words is structured within specific politicoeconomic contexts.

Figure 1 (p. 8) shows four possible politicoeconomic contexts within which industrialism may take root, develop and mature.

Figure 1
The politicoeconomic contexts of industrialism

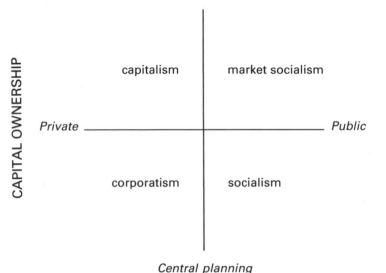

RESOURCE ALLOCATION
Market forces

CAPITAL OWNERSHIP

capitalism | market socialism

Private ———————————— *Public*

corporatism | socialism

Central planning

These are 'capitalism', 'market socialism', 'corporatism' and 'socialism'. Capitalism exists, for example, where a society's capital resources are predominantly privately owned, though not necessarily by individuals, and where its economic resources, including its land, labour, capital, goods and services, are allocated primarily by market forces or the price mechanism. Under socialism, a society's capital resources are mainly in public or common ownership and resource allocation is principally by central planning or governmental direction. Industrial societies like those of western Europe are basically capitalist but they contain elements of socialism, market socialism and corporatism within them, just as socialist societies like those in eastern Europe have elements of capitalist activity within them. The essence of this typology, however, is that each industrial society, when described as capitalist, market socialist, corporatist or socialist, is predominantly of one type.

Following Turner (1975), it is the establishment of a market economy both for capital and consumer goods and for people's labour which characterizes capitalism. This market depends on impersonal, calculative and contractual relationships which 'spread beyond national frontiers to link may countries together into an international market system'.[18] Further, while certain social interests, including those of government, control the economic means whereby income and wealth are created and distributed under capitalism, other socioeconomic groups merely possess the capacity to work under the direction of others. It is these groups who comprise the working population under capitalism. Very few within their ranks own any industrial capital and a majority work under a contract of service with firms and other enterprises. But their labour skills are vital to the productive process.

From the preceding analyses, it is clear that Britain is both an industrial society and a capitalist one. Amongst other things, this has implications for how its wealth is produced; how its work is organized; how its economic resources both material and human are used and allocated; how those owning them are rewarded; and how relations between employers and employees are structured. Industrialism and capitalism, in short, are the twin socioeconomic institutions out of which Britain's system of production, distribution and exchange has developed and matured. Personnel management within enterprises is a product of these institutional forces. It helps both to maintain them and, to some extent, to modify them. Moreover, as industrial capitalism changes, so too do the nature and practices of personnel management.

The changing structure of the labour force

Under industrial capitalism, the size, distribution, quality and skills of the labour force are vital elements in the productive process. The labour force consists of those in employment, that is, those individuals working under a contract of employment for others, the self employed and those in the armed services.[19] Since capitalist industrial society is one which is work based, and one in which certain groups make use of the labour and work of others, the structure of the labour force reflects both the priorities and the dynamics of the industrial system which it facilitates.

Personnel in Context

Table 1
Growth of the British labour force 1851–1989

Year	Male 000's	Female 000's	Labour force 000's	Total population 000's	Activity rate per cent
1851	6,554	2,819	9,373	20,808	45.0
1921	13,655	5,701	19,356	42,769	45.3
1951	16,034	7,745	23,479	48,854	48.1
1981	12,031[1]	9,052[1]	23,472	54,286	43.2
1986	11,717[1]	9,408[1]	24,053	54,900	43.8
1989	12,006[2]	10,887[1]	26,955[2]	57,065[2]	47.2[2]

[1] employees only: self employed and armed forces excluded
[2] figures for the UK
Sources: MITCHELL B R and DEANE P. *Abstract of British historical statistics*, CUP 1971 and *Employment Gazette*, various

Table 2
The occupational distribution of the British labour force 1911–88

| Occupational groups | Occupational groups as percentage of labour force | | | | | | |
	1911	1931	1951	1961	1971	1981	1988
Employers and proprietors	6.7	6.7	5.0	4.8	3.6	7.4	9.9
All white collar workers	18.7	23.0	30.9	35.9	42.7	48.6	51.9
All manual workers	74.6	70.3	64.3	59.3	54.7	44.0	38.2
Total labour force	100.0	100.0	100.0	100.0	100.0	100.0	100.0

Sources: PRICE R and BAIN G S, 'Union growth revisited: 1948–1974 in perspective', *British journal of industrial relations*, November 1976 and *Labour force surveys* (various)

Table 1 above, shows that the British labour force grew from just over nine million in 1851 to almost 27 million in 1989. In the years shown, the labour force activity rate never fell below 43.2 per cent, reaching a peak of 48.1 per cent in 1951. The occupational distribution of the labour force has also changed. As indicated in Table 2, the proportion of those described as 'employers and proprietors' declined from almost seven per cent of the labour force in 1911 to under four per cent in 1971, rising to almost 10 per cent in 1988. Similarly, between 1911 and 1971, the proportion of those in white collar employment increased from 18.7 to 42.7 per cent, while the proportion of those in manual employment decreased from 74.6 to 54.7 per cent. By 1988 other changes had taken place with those in white collar employment accounting for over 50 per cent of the labour force compared with 38 per cent in manual employment, as well as increases in the proportion of the self employed.[20]

These major changes in the occupational distribution of the labour force are reflected in corresponding changes in its industrial distribution. Table 3 shows, for the period 1901–89, that those industries where the proportion of those working declined were agriculture, mining and quarrying, manufacturing, and transport. The industries where the proportion increased were professional and miscellaneous services, including public administration and defence.

Table 3

The industrial distribution of the British labour force 1901–89

Industrial groups	Industrial groups as percentage of labour force						
	1901	1911	1931	1951	1971	1981	1989
Agriculture, mining and quarrying	14.8	13.6	11.8	8.8	4.4	3.3	2.2
Manufacturing	37.5	36.4	34.3	37.6	34.3	30.6	21.4
Construction	7.5	5.3	5.5	6.4	7.2	7.4	6.6
Gas, electricity, water	0.4	0.6	1.2	1.6	1.4	1.5	1.8
Transport	8.7	7.8	8.2	7.7	6.7	6.1	5.8
Professional and miscellaneous services	31.1	36.3	39.0	37.9	46.0	51.1	62.2
Total	100.0	100.0	100.0	100.0	100.0	100.0	100.0

Sources: HUNTER L C and ROBERTSON D J. *Economics of wages and labour*, Macmillan 1969 and DEPARTMENT OF EMPLOYMENT, *The changing structure of the labour force*, DE 1976 and *Economic Trends*, December 1989

Put another way, as shown in Table 4 (p. 12), the primary sector of the economy, that is, agriculture and mining and quarrying, accounted for only two per cent of the labour force in 1989 compared with 14.8 per cent in 1901. At the same time, the proportion of those working in the secondary sector, or in all manufacturing industries, fell from 45.4 per cent of the total in 1901 to 32.6 per cent in 1989. These two sets of changes were accompanied by a rise in the proportion of those working in the tertiary or service sector which increased from 39.8 per cent of the total in 1901 to 68 per cent by 1989.

Personnel in Context

Table 4
The sectoral distribution of the British labour force 1901–89

Sectors	Sectors as percentage of labour force						
	1901	1911	1951	1971	1981	1985	1989
Primary	14.8	14.6	8.8	4.4	3.3	2.6	2.2
Secondary	45.4	40.3	45.6	42.9	39.5	32.6	29.8
Tertiary	39.8	45.1	45.6	52.7	57.2	64.8	68.0

Source: As Table 3 on p. 11.

The labour force can also be classified by public sector and private sector employment. Amongst other things, Table 5 shows that the relative size of the public sector labour force grew considerably since the turn of the century up till the late 1970s, whilst that of the private sector decreased. By the late 1980s, the size of the public sector had declined again, accounting for about 23 per cent of the labour force compared with 5.8 per cent in 1901. Distributive

Table 5
The public sector labour force in Britain 1901–89

Year	Armed services	Central government	Local government	Public corporations	Total public sector labour force	Public sector as percentage of total labour force
	000's	000's	000's	000's	000's	Per cent
1901	423	160	375	—	958	5.8
1950	690	1,102	1,422	2,383	5,597	24.3
1970	372	1,533	2,559	2,016	6,480	26.4
1978	318	2,020	2,932	2,061	7,331	29.3
1984	326	2,009	2,884	1,661	6,880	28.7
1989	308	1,995	2,934	844	6,081	23.1

Sources: HUNTER L C and MULVEY C, *Economics of wages and labour,* Macmillan 1981 and *Economic Trends,* March 1985 and December 1989

changes also took place within the public sector labour force during the 1978–89 period. Between 1978 and 1989 for example, both the absolute and relative size of those employed in central government and the public corporations fell, whilst those in local government first declined and then rose.

Changes in the sex distribution and age distribution of the labour force between 1921 and the late 1980s are shown in Tables

Table 6
The sex distribution of the British labour force 1921–88

Year	Males as percentage of labour force	Females as percentage of labour force	Married females as percentage of females in labour force
1921	70.5	29.5	12.9
1951	69.2	30.8	38.2
1961	67.5	32.5	50.2
1971	63.4	36.6	63.1
1981	61.9	38.1	70.3
1986	58.7	41.3	70.1
1988	57.2	42.8	69.9

Sources: DEPARTMENT OF EMPLOYMENT, *The changing structure of the labour force,* DE 1976 and *Social Trends,* HMSO 1990

Table 7
The age distribution of the British labour force 1921–91

Year	Age groups as percentage of labour force by year				
	Under 20	20–24	25–44	45–65	Over 65
1921	18.7	14.5	38.9	23.8	4.1
1931	19.7	12.0	39.3	25.1	4.0
1951	11.0	11.6	42.8	30.8	3.7
1961	10.9	10.4	39.2	36.3	3.2
1971	8.6	12.3	38.6	37.2	3.2
1981	7.1	11.6	42.7	35.4	3.1
1991[1]	8.2	12.3	48.1	30.2	1.2

[1] estimate
Source: As in Table 6 above

6 and 7. In 1921, for instance, males made up 70.5 per cent of the labour force and females 29.5 per cent. By 1988, the proportion of males had fallen to 57.2 per cent, while the proportion of females had risen to 42.8 per cent. But whereas married females comprised only 12.9 per cent of all females in the labour force in 1921, they made up over 70 per cent of all working females by 1988. The main feature of the changing age distribution of the labour force between 1921 and 1991 is the steady decline in the proportion of those under 24 doing paid work and the

corresponding increase of those aged between 25 and 44. The proportion of those over 65 years of age working during these years steadily declined.

Under industrial capitalism, employer and market demand for labour is never constant. As the structure of the market economy changes so too does the structure of the labour force. Moreover, apart from the 20 or so years immediately following the second world war, the supply of potential workers to the labour market in Britain, ie its working population, has normally exceeded the actual demand for their services, as shown in Table 8.

Table 8
Unemployment as a percentage of the British working population 1921–90

Year	Percentage of working population unemployed
1921	16.6
1931	21.1
1951	1.2
1961	1.5
1971	3.5
1981	10.2
1986	13.9
1990	8.3

Sources: BEVERIDGE W H, *Full employment in a free society,* Allen and Unwin 1944 and *Employment Gazette,* various

It has been estimated, for example, that 'on average over the 50 years or so before 1914 unemployment seems to have been of the order of 5 per cent'.[21] In the interwar years, it ranged between 10 and 22 per cent of the working population. Only during the 1940s, 1950s and early 1960s was unemployment historically low. Since then unemployment as a proportion of the working population has steadily risen again, from around the two per cent level, to over three per cent in the early 1970s, to over six per cent by the late 1970s, and to about 14 per cent by the mid 1980s, falling again to eight per cent by 1990.

Historically, with labour supply fairly tight and with the market for jobs plentiful, personnel management as a managerial function has tended to be relatively 'soft' and welfare centred. But as labour demand tightens and unemployment rises in response to economic and technological changes, so the control functions of personnel management tend to predominate. The state of the labour market also affects management's relations with the trade unions. When unemployment is low, union power increases and the personnel role is a defensive one. With unemployment rising, union power diminishes and personnel management becomes more assertive.

Management, ownership and control

It is the task of those who manage organizations 'to organize the use of resources (including the work of others) towards the objectives of an enterprise'.[22] In the centuries preceding the industrial revolution, those controlling the manufacturing process were unable to cope with the problem of organizational size. This arose from the difficulties of managing which large scale enterprises presented. Up to the end of the eighteenth century at least, Pollard (1968) argues that managing was a function of direct involvement by ownership, 'and if it had to be delegated either because of the absence of the principals or because of the size of the concern, then the business was courting disaster'.[23]

In the early stages of the industrial revolution, each capitalist entrepreneur or individual master was typically his own manager. But as firms grew larger, and as the second and third generations of owners retired from active control, 'the problem of management became increasingly a problem of personnel: the numbers and skills of the managers'.[24] Basically, the problems of managing industrial enterprises during the industrial revolution were the same in all industries. This meant, writes Pollard, that:

> labour recruitment and training, discipline, control over production, accountancy and accountability were the ingredients of a science which varied only in detailed application, not in principle, as between different sectors of the economy.[25]

Neither the speed with which a professional managerial cadre emerged within nineteenth century business enterprises nor its size should be exaggerated. In practice, it was not until the last quarter of the century that the joint stock company with external shareholders became a generally acceptable form of business organization, thus providing an increased demand for managerial skills in industry. Before then, incorporation with limited liability was not possible, except at great cost and at considerable administrative inconvenience. Until the third quarter of the century, it was the family firm or the small common law partnership with unlimited liability for all partners, 'and unlimited freedom for dominant personalities, that characterized British business organization'. Even by 1885, limited companies only accounted for between five and 10 per cent of all businesses and, 'apart from public utilities, were common only in shipping, iron and steel and cotton'.[26]

With family firms still the norm, the private company developed. This form of business organization, although legally unrecognized until 1907, provided limited liability for small businesses, but had few enough shareholders to keep enterprise control in family hands. During the last years of the nineteenth century, there was a boom in company flotations and amalgamations. Also, aided by a period of cheap money, new company registrations increased from 2,515 in 1893 to 5,148 in 1897.[27] By 1914, the typical form of industrial enterprise had radically changed from what it had been in the early phases of the industrial revolution. By then, the joint stock company, with unlimited liability and employing a growing number of professional managers, had replaced the single entrepreneur or partnership as the predominant form of business organization in Britain.

It was the expansion of the joint stock company as the typical form of business enterprise, in both Britain and the United States, that led Berle and Means (1968) to write their pioneering work *The modern corporation and private property*.[28] Their central argument is that as companies get larger their shareholders become less influential in corporate affairs, and that the control function of ownership is replaced by that of top management. Their reasoning is that if the largest shareholder or group of shareholders in big companies do not have a sufficient proportion of votes in company affairs, then those companies are managerially rather than owner controlled. They go on to suggest that managers become independent arbiters of the public good and emerge as a neutral managerial elite, socially responsible to their companies and society generally.

The 'managerialist' thesis of Berle and Means has been developed and modified by other writers such as Burnham (1962), Dahrendorf (1959) and Galbraith (1969).[29] Although they differ in their emphases, they all assert that a separation of ownership from control has taken place within large companies. They also argue that since the new managerial elite has a different relationship to private property, it has different interests and objectives from the old capitalist class which it has replaced and that it therefore pursues significantly different business policies. This is not to argue that managerialism is a homogeneous theory, though it has led some managerialists to suggest that since managers are not property owners, conflicts of interests between themselves and their employees no longer exist. Dahrendorf, though a managerialist, does not support this view. He argues that conflict between managers and workers develops, because what separates them is not property but the authority to make decisions within industrial enterprises.

'Non-managerialist' writers, on the other hand, either do not accept that a divorce of ownership from control exists within larger companies or, if they do, they minimize its importance. Crosland (1962) summarizes this viewpoint. In his view, ownership, particularly institutional ownership, is still sufficiently concentrated to ensure continued owner control of the larger companies. He also suggests that owner control is reinforced by an elaborate system of interlocking directorates and, even to the extent that top managers exercise control, they do so in the interests of the owning class.[30] In the opinion of the non-managerialists, therefore, there has been less a divorce of ownership from control within large companies than a 'managerial reorganization of the propertied classes into the more or less unified stratum of the corporate rich'.[31]

Recent research in Britain suggests that in terms of shareholdings there has been a divorce of ownership from control in the larger private enterprises. But it also shows that for managers generally 'the interests of owners are seen to take precedence over other groups who have claims on the resources of the enterprise'.[32] Management as a group, it seems, especially top management, must of necessity cooperate closely in corporate policy making with those representing shareholders' interests at board level. Moreover, managers are hardly neutral in the policy making and executive processes, since their prime legal responsibility is to

corporate shareholders, whoever they may be. Also, if management collectively is responsible for organizational efficiency and
effectiveness, then it cannot be neutral in its contractual relationships with employees. For example, a total higher pay bill for its
employees can only be achieved at the economic cost of lower
financial returns to the company's shareholders. Under industrial
capitalism, therefore, the large company may be structured differently from the small owner managed firm. But it is ultimately
judged by the economic criteria of the market place. It is management's collective responsibility to ensure that these market
criteria are met on behalf of shareholder interests.[33]

Another thing which happens as industrial capitalism matures
is that both production and employment become concentrated in
a small number of very large companies. In 1977, for example, it
was estimated that there were some 2,100 private enterprises
employing 200 or more employees in the United Kingdom (UK).
Fifty-seven per cent of them had 1,000 or more employees and
about a third of them, or 738 enterprises, had 2,000 or more
employees. This figure did not include all the companies employing
over 2,000 employees, since these 738 enterprises were groups of
companies, organized in pyramids of holding and subsidiary
bodies. Also, those enterprises whose turnover was greatest were
predominantly very large employers. In 1977, nearly two thirds of
these employed 2,000 or more people, whilst 155 enterprises
had 10,000 or more UK employees. This high concentration of
employment meant that over seven million people in the UK,
more than a quarter of the total labour force, were employed by
large private sector enterprises at that time. This compared with
some 11 million, including the self employed, in the small scale
private sector and about seven million in the public sector. By
1986, there were 3,810 companies employing over 200 employees
or some 8.5 million employees in total. Of these companies 54 per
cent were in the manufacturing sector and 46 per cent in non-
manufacturing.[34]

A further feature of industrial capitalism is the emergence of a
strong public sector. In Britain, this largely happened after the
second world war, consisting of the public corporations, such as the
nationalized industries and a number of other public enterprises,
central government, including the National Health Service, and the
local authorities. During the 1980s, however, due to governmental

policy, the public sector was reduced in size. A number of nationalized industries, such as gas, electricity and water, were privatized and sold back to the private sector. There were over two million employees in public corporations in 1978, reduced to under a million by 1990. Similarly, the size and scope of the civil service were reduced during these years, with certain elements hived off and contracted out to private businesses.[33]

All three major sectors of the economy, the large private sector, the small private sector, and the public sector, now employ large numbers of managers at all levels within their enterprises. In 1981 it was estimated that there were at least 2.5 million managers in Britain, comprising over 10 per cent of the labour force.[36] These professional managers are hardly a homogeneous group. But, whether in private or public industry, it is their responsibility to ensure the efficient and effective management of the organizational resources for which they are accountable, including their subordinate employees.

The emergence and growth of personnel management

According to Pollard, 'in many respects the rational and methodical management of labour was the central management problem in the industrial revolution, requiring the fiercest wrench from the past'.[37] It now became necessary for the new class of masters and entrepreneurs to recruit and mobilize an industrial labour force. In doing this, they generally subjected their workers to a harsh and rigorous work discipline which was both alien to their experience and threatening to their dignity as human beings. There was also a tendency for the new men of business to be very concerned with their own capital stake in their firms 'and to see labour as an adjunct to be hired and manipulated according to the needs of the enterprise'. Because of the nature of early industrialism, its fierce competitiveness and the way it contrasted with preindustrial society, the new industrial labour force 'was introduced to its role not so much by attraction or monetary reward, but by compulsion, force and fear'.[38]

In the early stages of the industrial revolution, labour administration was not even an embryonic science. Not until the third decade of the nineteenth century at least did common humanity begin to combine with enlightened self interest amongst a few of the larger and more honourable employers to make them aware of labour management in terms of anything other than coercion, punishment or monetary reward. Moreover, the early Factory Acts and the trade unions, introduced from outside business organizations to put pressure on employers to work with rather than against their workers, were bitterly opposed by manufacturers as a whole. With labour relatively cheap and plentiful, it was generally viewed by employers as an economic resource to be bought in the cheapest market and to be firmly directed and controlled. It was not a human resource to be managed fairly and with a sense of social responsibility and humane concern.

Crichton (1968) shows that it was only towards the end of the nineteenth century that a number of philanthropic entrepreneurs began to develop a genuinely paternalistic care and concern for their workers. 'They tended to be strongly nonconformist in belief, and concerned about individuals, even while they enforced tough discipline over time-keeping and output'.[39] The part played by employers in the development of what came to be known as factory 'welfare work' is reinforced by Niven (1967). She shows that the early welfare workers were mainly women who saw their work as a service to the factory, as well as to the community. It was two Quaker firms, Rowntrees and Cadburys, who made an especially strong impact on the emergence and growth of the welfare movement. Other firms which also developed a welfare approach to their workers included W D and H O Wills, W R Jacob, Hans Renold and Hudson Scott.[40]

Mary Wood was probably the first person to become an industrial welfare worker when she was appointed at the Rowntree works at York, in 1896. By 1914 it was estimated that there were probably between 60 and 70 welfare workers in Britain. The Factory and Workshop Act 1901 had given a boost to their work, since the welfare orders made under the Act established the need for record keeping and self inspection by employers. Nevertheless, the early welfare workers had a difficult task because it was not clear what they should do in order to raise standards of factory welfare. Most of them ensured that factory legislation was implemented and provided personal counselling to employees when requested. They also looked after amenities such as the canteens, recreation grounds and rest rooms provided by their employers.

Seebohm Rowntree had a clear image of the welfare function. For him, welfare workers were representatives of the directors and of the employees. In their first role they were expected to devise improvements in conditions of work and to keep the personal element 'prominent in their relations with employees'. As representatives of the employees, he wrote:

> it is the duty of the social helpers to be constantly in touch with them, to gain their confidence, to voice any grievances they may have either individually or collectively, to give effect to any reasonable desire they may show for recreative clubs, educational classes, etc and to give advice in matters concerning them personally.[41]

By this view, welfare workers were seen to be intermediaries between employer and employees and were not to be subordinated to either, even if they were seen to serve both.

The first world war gave an added impetus to welfare work. With labour scarce and high productivity required for the war effort, employee welfare became a major concern for those in charge of factory production. In 1915 the Government appointed a Health of Munition Workers' Committee which, in the following year, recommended that welfare supervisors should be appointed in all factories employing women. As a result, several hundred women were recruited as welfare workers to munition factories alone between 1916 and 1918. Sidney Webb estimated that about 600 women were engaged in welfare work in 1917. By the end of the war this had risen to 1,000. The duties of these female welfare supervisors are described in the final report of the Health of Munition Workers' Committee in 1918. They included: engaging workers; keeping records; investigating the causes of absence and low output; investigating dismissals; advising on working conditions, discipline and night supervision; visiting the sick; arranging feeding, housing and transport; administering thrift and benevolent funds; and organizing some forms of training.[42]

In the light of these developments, and the steady emergence of the welfare function within some companies since the turn of the century, Seebohm Rowntree invited firms to send representatives to a conference of welfare workers and employers at York in June 1913. Twenty-nine firms sent 48 representatives, the majority of whom were welfare workers. According to Niven, the minutes of the meeting held on 7 June recorded that 'it was decided to form an Association of Employers interested in industrial betterment and of welfare workers engaged by them'.[43] This organization, the Welfare Workers Association, had 34 founding members, six firms and two employers joining as individuals. In late 1919, it amalgamated with the North Western Area Industrial Association bringing the membership of the new body, the Welfare Workers Institute (WWI), to 700.[44]

In the postwar recession, with unemployment steadily rising, the importance of welfare work began to decline, though it was not abandoned by the more progressive and enlightened employers. This decline was reflected in the fall of membership of the WWI, renamed the Institute of Industrial Welfare Workers (IIWW) in 1924, to 420 in 1927. Of these only 15 were men. Its membership did not rise again until the late 1930s when it reached 759 out of some 1,800 industrial welfare supervisors and labour managers in 1939, of whom about 40 per cent were men. By then the emphasis was shifting away from welfare work towards 'labour management'. This was reflected in another change of name of the IIWW to that of the Institute of Labour Management (ILM) in 1931.[45]

As Crichton points out, the second world war, like the first, immediately precipitated an increased demand for labour managers within factories, as Britain once again moved out of a recession into full employment in order to maximize industrial output and factory production. Experienced 'labour officers' or 'personnel officers' as they were increasingly called 'were seconded to Royal Ordnance Factories to set up labour departments there and train experienced assistants, or to the universities to provide emergency training programmes for new recruits'.[46] The report of the Chief Inspector of Factories for 1943 gave the number of personnel officers in factories employing over 250 workers as nearly 5,500 or three times as many as in 1939.[47] By the end of the war, Moxon (1946) claims that there were six areas of work being undertaken by personnel specialists. These were: employment; wages; joint consultation; health and safety; employee services and welfare; and education and training.[48]

It was during the war that the ILM first attempted to define the nature of personnel work which was now often referred to as personnel management. Its definition was as follows:

Personnel management is that part of the management function which is primarily concerned with the human relationships within an organization. Its objective is the maintenance of these relationships on a basis which, by consideration of the well-being of the individual, enables all those engaged in the undertaking to make their maximum personal contribution to the effective working of that undertaking.[49]

The ILM then went on to describe the specific areas with which personnel management was concerned. These included: methods of recruitment, selection, training and education and the proper employment of personnel; terms of employment, methods and standards of remuneration; working conditions, amenities and employee services; and the maintenance and effective use of facilities for joint consultation between employers and employees and between their representatives, and of recognized procedures for the settlement of disputes. In outlining the role of personnel officers, the ILM described them as 'those persons especially qualified by training and experience to advise on the formation of personnel policy'. It was their responsibility, claimed the ILM, to secure the understanding and application of that policy and 'the appropriate executive duties arising therefrom'.[50]

Unlike welfare work at the end of the first world war, personnel management continued to grow in importance after 1945. This was reflected in the change of name of the ILM to that of the Institute of Personnel Management (IPM) in June 1946. The growth of personnel management arose partly from the full employment policies of successive postwar governments resulting in tight labour supply and increased competition amongst employers for available labour. It was also because of the rising influence and power of the trade unions. This was especially so at employer level where domestic collective bargaining between managers and shop stewards often determined the actual pay and conditions of employees in the private sector, with industry wide or national bargaining providing minimum terms and conditions only. Consequently, the specialist personnel role not only became more firmly established within existing enterprises and sectors but also spread to the local authorities, the health service and nationalized industries, where hitherto its influence had been limited.

The increased importance of the personnel management function within enterprises was reflected by the growing number of personnel specialists in industry. It has been estimated that there were, by 1963, about 10–15,000 personnel managers in Britain, of whom approximately a third were members of the IPM.[51] Further evidence of the growth in the recognition and scale of the professional personnel function can be seen from Table 9.

Table 9
IPM membership 1956–89

Year	Total	Corporate members	Non-corporate members
1989	35,548	12,829	22,719
1985	25,096	8,188	16,908
1981	22,624	8,106	14,518
1976	18,554	9,281	9,273
1971	14,259	5,318	8,941
1965	6,510	3,166	3,344
1956	3,979	2,852	1,127

Sources: *IPM annual report for 1957–58 et seq,* IPM 1957–89

This shows that between 1956 and 1989 IPM membership increased from 3,979 to 35,548. This represented a 59 per cent increase between 1971 and 1981, confirming the view of Marks (1978) that personnel management in Britain dramatically extended its scope and influence during the 1960s and 1970s when, she claims, its practices spread 'throughout industry, commerce and the public services from the comparatively few enlightened sectors to the darkest corners in which people were employed'.[52] Between 1981 and 1989, IPM membership increased by a further 12,924 or 57 per cent.

Conclusion

It is not possible to understand the nature, activities and tasks of modern personnel management, as 'that part of management concerned with people at work and with their relationships within an enterprise',[53] without having regard to its cultural and historical contexts. Both as a general management activity and a specialist one, personnel management in Britain has developed out of industrial capitalism, with its advanced technologies, large scale enterprises, complex division of labour, concentrated patterns of capital ownership and market allocation of resources. Under industrial capitalism the labour force is a vital part of production and distribution within the economy. The constantly changing structure of the labour force mirrors the market priorities of the industrial system which it supports.

Personnel management has evolved and matured out of such institutional and historical forces. As British industrial capitalism has developed, largely in response to changes in its market, technological and politicoeconomic contexts, so too have personnel management practices and the emphasis and division of roles between line and personnel managers and within the specialist personnel function itself. The aims of personnel management are the effective recruitment, selection, rewarding, deployment, training, coordination, control and management of labour resources in organizations. Proper utilization and development of these resources is necessary if the corporate objectives, efficiency and effectiveness of private and public enterprises are to be achieved. When unemployment is low, personnel management tends to be more welfare centred, with specialist personnel managers having increased influence within organizations. With the economy slowing down and unemployment high, personnel management is more likely to be hard and control oriented, with line managers tending to take the initiative in personnel matters.

As industrialization proceeds, industrial organizations whether privately or publicly owned become large, impersonal and run by professional managers. These include general managers and managerial specialists, such as production, marketing, finance and personnel managers. Managing organizational resources is not a neutral function and managers, including personnel managers, cannot be impartial in the policy making and managerial process. The early welfare workers might have claimed to be intermediaries between management and employees and 'social helpers' of the employer. Modern personnel managers can only normally justify themselves where it is shown that they are contributing towards the economic efficiency and organizational effectiveness of the enterprises in which they work. It is by these criteria that they are judged by their managerial peers.

References and footnotes

1 LANDES D S. *The Unbound Prometheus* (Cambridge, CUP, 1969). pl.
2 *ibid.*
3 TURNER B A. *Industrialism* (Harlow, Longman, 1975). p15f.
4 *ibid.* p2.
5 ARON R. *18 Lectures on Industrial Society* (London, Weidenfeld and Nicolson, 1961). p73.
6 A society's 'capital' or its 'capital resources' are those real or financial assets having a monetary value. Real capital or capital goods are a physical stock of productive assets such as factories, plant, materials, machinery and so on. Money capital is the monetary value of assets such as Stock Exchange securities, titles to property and wealth, and expressions of debt used in the capital formation process.
7 ARON. *opcit.* p74.
8 See, for example, GOLDTHORPE J *and others. The Affluent Worker: Industrial Attitudes and Behaviour* (Cambridge, CUP, 1968); BEYNON H. *Working for Ford* (Harmondsworth, Penguin, 1973); BLAUNER R. *Alienation and Freedom* (Chicago, Chicago University Press, 1964); PAHL J M *and* PAHL R E. *Managers and their Wives* (Harmondsworth, Penguin, 1972); and WATSON T J. *The Personnel Managers* (London, Routledge and Kegan Paul, 1977).
9 KERR C *and others. Industrialism and Industrial Man*, 2nd ed. (Harmondsworth, Penguin, 1973). p56.
10 *ibid.* p280f.
11 *ibid.* p281f.
12 See BELL D. *The Coming of Post Industrial Society* (London, Heinemann, 1974) and TOURAINE A *The Post Industrial Society* (NY, Random House, 1971).
13 BROWN D *and* HARRISON M J. *A Sociology of Industrialization: an Introduction.* (London, Macmillan, 1978). p141.
14 A 'system' is a group of elements organized together for a purpose, such as a computer. Analytically, any system comprises a set of 'inputs' which are 'processed' to provide 'outputs' which, in turn, are part of the 'feedback' into that system. In the case of the computer, its inputs are raw data which are processed into usable information or outputs by its central processing unit.
15 BROWN *and* HARRISON. *opcit.* p141.
16 *ibid.* p144.
17 *ibid.* p22.
18 TURNER. *opcit.* p39.
19 This is sometimes called the 'employed labour force'. In this book, the term labour force is normally used.
20 See also FARNHAM D *and* PIMLOTT J. *Understanding Industrial Relations.* 2nd ed. (Eastbourne, Cassell, 1983). p9.
21 HUNTER L C *and* ROBERTSON D J. *Economics of Wages and Labour.* (London, Macmillan, 1961). p163.

22 CRICHTON A. *Personnel Management in Context.* (London, Batsford, 1968). p49.
23 POLLARD S. *The Genesis of Modern Management.* (Harmondsworth, Penguin, 1968). p35.
24 *ibid.* p127.
25 *ibid.* p78.
26 KEMPNER T *and others. Business and Society.* (London, Allen Lane, 1974). pp28 and 31.
27 *ibid.* p32.
28 BERLE A A and MEANS G C. *The Modern Corporation and Private Property.* 4th ed. (NY, Harcourt, Brace and World, 1968). The first edition was published in 1932.
29 See BURNHAM J. *The Managerial Revolution.* (London, Greenwood Press, 1962); DAHRENDORF R. *Class and Class Conflict in Industrial Society.* (London, Routledge and Kegan Paul, 1959); and GALBRAITH J K. *The New Industrial State.* (Harmondsworth, Pelican, 1969)
30 CROSLAND C A R. *The Conservative Enemy.* (London, Cape, 1962).
31 MILLS C W. *The Power Elite.* (NY, OUP, 1959). p147.
32 MANSFIELD R *and others. The British Manager in Profile.* (London, BIM, 1981). p16.
33 Research by the Stock Exchange shows a relative decline in individual shareholdings in public limited companies (PLCs) and a corresponding increase in institutional holdings by insurance companies and pension funds, as shown in the following table.

Percentage distribution of shareholdings in PLCs 1963–1981

	1963	1969	1975	1981
Individuals	54.0	47.4	37.5	28.2
Charities	2.1	2.1	2.3	2.2
Banks	1.3	1.7	0.7	0.3
Insurance companies	10.0	12.2	15.9	20.5
Pension funds	6.4	9.0	16.8	26.7
Unit trusts	1.3	2.9	4.1	3.6
Investment trusts	11.3	10.5	10.5	6.8
Companies	5.1	5.4	3.0	5.1
Public sector	1.5	2.6	3.6	3.0
Overseas	7.0	6.6	5.6	3.6
	100.0	100.0	100.0	100.0

Source: *The Observer,* 13 November 1983

34 DEPARTMENT OF TRADE. *Report of the Committee of Inquiry on Industrial Democracy* (Chairman, Lord Bullock). (London, HMSO, 1977). p6 and DEPARTMENT OF TRADE AND INDUSTRY. *Business monitor MA3.* (London, HMSO, 1989). p53.
35 See FARNHAM D. *The Corporate Environment.* (London, IPM, 1990).

36 This figure is obtained from the '10 per cent' sample of households and communal establishments included in the 1981 census. This sample incorporated 101,185 full time 'employers and managers' working in central government, local government and large establishments and 159,604 in small establishments. It also included another 12,638 'part time' employers and managers in the same organizational categories. See OFFICE OF POPULATION CENSUSES AND SURVEYS. *Census 1981. National report. Great Britain. part 2.* (London, HMSO, 1983). p6.

37 POLLARD. *opcit.* p189.

38 CHECKLAND. *opcit.* pp103f and 243.

39 CRICHTON. *opcit.* p15f.

40 NIVEN. *opcit.* p24ff.

41 Quoted in NIVEN. *ibid.* p23.

42 *ibid.* p44.

43 *ibid.* p36.

44 *ibid.* p61ff.

45 *ibid.* pp76, 84, 91 and 107.

46 CRICHTON. *opcit.* p35.

47 NIVEN. *opcit.* p100.

48 See MOXON G R. *Functions of a Personnel Department.* (London, IPM, 1946).

49 NIVEN. *opcit.* p107.

50 *ibid.* p108.

51 *ibid.* p152.

52 MARKS W. *Politics and Personnel Management.* (London, IPM, 1978). p1.

53 INSTITUTE OF PERSONNEL MANAGEMENT. *The Institute of Personnel Management.* (London, IPM, 1980). p1.

2

The organizational context

In preindustrial societies the organization of production is largely
governed by tradition. Work roles are allocated according to age,
rank, sex and acquired skills. Under industrial capitalism, by
contrast, formal and rational methods of allocating job tasks and
of organizing production replace traditional procedures. Before
we consider the managerial role in modern organizations, it is first
necessary to examine their diverse types, what is meant by
organizational objectives and policy making, their range of internal
structures and the nature of conflict within them.

Organizational typologies

The problem of defining formal organizations has concerned
many organizational theorists. Silverman (1970), for example,
summarizes the debate. He discusses the different characteristics
of organizations put forward by other writers and suggests that
organizations have at least three distinguishing features. First, they
are consciously created artefacts, serving certain purposes which
are normally stated when they are first formed. 'Their founders
further provide them with a set of rules which generally lay down
clear lines of authority and communication [to ensure] that these
purposes may be most readily attained', though in practice both
organizational purposes and their rules may be displaced over
time. Secondly, organizations are characterized by a pattern of
relationships which are taken for granted 'by the participants who
seek to co-ordinate and to control'. Lastly, much attention is paid
in organizations 'to the discussion and execution of planned
changes in social relations, and in the "rules of the game" upon
which they are based'.[1]

Various typologies of organizations have been proposed. Silver-

man, for example, distinguishes between 'environment-input typologies', 'environment-output typologies' and typologies based on
'intra-organisational factors'.[2] Eldridge and Crombie (1974) identify five organizational typologies.[3] These are: a functional typology, as in the studies of Blau and Scott (1963), Trist and others
(1963), and Katz and Kahn (1966);[4] a technological typology, as
provided by Blauner (1964), Woodward (1965 and 1970) and
Thompson (1967);[5] a regulatory typology as per Etzioni (1961);[6]
and a structural typology, as advanced by Ackoff (1970) and
Vickers (1970).[7] Eldridge and Crombie also consider 'total institutions' to be another type of organization, such as orphanages,
hospitals, prisons and monasteries, drawing heavily on the work
of Goffman (1968).[8]

Organizations can also be classified by their orientation and
ownership. Their orientation, for example, is indicated by the
basic goals which they seek to achieve. For Thomason (1981), the
basic goals or purposes of private business are to satisfy consumer
demand in the market place. The goals of public service organizations are to satisfy citizen need within the community. This is
'regardless of whether the citizen can translate that need into
effective demand or of whether any means can be found of charging
directly for the service'. Thus private and public organizations
have essentially different goals. They are distinguishable, says
Thomason, 'by the terms demand and need, and their derivative
objectives are characterized differently'.[9] The relationship between
organizational orientation and organizational ownership is shown
in Figure 2. Organizations can be directed towards profit and
revenue goals or welfare and community ones, whilst ownership
can be in either private or public hands. By this typology, there
are four categories of organizations: private businesses; public
corporations; public services; and voluntary bodies.

Private businesses, for example, dominate agriculture, manufacturing, distribution, many service enterprises and the financial
sector including the banks, insurance companies, pension funds
and Stock Exchange. They are profit oriented and privately owned.
Public corporations are revenue oriented and publicly owned and
include all the trading and commercial activities of the public
sector industries. The public services are welfare and community
oriented and publicly owned. In most cases the financial resources
for public service organizations, such as in health care, edu-

Figure 2
Organizational types by orientation and ownership

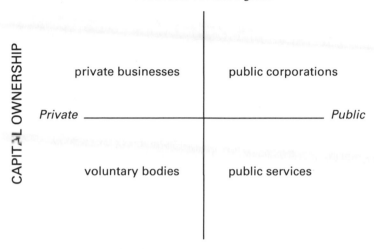

ORIENTATION
Profit and revenue goals

CAPITAL OWNERSHIP

private businesses | public corporations

Private ─────────────────── *Public*

voluntary bodies | public services

Welfare and community goals

cation, public housing and personal social services, come from taxation rather than from direct charges on individual clients. Voluntary bodies are welfare oriented and privately owned. They include the churches, charitable trusts, trade unions, employers' associations, professional bodies, producer cooperatives and so on.[10]

Objective setting, planning and policy making

Objective setting in organizations is a key managerial task which derives out of an organization's purposes. Figure 3 on page 32 shows the three levels where objective setting takes place: corporate level; executive level; and operational level. They approximate to the senior, middle and supervisory levels of management. The corporate objectives of private businesses and voluntary bodies, for example, are normally set by their governing bodies, taking

Figure 3
Objective setting, planning and policy making

account of their legal requirements and the advice of senior executive managers. Similarly, the corporate objectives of public corporations and the public services are set by their governing bodies, taking account of their organizational purposes as established by Parliament. Executive and operational objectives, in turn, are set lower down organizational hierarchies by managerial staff, acting within the framework of corporate purposes and corporate objectives. Corporate objectives tend to be long term, executive objectives medium term and operational objectives short term.

A distinction needs to be made between objective setting and planning, on the one side, and policies, programmes, procedures and rules on the other. For O'Shaughnessy (1968), 'objectives emphasize aims and are stated as expectations, but policies emphasize rules and are stated in the form of directives'.[11] Thus a corporate production objective in a manufacturing organization might be to achieve low unit costs from long production runs. A resultant corporate policy would be not to produce one-off jobs unless they are authorized by senior management. A corporate personnel objective might be to establish good working relationships with the trade unions and their representatives. The corresponding personnel policy would be to create and maintain effective consultative, negotiating and communication machinery with the relevant unions.

Plans are proposed courses of action directed towards achieving a set of formally stated objectives. At corporate level they are the horizontal link between objectives and policies. Below corporate level they link objectives, programmes, procedures and rules horizontally and integrate with other plans vertically. Policies are general guidelines for actions which are likely to be repeated in organizations, while programmes provide guidelines for actions within specific projects. Procedures, in turn, are more detailed guidelines for action, setting out the chronological sequence of steps or tasks to be taken in particular activities. Rules are authoritative statements or instructions issued by management of specific actions that must or must not be taken in given situations. They leave little room for individual discretion. Policies, programmes, procedures and rules, each in their own way, aim to ensure consistency of action by individual job holders in given organizational circumstances.

There are certain advantages in setting formally stated objectives within organizations, whether at corporate, executive or operational level. First, where written objectives are absent, there is a danger that action might be taken in pursuit of ends which do not contribute to organizational effectiveness. Secondly, explicit criteria for judging organizations and intraorganizational performance are provided. Thirdly, since objectives are normally based on forecasts, it is by considering the progress of an organization and its subunits that setbacks and future opportunities can be anticipated. Fourthly, formal objectives facilitate communication within organizations and lessen the risk of internal misunderstanding. Lastly, where objectives are made explicit, any conflicts amongst them can be identified and attempts made to reconcile them.

In practice, every organization has multiple corporate objectives, so it is difficult to specify which is the most important category of objective in each case. Basically, however, senior management has to consider its 'first order' objectives and 'second order' objectives in turn. First order corporate objectives are normally economic, since organizations have to be economically and financially viable. In the private sector, the objective may be profit. This is not to argue that all private businesses are, as in classical economy theory, profit maximizing organizations. But it does suggest that they must achieve at least a satisfactory profit, or a reasonable return on their financial capital, if they are to meet their shareholders' expectations and to have some degree of organizational success and stability. As the Chairman of Imperial Chemical Industries told the Company's shareholders at their Annual General Meeting in 1983:

> our first and overriding aim is an increase in profits. It is only through success in that key factor that we can properly meet the justifiable expectations of you, our shareholders, our employees, and our customers.[12]

Even in non-profit making organizations, such as in the public services and voluntary bodies, an efficiency objective is necessary if the best possible services are to be provided within the limited economic resources available.

Second order corporate objectives are much more varied. They include, for example, 'functional', 'service' and 'social' objectives. Functional objectives, for instance, relate to such areas as production, marketing, finance and personnel. Thus a production objective might be to provide an improved range of products to customers; a marketing objective to move into new market areas; a financial objective to raise new sources of investment funding; and a personnel objective to recognize trade unions for collective bargaining purposes among certain categories of employees. Service objectives concern the basic aims which organizations claim to achieve. Thus a building firm might claim that it aims to provide houses for those buying them; a hospital health care for those who are ill; an insurance company protection for its policy holders; and an institution of higher education, a learning community for staff and students.

The social objectives of organizations are normally aimed at either their employees and/or the general public. An organization might, for example, have the objective of being a fair, reasonable and model employer and of providing a healthy and safe working environment for its employees. Organizations might also have objectives aimed at protecting the ecological environment, at contributing to charitable bodies and at serving their local communities.[13]

In practice there appears to be a large element of bargaining both within and between managerial groups when objective setting takes place. Objective setting at corporate, executive and operational levels is essential, however, since the proper selection and implementation of appropriate objectives contribute to organizational effectiveness. As Drucker (1974) argues, organizational efficiency is an input–output concept and demonstrates the ability to get things done correctly within organizations. Organizational effectiveness, on the other hand, is the ability of those in authority to choose appropriate organizational objectives. In Drucker's words: it is 'effectiveness rather than efficiency [which] is essential in business. The pertinent question is not how to do things right but how to find the right things to do, and to concentrate resources and efforts on them'.[14]

Private businesses

Any individual may set up in business, with a view to making a profit, without any legal formality providing s/he trades in their own name. Where an individual trades under another name, s/he is required to register the business under the Registration of Business Names Act 1916. Sole traders may or may not employ others in their business and their liabilities for any trading debts are unlimited. This means that any part of a sole trader's property or assets may be used to pay off unpaid debts incurred by the business in the proprietor's trading activities. Because a sole trader's access to financial capital is strictly limited, most such businesses tend to be small. They are normally confined to activities such as taxi-driving, retail shops, jobbing building and keeping guest houses.

Among professional workers, such as accountants, dentists, doctors and solicitors, partnerships are fairly common. A partnership is defined in law by the Partnership Act 1890 as persons carrying on business in common with a view to making a profit. A partnership is required to register its business name, unless it consists only of the names of the partners, and is normally limited to a maximum of 20 persons. Partnerships generally employ people and all partners have a duty to take part in managing the undertaking. As with sole traders, the financial liability of partnerships is usually unlimited, except under the provisions of the Limited Partnership Act 1907. This enables limited liability to be extended to some partners, confined to the amount of their investment in the business, but they have no right to engage in its managerial functions. Limited partnerships are also required to be registered with the Registrars of Companies. As with sole traders, partnerships do not continue in perpetuity. When key partners die or retire, the partnership comes to an end.

The most common form of private business organization in Britain is the registered company. There were about 970,000 of these in 1989. It is the Companies Acts which provide the basic legal regulation of these enterprises. These Acts enable the legal incorporation of private businesses by creating a legal entity, or corporate body, which is separate and distinct from the personality and existence of any individual who is a member of the organization. As Thomason (1975) says it is 'this legal fictional body which employs people, or which holds and owns property or enters into commercial contracts'.[15] The Companies Acts lay down rules for the constitution, management and dissolution of such organizations, though they leave their internal management largely to a company's directors, subject to specific safeguards for their shareholders. The Registrars of Companies for England and Wales and for Scotland issue certificates of incorporation and changes of name. They are also responsible for company registrations and for the safe custody of documents required by statute.

There are two main types of company as shown in Table 10, the private limited company and the public limited company. Private companies are far more common than public companies but their financial capital per enterprise is much smaller. Both private and public companies provide limited liability for their shareholders. This means, like the limited partnership, that if the company is wound up, the liability of individual shareholders is limited to the amount of their original shareholding. Normally shareholders receive an annual share of corporate profit which is called a dividend.

Table 10
Number of companies on British registers 1983–89

	1983	1984	1985	1986 (000's)	1987	1988	1989
Public companies	3.4	3.7	4.3	5.1	5.2	6.6	9.8
Private companies	852.4	891.3	863.8	848.8	868.0	910.8	968.0
All companies	855.8	895.0	868.1	853.9	873.2	917.4	977.8

Source: DEPARTMENT OF TRADE, *Companies in 1988–89*, HMSO 1989

A private company is formed when a number of documents are approved by the appropriate Registrar of Companies. These are: the memorandum of association stating the company's name, objectives and share structure; the articles of association setting out the internal rules of the company; and a declaration that the company is complying with the Companies Acts. It is also necessary to provide a written statement showing the nominal share capital of the company and the ways in which its shares are organized. A private company must have at least two shareholders with a maximum of 50 and is precluded from issuing shares to the general public. Restrictions are also placed on the rights of individuals to transfer their shares.

A public limited company (PLC) is one which does not restrict its share transactions or its number of shareholders, though it must have a minimum of seven. The shares of PLCs are bought and sold on the open market through the Stock Exchange. A PLC must have more than one director and before such an enterprise is formed, it is required to issue a prospectus stating its proposed directors and the details of its financial structure. As can be seen from Table 10, the number of PLCs in Britain increased from some 3,500 in 1983 to almost 10,000 by 1989. This reflects the increased significance of business growth in the large corporate sector recently. Further, (see Table 11) the largest PLCs in Britain are highly capitalized organizations, with equity valued in millions of pounds. They are very powerful enterprises, employing millions of people and commanding vast capital resources.

Since the end of the second world war, an important feature

Table 11
Ten highest equity PLCs 1989

Company	Market capitalization 1 July 1989 £ million
British Petroleum	17,291
British Telecommunications	15,207
Glaxo Holdings	10,164
British American Tobacco Industries	9,963
Imperial Chemical Industries	8,648
Hanson	8,370
British Gas	8,264
BTR	6,756
General Electric	6,756
Cable and Wireless	5,243

Source: ALLEN M (ed), *The Times 1000 1989–90*, Times Books 1989

of the large corporate sector has been the concentration of manufacturing output in a small number of very large enterprises. The increasing share of output accounted for by the largest 100 manufacturing enterprises in Britain is paralleled by the growing proportion of the labour force employed by them. This appears to be more pronounced in Britain than in most other industrial countries, including those of the EC. According to a Department of Trade report (1977), known as the Bullock Committee of Inquiry on Industrial Democracy, figures for the share of total output and of total employment accounted for by enterprises with over 1,000 employees were consistently higher for Britain than those for other EC countries, for the United States and for Sweden.[16]

An examination of the pattern of share ownership of quoted ordinary shares in British PLCs shows that the shares owned by individuals, executors and trustees resident in Britain accounted for only 28 per cent of the total in 1981, compared with 42 per cent in 1973 and 59 per cent in 1963. The shares owned by British financial institutions, such as insurance companies, pension funds, banks, and other investment trusts and so on, rose from 28 per cent in 1963, to 42 per cent in 1973 and to 58 per cent in 1981. Charities, non-financial companies, the public sector and overseas shareholders comprised the rest or about 15 per cent of the total.[17] Since the 1950s, the larger quoted British PLCs in manufacturing, distribution and other services have increasingly depended on internal sources for funding, that is, from retained profits and provisions for depreciation. The next most important source of funds has been the banks and other borrowing. The importance of new share issues appears to have been relatively modest.

In Britain, of the 4,000 or so enterprises employing 200 or more people in the late 1980s, it is estimated that one in six of them were controlled from overseas. These multinational corporations (MNCs) consist of affiliated firms based in several countries. Typically, they are linked by ties of common ownership; draw on a common pool of resources, such as financial capital, information and trade names; and respond to a common business strategy. Such firms account for a substantial proportion of world trade, much of it taking place by internal transfers between trading subsidiaries of the same organizations. MNCs are found especially in manufacturing, oil, banking, mining and pharmaceuticals. About 70 per cent of the MNCs sited in Britain are overseas subsidiaries of United States enterprises, with another 10 per cent controlled by enterprises incorporated in member states of the EC. Clearly, MNCs are very powerful enterprises. They control very large financial and capital resources. They employ significant numbers of people. And they command critical power in consumer markets.[18]

Public corporations

Public corporations are defined as 'public trading bodies which have a substantial degree of financial independence of the public authority which created them'.[19] They are commonly assumed to be identical with the nationalized industries. But this is not strictly accurate. All the nationalized industries are public corporations, but not all public corporations, such as the Bank of England, the British Broadcasting Corporation, or the Independent Broadcasting Authority for example, are nationalized industries (see Table 12). Although the majority of public corporations are treated in an identical way in public expenditure white papers to the nationalized industries, they are not normally revenue earning bodies. Further, some public corporations such as the Commonwealth Development Corporation are closely integrated into

Table 12

Main public corporations other than the nationalized industries 1990

Corporation	Vesting year
Audit Commission	1983
Bank of England[1]	1946
British Broadcasting Corporation	1927
Commonwealth Development Corporation	1948
Covent Garden Market Authority	1961
Crown Suppliers[1]	1976
Development Board for Rural Wales[1]	1977
English Industrial Estates Corporation	1986
General Practice Finance Corporation	1966
Highlands and Islands Development Board	1965
Independent Broadcasting Authority[1]	1972
Land Authority for Wales	1976
Local Authority Airport Companies	1987
Local Authority Bus Companies	1986
New Town Development Corporations[2]	1946
Northern Ireland Housing Executive[1]	1971
Northern Ireland Transport[1]	1968
Oil and Pipeline Agency	1985
Passenger Transport Executives	1975
Pilotage Commission	1979
Royal Mint	1975
Scottish Development Agency	1975
Scottish Special Housing Association	1937
Trust Ports (Northern Ireland)	1974
UK Atomic Energy Authority	1986
Urban Development Corporations	1981
Welsh Development Agency	1976
Welsh Four Channel Authority	1981

[1] succeeded an existing corporation
[2] these are being dissolved and their assets transferred to the Commission for New Towns
Source: CENTRAL STATISTICAL OFFICE, *Economic trends*

government department spending programmes for expenditure purposes.

Many British nationalized industries were formed between 1946 and 1950. These included those in airways, coal, electricity, gas, railways and transport. The iron and steel industry was also nationalized at that time, was denationalized in 1953 but was taken back into public ownership in 1967. Further nationalization took place during the 1970s when, in response to Britain's continued industrial decline, another group of organizations came into public ownership during the Wilson and Callaghan Labour Governments. These included British Aerospace, British Leyland, British Ship-builders, the British National Oil Corporation and Rolls Royce. In general Labour governments have tended to favour nationaliz-ation, Conservative governments to oppose it. During the first Thatcher administration from 1979 till 1983, for example, a number of nationalized corporations were 'privatized' by being returned, partly or wholly, into private ownership. These included: Amersham International; Associated British Ports; British Aero-space; British Rail Hotels; Cable and Wireless; and the National Freight Corporation.

Table 13
The nationalized industries 1989: capital and employees

Industry	Capital employed £000's	Employees No.
British Coal Corporation	3,814,000	135,900
British Railways Board	1,906,900	154,748
British Shipbuilders	41,847	8,642
British Waterways Board[1]	24,742	3,200
Electricity Council[2]	16,271,500	131,398
North of Scotland Hydro-electric Board[2]	615,655	3,835
Post Office	2,257,300	198,217
Scottish Transport Group	167,335	10,253
South of Scotland Electricity Board[2]	2,534,544	11,879

[1] 1985 figures   [2] subsequently privatized
Source: ALLEN M (ed), *The Times 1000 1989–90*, Times Books 1989

Table 13 shows Britain's nationalized industries in 1989, together with their capital employed and number of employees. They occupy a strategic position in the national economy and they provide a variety of essential goods and services to the public.

It was the intention of the Thatcher Government, reelected in 1983 and 1987, to denationalize a number of key public corpor-ations and return them to private shareholders. These included: British Telecom, British Airways, Rolls Royce, as many as possible of Britain's airports, 'and substantial parts of British Steel, of British Shipbuilders and of British Leyland'.[20] The Government also aimed to introduce substantial private capital into the National Bus Company and to privatize the British Gas Corporation. By 1990, only a handful of nationalized industries remained. In addition to the above enterprises, the following had been privatized: Enterprise Oil (1984); the regional water authorities (1990); and the Central Electricity Generating Board and Area Electricity Authorities (1990).

Public corporations have five main features. First, their assets are publicly owned, they are managed by government appointed executives and they are monitored by government departments. Secondly, they are not subject to company law but have a separate legal status enabling them to sue, to be sued, to enter into contracts and to acquire property in their own name. Thirdly, they are independently financed, sometimes obtaining their current revenue from the sale of their goods or services, with most of their capital expenditure being raised by borrowing either from the Treasury or from the public. Fourthly, they are exempt from the normal parliamentary financial control exercised over government departments. Fifthly, their boards are usually appointed by a secretary of state and their employees are not civil servants.

The independent legal status of public corporations was originally designed to give them some degree of commercial flexibility which is not possible in government departments. In practice, however, governmental control over the activities of public corporations is ultimately ensured by the statutory powers conferred on their responsible ministers. Ministers appoint their boards, for example, and determine their terms of appointment. Ministerial approval is also required for capital investment plans. It is ministers, too, who have the authority to sanction the raising of financial capital from external sources. Most important of all, ministers are empowered, after appropriate consultations with their boards, to direct them in ways considered to be necessary in the public interest. In short, government uses the public corporations, but especially the nationalized industries, 'to achieve their overall economic objectives and thus determine their industries' pricing and investment policies on much wider criteria than those which may be wanted by the boards for commercial reasons'.[21]

The public services

There are three major public services in Britain; the civil service; the National Health Service; and the local authority services, including the police services. They employ in total some six million people, or about 23 per cent of the British labour force, and provide the general public with a wide range of services which, while funded collectively through national insurance, taxation and local rates, are often consumed personally by individual citizens. The services provided include: central government administration; national defence; agencies of law enforcement; health care; recreational facilities; consumer protection; education; fire protection; environmental health services such as refuse collection; street cleaning and refuse disposal; personal social services; and public transport and highways.

The civil service is the administrative arm of central government and consists of over 20 government departments and a number of departmental and non-departmental agencies (NDAs).[22] Departmental agencies, such as the Boards of Inland Revenue and Customs and Excise within the Treasury, are units administering bodies of self contained work and enjoying a degree of autonomy within their departments. NDAs, such as the Advisory Conciliation and Arbitration Service, the Equal Opportunities Commission and the former Manpower Services Commission, are outside the traditional departmental framework of the civil service. Their work is normally regarded as unsuitable for the typical government department. They too have a degree of autonomy and independence from governmental control and some insulation from parliamentary scrutiny. In 1989 there were 395 executive, 969 advisory, 64 tribunal and 127 other such bodies.

Each government department is headed by a minister. The most important departments, such as Defence, Employment and Education and Science, have ministers of cabinet rank, called secretaries of state. In turn, each departmental minister is assisted by second rank or junior ministers of state and by third rank parliamentary secretaries, who collectively form a ministerial team. Each major civil service department is a hierarchy where work is allocated to smaller units or divisions, subdivided into branches. Divisions are normally headed by an under secretary, with branches being the responsibility of an assistant secretary. Some divisions

Personnel in Context

and branches have line functions concerned with the major work of their departments. Others have staff functions concentrating on managerial matters such as finance and personnel. Although most of the major ministries are located in London, 75 per cent of all civil servants work outside the Greater London area.

The National Health Service (NHS) was created by the National Health Service Act 1946. It is based on the principle that medical care and comprehensive health services should be readily available and supplied, largely free of charge, to anyone normally resident within the UK. Up till 1974, hospitals were administered through the health ministers and regional hospital boards (RHBs); the family doctor and dental services through local executive councils; and all other health services through county and county borough councils. In 1974, the health services in England were unified by the creation of 14 regional health authorities (RHAs), which replaced the RHBs, and 90 area health authorities (AHAs). There were equivalent changes in other parts of Britain. In 1982, the English AHAs were abolished and the 14 RHAs are now complemented by 191 district health authorities locally.

According to the Report of the Royal Commission on the National Health Service (1979), chaired by Alec Merrison, 'politicians and public alike are agreed on the desirability of a national health service in broadly its present form, but agreement often stops there'.[23] The Commission identified what it considered the objectives of the NHS to be. These are that the NHS should:

> encourage and assist individuals to remain healthy;
> provide equality of entitlement to health services;
> provide a broad range of services to a high standard;
> provide equality of access to these services;
> provide a service free at the time of use;
> satisfy the reasonable expectations of its users; [and]
> remain a national service responsive to local needs.[24]

The Commission conceded that these objectives sometimes conflict. Also, because each objective is costly to pursue and resources are limited, the NHS continually faces the problem of choice amongst its objectives, and between different ways of achieving them.

In addition to doctors and dentists, the NHS employs a wide range of other personnel. These include: 485,000 nurses and orderlies; 175,000 ancillary staff such as porters, domestics, gardeners and cooks; 132,000 administrative and clerical staff; 58,000 professional and technical workers such as hospital pharmacists, hospital opticians and laboratory technicians; and 22,000 ambulance personnel. The costs of employing staff and other current expenditure are almost totally borne by the Exchequer. Each financial year, about 86 per cent of NHS current expenditure is provided through general taxation, some 11 per cent through national insurance contributions and about three per cent from prescriptions and other charges. Only some six per cent of NHS spending is capital expenditure.

Figure 4
Local government structure in England and Wales 1990

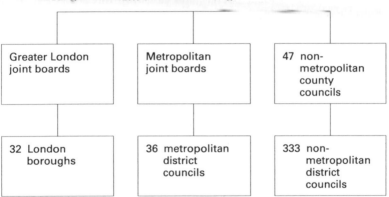

In 1989, the government published a white paper proposing radical reforms of the NHS. The proposed reforms were aimed at enabling a higher quality of patient care to be obtained from the resources which the nation provides for the NHS. In presenting its plans, the government claimed that it wished to give patients better health care and greater choice of the services available. The proposals included: delegating as much decision making as possible to where patient care is delivered; giving hospitals self-governing status to manage their own budgets and determine patient care policies; and introducing an internal market encouraging hospitals to compete for patients. General practitioners would be encouraged to manage their own budgets and provide better patient care at lower costs. The general thrust of the white paper was to promote greater economic efficiency and effectiveness in health care provision by using internal market mechanisms and private sector business methods. These initiatives reflected similar changes in other parts of the public sector which emphasized market values rather than welfare ones.

In seeking the more efficient managing of NHS resources, the government wanted better use made of staff, better management information systems and greater involvement of doctors and nurses in managing the services. The government also sought greater pay flexibility to allow managers to relate pay rates to local markets and to reward individual performance. This, combined with local conditions of service arrangements, would enable managers to devise employment packages locally and which would be best suited to local needs, thus assisting the achievement of better value for money in the service.

In 1990, there were 448 local authorities in England and Wales and 65 in Scotland. These consisted of 47 top tier or county authorities in England and Wales and 401 lower tier district or borough authorities (see Figure 4). During 1986, the Thatcher Government abolished the Labour controlled Greater London Council (GLC) and the six Metropolitan county councils of Greater Manchester, Merseyside, South Yorkshire, Tyne and Wear, West Midlands, and West Yorkshire. In Scotland, there are nine top tier authorities or regional councils and the three all purpose island councils of Orkney, Shetland and the Western Isles. The nine regions, in turn, are divided into 53 lower tier district councils. Councils in Britain consist of elected councillors working in cooperation with the professional officers employed by the authorities. Their joint task is to ensure the efficient and effective provision of the wide range of services, laid down by law, which the authorities are required to provide.

Those local authority services which are planned over a wide area are generally the responsibility of county authorities. These include consumer protection, fire services, highways and traffic, and strategic planning. In the metropolitan areas some of these services are run by joint boards. These comprise representatives from district councils now that the GLC and the other metropolitan counties have been abolished. Services requiring the economic use of highly specialized staff, such as education, libraries and personal social services, are provided by either the shire county councils or metropolitan district councils. Essentially local services, including cemeteries, development control, environmental health and housing, are usually allocated to district authorities. Other local government services, such as art galleries, museums and provision for physical recreation, are provided through either district councils or county authorities. In these cases, the authorities decide the allocation of services between themselves.

Local government expenditure accounts for about 25 per cent of public expenditure. It consists of both capital spending and recurrent items. Central government has always sought to influence the level of spending through controls over borrowing, grants and by persuasion. The Local Government Finance Act 1988 changes the way in which local authorities obtain their revenue. First, the domestic rating system was abolished and the community charge was introduced to England and Wales, though it was imposed in Scotland in 1987. Second, the business rate became a nationally determined tax distributed to local authorities on a *per capita* basis. Third, the block grant, introduced in 1981, was replaced by a new revenue support grant based on the central government's standard rate of expenditure. Although the local authorities can still determine their own level of expenditure, there are limits on their capital expenditure and central government has the power to cap the community charge. Seventy-five per cent of local authority revenue comes from central government sources.

The increased control of local government finance was accompanied by further political centralization during the 1980s. Some 70 pieces of legislation altered the powers which local authorities could exercise and many *ad hoc* bodies were created to by-pass local councils such as housing trusts and development corporations. Though local government is still important in meeting the needs of the community, its role is becoming increasingly that of enabling a mixture of private, voluntary and public provision of services locally. This will inevitably affect its organization and management, and its relationship with central government and the private sector.

Structuring organizations

According to Drucker (1974) organizational 'structure is a means for attaining the objectives and goals of an institution'.[25] It is the means for allocating work responsibilities, providing a framework for operations and performance assessment, and providing mechanisms for processing information and assisting decision making within organizations. Child (1977) goes further by setting out the essential components of organizational structure as follows:

(1) The allocation of tasks and responsibilities to individuals, including discretion over the use of resources and methods of working. Structural features concerned here are the degree of job specialization and definition.
(2) The designation of formal reporting relationships, determining the number of levels in hierarchies and the spans of control of managers and supervisors.
(3) The grouping together of individuals in sections or departments, the grouping of departments into divisions and larger units, and the overall grouping of units into the total organization.
(4) The delegation of authority together with associated procedures whereby the use of discretion is monitored and evaluated.
(5) The design of systems to ensure effective communication of information, integration of effort, and participation in the decision-making process.
(6) The provision of systems for performance appraisal and reward which help to motivate rather than alienate employees.[26]

Deficiencies in any aspects of organizational structure can lead to serious organizational consequences including low morale, poor decision making, intraorganizational conflict and rising costs.

The classical approach to structuring organizations is to create bureaucracies. Bureaucracy is characterized by a high degree of specialization amongst jobs and departments, by formal procedures and paperwork, and by extended managerial hierarchies with marked status distinctions. Official business is conducted in accordance with stipulated rules characterized by three main features. First, the duty of each official is defined in terms of impersonal criteria. Secondly, officials are given the authority necessary to carry out their assigned functions. Thirdly, the means of compulsion at their disposal are strictly limited and the conditions under which their use is legitimate are clearly defined. Higher office holders have the duty of supervision, while lower office holders are expected to comply with the instructions of their superiors. Official business is normally conducted on the basis of written documents. Bureaucratic organizational structures, which continue to be very common in both private and public industry today, aim to achieve organizational control by ensuring a high level of predictability in people's behaviour at work.

Though bureaucracies continue to be commonplace, a wide variety of organizational structures is used depending upon the various internal and external pressures acting on a particular

Figure 5
The major factors influencing organization design and performance

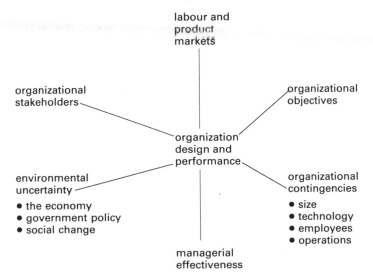

enterprise. These are highlighted in Figure 5. The environmental uncertainty facing organizational decision makers is of crucial influence. Turbulent markets and rapid change within markets are characteristic of organizational and business activity in the modern economy. Obviously, the degree of environmental uncertainty varies amongst organizations. Some governmental agencies and monopolistic firms change only slowly and are structurally little different from what they were in the past. But for many organizations, cost of living adjustments, devaluations, political fluidity and inflation are at the root of uncertainty and change. Such environmental instability also affects employee attitudes within organizations. Generally, employees tend to be less deferential than in the past, have higher expectations in their work and want more say in organizational decision making.

The multiplicity of factors influencing organization design and performance has led some organizational theorists to stress the importance of the 'structural contingencies' of organization. Hunt (1981), for example, defines contingency theory as 'attempts to understand the multivariate relationships between the components of organizations and to designing structures piece-by-piece, as best fits the components'.[27] Choosing a design for the whole organization is seen by contingency theorists to be too restrictive. Organizational subunits may be shaped from a design continuum, they argue, depending on the circumstances. 'Single design types, neatness, symmetry, and permanence are not indicative of "good" design'.[28] Some of the contingencies acting on job design and enterprise structure include: corporate objectives; type of environment; diversity of operations; size of units; technology; and the employees involved. Too much can be expected of structure alone, however, since 'even a well-conceived organizational design cannot be expected to cope with problems such as deep-seated conflicts'.[29]

In outline, managers have four sets of decisions to make when designing or modifying organizational structures: how to structure individual jobs; how to distribute jobs vertically; how to group activities horizontally; and how to facilitate coordination, integration and control within their organizations. In shaping the jobs which individuals do, for example, managers need to decide how specialized a job should be and how much discretion a job holder should have in doing it. Recently, attempts have been made to humanize certain jobs and organizational structures. In other instances, especially among professional workers, the highly formal approach to job definition has long ceased to be appropriate. In deciding how to distribute jobs vertically, managers face the dilemma of balancing the number of hierarchical levels within an organization with the spans of control required by managerial staff. 'Tall' organizations bring considerable disadvantages, eg communication failure and low motivation among subordinate employees. 'Flat' organizations, on the other hand, widen the spans of managerial control. Managers need to achieve a balance, especially in large organizations, between an appropriate organizational height and a relevant span of control.[30]

The activities of people within organizations can be grouped horizontally in a number of ways. The main forms of horizontal differentiation within organizations are: functional structures; product structures; divisional structures; and mixed structures. Functional groupings, for example, put work activities into separate departments. They provide specialist contributions to the common product or service and its customers. The functional model is particularly appropriate where an organization provides a single range of products or services in a domestic market. An example of a functional structure is shown in Figure 6. Under such groupings, a high degree of centralized decision making takes place. The major structural question is whether a 'line' and 'staff' structure, or a 'functional' authority one, is more appropriate. Line functions are those which seek to achieve the objectives of an organization, while staff functions support them. It has to be determined, for example, whether the head of personnel can tell the head of production what to do on personnel matters (functional authority) or whether s/he can only advise (line and staff authority).

Difficulties arise with functional structures when an organization begins to diversify its products, markets or services. In this case, a product structure is more appropriate, since it brings people together who are contributing to a common product or service. An example of a product based structure is shown in Figure 7. While functional structures are primarily hierarchical, a product structure is primarily technological, suggesting a flow of work horizontally across functional areas. As Child points out, in stable conditions functional structures may be advantageous. But 'in conditions demanding some change and active problem solving, a product form [of organization] may prove superior because it encourages more intensive communication, confrontation of issues and integration of effort'.[31]

Where highly centralized structures are ineffective, divisional structures are more appropriate. These were first developed in the United States and subsequently spread to Europe and Britain. Divisional structures reduce large organizational size to manageable terms. In the private sector, for example, divisional structures have two main characteristics, as indicated in Figure 8. First, the corporate head office is mainly concerned with strategic planning,

Figure 6
Functional organizational structure

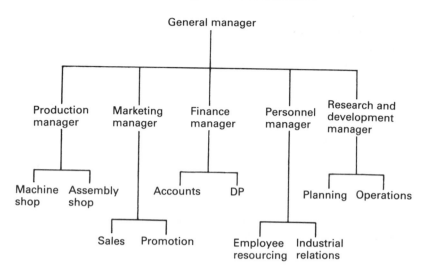

Figure 7
Product organizational structure

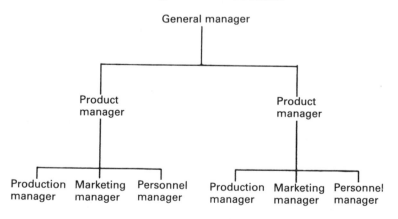

Figure 8
Divisional organizational structure

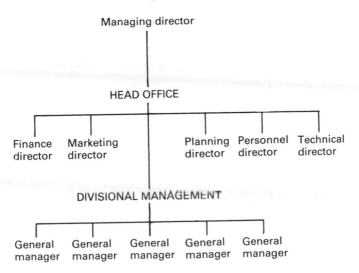

overall financial control and policy appraisal. Secondly, profit responsibility is assigned to general managers at divisional level which are essentially self contained business units. Divisions can be either geographically or product based. Where a divisional structure is adopted, however, the problem of how best to group activities within divisions still arises. This in turn can be done on a functional basis, a product basis or some mixture of the two.

Mixed structures are of two main types: project team structures and grid structures. According to Hunt, 'the common characteristic of mixed structures is a lateral grid which is superimposed on the vertical hierarchy'.[32] The main difference between a project team and a grid structure is the time period which, in a project team, is limited. Grid structures, by contrast, tend to be more permanent and they are generally applied to the whole of an organization. The principles of a mixed structure are indicated in Figure 9. The solid vertical lines illustrate the line accountability of individuals, while the dotted lines show their project team accountabilities. In such cases, groups of functional specialists are allocated to project teams, under the direction of project managers.

Figure 9
Mixed organizational structure

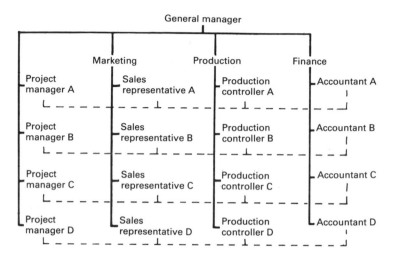

Coordination and integration become major problems facing managers as a corporate team when organizations grow and are divided into subunits. Poor coordination is commonly found in manufacturing industry, for example, between marketing and production and between production and personnel. Appropriate structural devices such as team building have been devised to promote better organizational integration. The main organization design decisions affecting managerial control are, as Child indicates, 'first, how far to delegate decision-making, second, how much to formalize procedures and working practices and third, how much emphasis to place on direct supervision'. Rather than control being directed vertically downwards through organizations, there is now wider recognition that employees should be encouraged to achieve self control 'on the basis of agreements with management to meet certain objectives or performance standards'.[33]

Conflict in organizations

There are two main theories analysing the nature of conflict in organizations. One, the traditional view, argues that there are no basic conflicts within enterprises but only frictional and limited ones which are purely temporary in nature. Any fundamental conflicts which emerge, such as between managers and subordinates or between employers and unions for example, are seen to be aberrant and deviant conditions. The second view is that organizations are no different from other social institutions, such as the family, the churches, party politics and international relations. In all these cases, it is argued, differences of interest inevitably arise between individuals and groups which need to be, first, recognized and, secondly, managed in order to maintain some degree of internal consensus and social stability. Coser (1965) goes further by suggesting that 'conflict may serve to remove dissociating elements in a relationship and to re-establish unity'. He also argues that conflict 'has stabilizing functions and becomes an integrating component of the relationship'.[34]

In an organizational context, Reddish (1966) stresses the first viewpoint and Dahrendorf (1959) the second. In his evidence to the Royal Commission on trade unions and employers' associations, for example, Reddish writes:

> We reject the idea that amongst the employees of a company there are 'two sides' meaning the executive directors and managers on the one hand and the weekly-paid employees on the other. Executive directors are just as much employees of the company as anyone else. We are all in the same side, members of the same team.[35]

For Dahrendorf, managers have both the right to manage and the duty to do so. This requires them to make decisions as to who does what, when and how in enterprises, with subordinates being expected to accept managerial decisions if organizational objectives are to be achieved. In his view, irrespective of the particular persons in positions of authority, 'industrial enterprises remain imperatively coordinated associations the structures of which generate quasi-groups and conflicting latent interests'.[36]

Fox (1966) describes the first view as a unitary frame of reference and the second as a pluralistic one, though in his later writings (1971, 1973 and 1974), he appears to use the terms 'perspective', 'view', 'approach' and 'ideology' interchangeably.[37] For Fox an industrial enterprise as a unitary system has a number of features. Management is its sole source of authority and its one focus of loyalty, with everyone striving towards a set of common corporate objectives. Management's right to manage goes unchallenged and there are no oppositionary groups or factions threatening or disturbing managerial rule. This model of organization, he says, is closest to that of a professional football team where 'team spirit and undivided management authority coexist to the benefit of all'.[38]

The unitary frame of reference clearly denies the validity of conflict in organizations whether between managers and subordinates or between others. For individuals holding this perspective any conflict which emerges within enterprises is:

> either (a) merely frictional, e.g. due to incompatible personalities or 'things going wrong', or (b) caused by faulty 'communications', e.g. 'misunderstandings' about aims or methods, or (c) the result of stupidity in the form of failure to grasp the communality of interest, or (d) the work of agitators inciting the supine majority who would otherwise be content.[39]

Conflict within organizations, in short, is viewed as being disruptive of internal harmony and is seen to result from the antisocial behaviour of disloyal elements.

Those holding the pluralist viewpoint, in contrast, accept the existence of rival sources of leadership and authority within organizations including work groups, trade union leaders and other internal and external influences. They also accept that the degree of common purpose and internal consensus existing within enterprises is of a very limited nature. In the sense that organizational subgroups are mutually dependent and interdependent on one another, there is a narrow common interest in the long term survival of the whole of which they are a part. But this has little impact on the day to day conduct of organizational participants and enterprise relationships. Further, it 'cannot provide that harmony of operational objectives and methods for which managers naturally yearn'. The implication for management, says Fox, is that it must 'face the fact that there are other sources of leadership, other focuses of loyalty, within the social system it governs, and it is with these that management must share its decision-making'.[40] Conflict, in other words, is seen to be endemic within organizations and has to be recognized and managed by those in authority and holding organizational power.

Margerison (1969) provides a useful behavioural model for analysing the different types of conflict which manifest themselves in enterprises.[41] He distinguishes between distributive, structural and human relations conflict and identifies the main means by which each might be resolved.

Figure 10
Conflict and conflict resolution within organizations

	Type of conflict		
	distributive	structural	human relations
Manifestation of conflict	strikes and restrictive practices	demarcation disputes and challenges to managerial authority	interpersonal conflict and individual alienation
Method of conflict resolution	collective bargaining	structural analysis of sociotechnical system	man management analysis and development of individual attitudes

Source: MARGERISON C J, 'What do we mean by industrial relations? A behavioural approach', *British journal of industrial relations*, July 1969

Distributive conflict, for example, arises out of the competition which takes place for organizational resources, especially between management as custodians of owner interests and employees as wage and salary earners. But it also occurs between different managerial groups, particularly when internal resource allocation is being determined. Structural or social conflict, normally between management and work groups, but also between different work groups, emerges out of the complex organizational, technological and authority relationships existing within modern industrial enterprises. Human relations conflict can be either interpersonal or created by the boring and monotonous working conditions experienced by some subordinate employees. Figure 10 above shows that different methods for resolving industrial conflict are necessary, depending upon whether it is distributive, structural or human relations in nature.

Conclusion

Organizations of various kinds pervade modern society. They vary widely in their forms of ownership, structure, size and orientation, though there is a tendency towards the growth in numbers of large bureaucratic enterprises, on multiple sites. Managing them is a formidable task, particularly coordinating and integrating their myriad activities and functions. It is management's task to determine their objectives, to plan how to achieve them and to provide appropriate policies and guidelines for those supervising their day to day activities. It is management's task, too, to identify and manage the various conflicts which emerge within industrial capitalist enterprises, if organizational efficiency and effectiveness are to be achieved. It is here that the skills, knowledge and training of personnel specialists have a vital contribution to make.

References and footnotes

1   SILVERMAN D. *The Theory of Organizations*. (London, Heinemann, 1970). p14.
2   *ibid*. pp15–23.
3   ELDRIDGE J E T *and* CROMBIE A D. *A Sociology of Organizations*. (London, Allen and Unwin, 1974). pp37–56.
4   BLAU P *and* SCOTT W R. *Formal Organizations*. (London, Routledge and Kegan Paul, 1963); TRIST E L *and others*. *Organizational Choice*. (London, Tavistock, 1963); and KATZ D *and* KAHN R L. *The Social Psychology of Organizations*. (NY, Wiley, 1966).
5   BLAUNER R. *Alienation and Freedom*. (Chicago, Chicago University Press, 1964); WOODWARD J *Industrial Organization: Theory and Practice*. (London, OUP, 1965) and (ed). *Industrial Organization: Behaviour and Control*. (London, OUP, 1970); and THOMPSON J D. *Organizations in Action*. (NY, McGraw-Hill, 1967).
6   ETZIONI A. *A Comparative Analysis of Complex Organizations*. (NY, Free Press, 1961).
7   ACKOFF R. *A Concept of Corporate Planning*. (NY, Wiley, 1970);

and VICKERS G. *Freedom in a Rocking Boat*. (Harmondsworth, Allen Lane, 1970).

8   GOFFMAN E. *Asylums*. (Harmondsworth, Penguin, 1968).

9   THOMASON G. *A Textbook of Personnel Management*. 4th ed. (London, IPM, 1981). p9.

10   In this chapter, discussion is focused on private businesses, public corporations and the public services. Little comment is made on voluntary bodies as an organizational type, since they are such a small part of the organizational sector.

11   O'SHAUGHNESSY J. *Business Organization*. (London, Allen and Unwin, 1968), p24.

12   HARVEY-JONES J. quoted in *The Guardian*, 22 April 1983. p20.

13   Some organizations, for example, provide sabbatical leave for a small number of senior managers to enable them to work on externally directed community projects and similar activities.

14   DRUCKER P F. *Managing for Results*. (London, Pan, 1964). p18.

15   THOMASON G. *A Textbook of Personnel Management*, 1st ed. (London, IPM, 1975). p87.

16   DEPARTMENT OF TRADE. *Report of the Committee of Inquiry on Industrial Democracy*. (Chairman, Lord Bullock). (London, HMSO, 1977). p8.

17   *ibid* and STOCK EXCHANGE. *The Stock Exchange Survey of Share Ownership*. (London, 1982).

18   See, for example, DEPARTMENT OF TRADE. *opcit*. pp5 and 7.

19   BUTLER D *and* SLOMAN A. *British Political Facts 1900–1979*. 5th ed. (London, Macmillan, 1980). p363.

20   CONSERVATIVE PARTY. *The Conservative Manifesto 1983*. (London, Conservative Central Office, 1983). p16.

21   FARNHAM D *and* McVICAR M. *Public Administration in the United Kingdom*. (London, Cassell, 1982). p255.

22   The main government departments are: Agriculture, Fisheries and Food; Cabinet Office; Central Office of Information; Lord Chancellor's Department; Defence; Education and Science; Employment; Energy; Environment; Foreign and Commonwealth Office; Home Office; Health and Social Security; National Savings; Northern Ireland Office; Scottish Office; Trade and Industry; Transport; Treasury; and Welsh Office.

23   ROYAL COMMISSION ON THE NATIONAL HEALTH SERVICE. (Chairman, Sir Alec Merrison). *Report*. (London, HMSO, 1979). p9.

24   *ibid*.

25   DRUCKER P F. 'New templates for today's organizations'. *Harvard Business Review*. January–February, 1974. p52.

26   CHILD J. *Organization: a Guide to Problems and Practice*. (London, Harper and Row, 1977). p10.

27   HUNT J. *Managing People at Work*. (London, Pan, 1981). p189.

28   *ibid*.

29   CHILD. *opcit*. p23.

30 This issue is further explored in chapter 3 below.

31 CHILD. *opcit.* p80.

32 HUNT. *opcit.* p209.

33 CHILD. *opcit.* p135.

34 COSER L A. *The Functions of Social Conflict.* 2nd impression. (London, Routledge and Kegan Paul, 1965). p80.

35 REDDISH H. 'Written memorandum of evidence to the Royal Commission on trade unions and employers' associations' in BARRETT B *and others. Industrial Relations and the Wider Society.* (London, Collier Macmillan, 1975). p299.

36 DAHRENDORF R. *Class and Class Conflict in Industrial Society.* (London, Routledge and Kegan Paul, 1959). p259.

37 See FOX A. *A Sociology of Work in Industry.* (London, Collier Macmillan, 1971); 'Industrial relations: a social critique of pluralist ideology' in CHILD J (ed). *Man and Organization.* (London, Allen and Unwin, 1973); and *Man Mismanagement.* (London, Hutchinson, 1974).

38 FOX A. *Royal Commission on Trade Unions and Employers' Associations Research Papers: 3 Industrial Sociology and Industrial Relations.* (London, HMSO, 1966). p3.

39 *ibid.* p12.

40 *ibid.* p8.

41 MARGERISON C J. 'What do we mean by industrial relations? A behavioural approach'. *British Journal of Industrial Relations.* Vol VII, No 2, July 1969.

3

The managerial context

In Britain and the United States, there is no agreed definition of 'management'. As Hunt (1981) says, 'one of the problems of theories of management has been confusion over the term *management*'.[1] Harbison and Myers (1959), for example, define management as 'the hierarchy of individuals who perform specified critical functions in an organization. Management thus connotes both people and tasks'.[2] They present a threefold concept of its development in industrial society: as an economic resource, a system of authority and a social elite. More recently, Mant (1977) provides three meanings of management: the activity of running things; the ideology of management; and the people paid to run things.[3]

The term 'management' is usually used in two main senses. First, it is used as a collective term to describe those people responsible for subordinate employees and other resources within organizations. As the Trades Union Congress (1966) puts it, 'the function of management is to run an enterprise in such a way as to achieve whatever objectives it sets itself'. To do this, management as a group, and individually, have to take a series of day to day decisions, each having repercussions on the various functions of the enterprise.[4] Secondly, the term is also used to describe and analyse the jobs, activities and tasks which managers actually do. For analytical purposes in this chapter, therefore, it is useful to distinguish four aspects of management: what managers do (managerial work); how they do it (the managerial process); and how they are organized within enterprises (management levels and management functions). These concepts focus on management as a series of interrelated activities. Some are individual activities but most are group ones. Few managers work alone, most work in or with groups.

Managerial work

Classical management theorists, such as Fayol (1949), Urwick (1947) and Brech (1975), view managers as rational decision makers whose main activities are planning, organizing, directing, coordinating and controlling organizational resources.[5] Another group of writers see managerial decision making being influenced by a variety of internal and external factors. These include shareholders, employees, consumers, the community and government. Management attempts to balance the conflicting interests of these various stakeholders in the enterprise. As Falk (1963) writes: 'it is virtually impossible to isolate any of these [participants]. Management, if it accepts its twentieth century functions, is caught up in a mesh of widening responsibility'.[6]

Recent studies of the managerial role are more cautious about its so called rational, neutral or mediatory functions. Drucker (1977) argues that there are five basic operations in the manager's work which together 'result in the integration of resources into a viable growing organism'. These are: setting objectives; organizing; motivating and communicating; establishing targets and yardsticks; and developing people, including themselves.[7] More succinctly, Stewart (1979) suggests that the manager's job can be broadly defined 'as "deciding what should be done and then getting other people to do it".' The first task involves setting objectives, planning and creating an organizational structure. The second consists of motivating, controlling and developing people. 'The two tasks are separated for convenient analysis, but in practice they may often overlap'.[8]

A number of studies of managerial work have been undertaken in both the United States and Europe, such as by Carlson (1951), Sayles (1964), Mintzberg (1973 and 1975), and Stewart (1967, 1976 and 1982).[9] Mintzberg, for example, shows how managers perform crucial political and interpersonal roles in organizations. He integrated existing research with his own survey of the activities of five chief executives. His combined study covered all levels of managers including supervisors, sales managers, administrators and senior executive managers. Mintzberg concludes that there is considerable similarity in the behaviour of managers at all levels. They all, he argues, derive their status from the formal authority which they have over organizational resources. This involves them in a set of interpersonal relations with peers, subordinates and superiors which in turn provide them with the information they need to make decisions.

Figure 11
Managerial roles

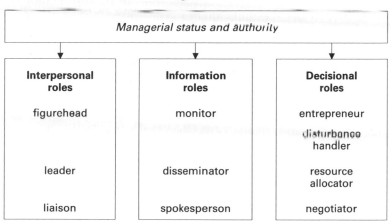

Source: MINTZBERG H, 'The manager's job: folklore and fact', *Harvard Business Review*, July–August 1975

As indicated in Figure 11, these different aspects of a manager's job cause each manager to be involved in a series of 'interpersonal', 'informational' and 'decisional' roles, which Mintzberg defines as 'organized sets of behaviors'. Three interpersonal roles, for example, help managers keep their organizations running smoothly. Though the duties associated with these roles are often routine, managers cannot ignore them. As a figurehead, for example, the manager performs certain ceremonial duties. As a leader, the manager hires, instructs and encourages subordinates. The manager also plays a liaison role by dealing with people other than subordinates or superiors, such as managerial peers, suppliers or clients.

Mintzberg suggests that receiving and communicating information are perhaps the most important aspects of a manager's job. A manager needs information to make balanced decisions and others depend on information provided by managers. There are three informational roles in which managers gather and disseminate information. The first is the monitor role where the manager continually looks for information which can be used to his or her advantage. This usually enables the manager to be the most informed member of his or her group. Secondly, in the disseminator role, the manager distributes information to subordinates which would otherwise be inaccessible to them. Finally, as spokesperson, the manager transmits some of the information he or she has collected to individuals outside the managerial subunit or the organization.

Information is also a basic input to managerial decision making. According to Mintzberg, there are four decisional roles which the manager adopts. In the role of entrepreneur, for example, the manager tries to improve the position of his or her managerial subunit. As an entrepreneur, the manager initiates change. In the role of disturbance handler, the manager responds to situations which are beyond his or her control such as strikes, customer bankruptcy, poor cash flow and so on. As a resource allocator, the manager is responsible for deciding how and to whom the resources of the organization and the manager's own time are to be allocated. Additionally, the manager screens all important decisions made by others in the work subunit, before they are acted upon. The fourth and last decisional role is that of negotiator. Managers spend a lot of their time negotiating, since it is they alone who have the information and authority that organizational negotiators require.

Mintzberg's work is particularly interesting because it highlights the uncertain and turbulent environment in which most managers operate. Events and situations, he stresses, are only partially predictable and the manager often deals with them on an *ad hoc* basis. In his view, managers have neither the time nor the inclination to be reflective thinkers. Above all, they are 'doers' coping with often unexpected challenges and unforeseen circumstances. Thus Mintzberg's analysis of the managerial role offers a useful reminder that managers normally operate in a changing environment and in varying situational contexts.

Mintzberg's American studies are supplemented by those of Stewart in Britain. She provides a typology of managerial jobs, based on the patterns of contact which they require (Stewart 1976). Stewart identifies 12 types of managers' jobs (see Figure 12) divided into four groups and three divisions. The four groups are distinguished by the time spent in contact with other people.

The 'Hub' group which is the most common type of job involves a wide variety of contacts. The 'Peer dependent' group spend most of their time with people at the same level. The 'Man management' group have almost all their contacts with subordinates or bosses. The 'Solo' group have little contact with other people. The three divisions are distinguished according to the importance of internal and external contacts in each job.[10]

Figure 12
Types of managerial jobs

Characteristics	internal contacts	internal/external contacts	external contacts
Hub (H)	HO	H1	H2
Peer dependant (PD)	PDO	PD1	PD2
Man management (MM)	MMO	MM1	MM2
Solo (S)	SO	S1	S2

Source: STEWART R, *Contrasts in Management*, McGraw-Hill 1982

Stewart's second typology of managerial jobs distinguishes them according to the pattern of activities they impose on managers. She calls these 'systems maintenance', 'systems administration', 'project' and 'mixed'. According to Stewart, the first two types of managerial work pattern are found largely in junior and middle management jobs. 'Managers at any level can have jobs with the third type', while the fourth type applies mainly to senior managerial jobs.[11] In summary, what emerges from Stewart's and similar studies is that managerial work 'is one of fragmented activity, incomplete tasks, interruptions, variety and unpredictable events'.[12]

The managerial process

In setting out to develop a 'science of management', Fayol (1949) divided business operations into six activities, all closely dependent on one another. These were: technical; commercial; financial; security; accounting; and managerial. He focused on management which he defined in terms of five elements: planning; organizing; commanding; coordinating; and controlling.[13] Although 'recent studies have suggested that managers do *not* plan, organize, direct and control in the way proposed by traditional theorists',[14] this breakdown of the managerial process into five basic components remains useful for two reasons. First, these activities are common in varying degrees to all managerial roles. Secondly, the classification provides an analytic breakdown of the essential elements in the total managerial process in every organization.

1 Planning

Planning means devising a course of action enabling an organization to meet its stated objectives as determined by management. There are three main categories of managerial planning: corporate, executive and operational. Corporate plans are normally long term and are determined by senior management. In outline, corporate planning involves: finding means to implement corporate objectives; determining policies necessary to achieve specific objectives; and establishing an organizational framework ensuring that managerial policies are carried out. Executive and operational plans, by contrast, provide the details of how corporate plans are to be achieved in practice and are the responsibility of middle and supervisory management. A simplified model of the corporate planning process is provided in Figure 13 on page 67.

Corporate planning has become an important activity for senior managements in recent years, in both private businesses and the public sector. Defining long term corporate objectives in specific terms, and determining the means to achieve them, provides a basic long range framework into which other planning fits. With current external uncertainties, effective corporate planning greatly influences the performance, survival and growth of many enterprises.

There is no general agreement about the essential characteristics of corporate planning, but five basic attributes stand out. First, corporate planning is concerned with asking fundamental questions about the nature of a business or the services provided to customers or clients, such as 'what business are we in and where are we going?'. Secondly, it provides a framework for more detailed planning and day to day managerial decisions. Thirdly, it involves a longer time scale than other planning. Fourthly, it provides a sense of coherence and direction to managerial decisions and actions over time. Fifthly, it is a top level activity demanding firm

Figure 13
The corporate planning process

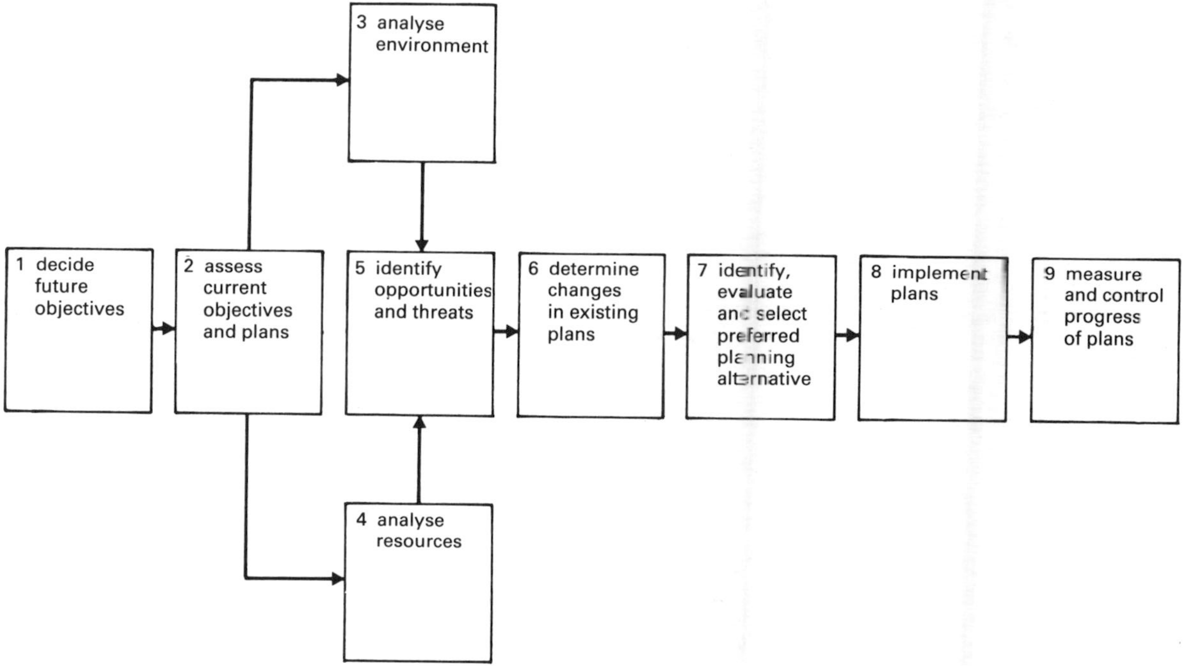

1 decide future objectives

2 assess current objectives and plans

3 analyse environment

4 analyse resources

5 identify opportunities and threats

6 determine changes in existing plans

7 identify, evaluate and select preferred planning alternative

8 implement plans

9 measure and control progress of plans

commitment from senior management in order to generate further commitment by staff at lower organizational levels.

In determining formal corporate plans, senior management undertakes a number of interconnected activities as outlined in Figure 13. First, it decides future corporate objectives as the necessary first step in the total planning process. Secondly, it assesses current objectives and plans. Thirdly, senior management then analyses which aspects of the environment are most likely to have the greatest impact on the enterprise's ability to achieve its future objectives. Fourthly, it analyses enterprise resources in order to identify the competitive advantages and disadvantages of the enterprise. Fifthly, assessing current objectives and plans, analysing the environment and analysing its resources come together in managerial identification of corporate opportunities and threats. Sixthly, it is then possible for senior management to determine any changes required in existing corporate plans, if future objectives are to be achieved.

The seventh, eighth and ninth steps in the corporate planning process are: identifying, evaluating and selecting the best corporate planning alternative; implementing agreed plans; and measuring and controlling their implementation. Once corporate plans have been determined, for example, they have to be incorporated into executive and operational plans. Further, as implementation proceeds through each part of the enterprise, individual managers have to check progress against corporate plans at critical stages. In this way, they can assess whether the enterprise is moving towards its stated corporate objectives.

These basic steps in corporate planning are handled differently in various organizations. Large private businesses and public enterprises, for example, are likely to use professional planning staff to formulate their objectives and plans and to coordinate other planning activities. Small organizations, however, do not normally have specialist corporate planners. Nor do they necessarily formalize the planning process. Nevertheless, most organizations can apply these outline principles with positive benefits.

Executive and operational plans, in turn, derive out of the objectives and corporate plans of senior management. They are of two types: 'single use' and 'standing' plans. Single use plans are detailed courses of action which are not normally repeated, such as the setting up of a new warehouse or the building of a new school. They operate within specific programmes, projects and budgets. Standing plans, on the other hand, are standardized approaches for handling recurrent and predictable situations within organizations. They consist of detailed policies, programmes, procedures and rules.[15]

2 Organizing

Organizing involves mobilizing the material and labour resources of an organization to put managerial plans into effect. Once management has established its corporate objectives, and has developed plans to achieve them, it must design and develop an appropriate organizational framework enabling job holders to carry out their work activities in practice. There are two main elements in the organizing process: structuring the organization, as discussed in the previous chapter,[16] and allocating authority within it.

Power and authority are necessary elements in both organizational and everyday life. Power is the ability of individuals or groups to influence or change the behaviour of others. By contrast authority is legitimate or accepted power, based on the willingness of those without formal power, such as subordinate employees, to accept the decisions of power holders such as managers when required to do so. According to Barnard (1968) individuals accept managerial authority in the following circumstances: when they believe it is not inconsistent with the purpose of an organization; when they believe it to be in their personal interests to do so; and when they understand the communication made to them.[17]

French and Raven (1959) claim that there are five sources or bases of social power: reward power based on one person being able to reward another; coercive power based on one person being able to punish another; legitimate power or authority based on subordinates accepting the power of superiors or those in command positions; expert power based on a belief that one person has specialist knowledge that the other does not have; and referent power based on one person wishing to identify with or imitate another.[18] Each of these power bases is inherent in managerial roles and positions. In exercising their power both individually and collectively, managers can adopt either an authoritarian or a more participative style. In the first case managers make decisions unilaterally. In the second case they apply a more consultative and integrative approach. Which style is used depends on personal, group, organizational and power factors in each case.

It is largely through the line and staff structure that formal managerial authority is exercised. Line authority is the standard chain of command which extends down the various levels in the managerial hierarchy to the point where day to day activities and tasks are carried out by non-managerial employees. It is that part of the organization directly responsible for achieving corporate managerial objectives.

Staff authority relates to individuals or groups whose main functions are to provide services and advice to line management or who perform an auditing or monitoring function. Staff positions differ from line positions in their sources of power. While line managers have formal authority to tell others what to do, staff members provide only advice and counselling, thereby exerting expert power over those in authority. Where staff departments do have formal authority over line members, within the limits of their own function, this is called 'functional authority'. It arises from the need to have a degree of uniformity and specialist expertise in carrying out certain organizational activities. In the personnel function, for example, this often includes industrial relations and managing personnel systems generally.

Delegation is the assigning by managers of the formal authority and responsibility for carrying out specific tasks and duties to subordinates. Effective delegation, it is claimed, enables managers at all levels to use corporate resources efficiently, frees them for more important tasks, improves the quality of decision making and encourages individual initiative. Classical guidelines for effective delegation include giving subordinates the necessary authority and responsibility and following the 'scalar' and 'unity of command' principles. These maintain that there should be a clear line of authority running from the top of the organization to the bottom and that each role holder should report to only one superior. The size and complexity of many modern organizations, however, mean that these classical guidelines do not apply in all cases: much depends on the contingencies of the situation. Barriers to effective delegation include the reluctance not only of some managers to delegate to their subordinates but also of subordinates to accept delegated authority from their managers.

The delegation of individual or personal authority by managers is closely related to the decentralization of collective or group authority within enterprises. Decentralization and centralization refer to the extent to which authority is either passed down to lower organizational levels or retained at the top. The greater the degree of delegated authority, the more decentralized the organization is. The advantages of decentralization are similar to those of managerial delegation. But total decentralization, with no coordination from the top, is clearly undesirable. In determining the amount of decentralization necessary within an organization, senior management take a number of factors into account. These include: the state of the market and the availability of resources of the enterprise; the size and rate of growth of the organization; and internal factors such as its history, the quality of lower management and the cost and risks of decentralization.

3 Direction

Direction by management provides instructions for subordinate employees enabling them to do their work and job tasks to set standards. There are three aspects to directing employees: leading them; motivating them; and communicating with them. It is through leadership skills, for example, that managers seek to harness the effort and teamwork of all employees. Early theorists believed that effective leadership depended on the leader's referent power, that is, the leader's individual traits or personal characteristics. Other researchers such as Likert (1961) and Porter and his colleagues (1975) focus on leadership style to explain effectiveness within groups.[19] Later theories take a broader approach. They examine, for example, the importance of leadership style and situational factors such as leader–member relations, task structure and leader power.[20] Other research, such as by Vroom and Yetton (1973) for instance, indicates a positive relationship between participative leadership styles and employee productivity and satisfaction.[21]

Motivating employees and job satisfaction are central to understanding organizational effectiveness. They focus on the individual, the job and the work situation. Expectancy theory, for example, suggests that individuals direct strong effort towards their jobs when they expect that high performance leads to desired outcomes and that their efforts will result in high performance.[22] Job satisfaction and high performance, however, are not necessarily correlated. Satisfaction and performance are probably influenced by rewards. Rewards which are valued, for example, can increase job satisfaction but are only likely to influence job performance if they are explicitly tied to performance criteria.

Communication within management, and between management and subordinates, is an integral and vital part of direction. It is through communication channels that instructions, information, facts and ideas are transmitted from person to person and from group to group within organizations. Downward channels of communication transmit plans, policies and procedures from senior management to lower organizational levels. Upward channels carry information to senior management enabling them to monitor effectiveness and performance. Horizontal channels coordinate the actions of different departments and functions across enterprises. They also facilitate communication between managerial and staff representatives at different organizational levels. These formal channels of communication are normally supplemented by informal networks which arise spontaneously within all organizational hierarchies.

4 Coordination

Since management divides work into specialized functions or organizational subunits in order to increase productivity and efficiency, there is a corresponding need for these different work activities to be coordinated. Coordination is the process of integrating the objectives and activities of separate organizational subunits, departments or functional areas in order to achieve corporate objectives. Without effective coordination, individuals and departments lose sight of their organizational roles by pursuing their own interests at the expense of larger organizational ones. The need for coordination varies widely according to the degree of interdependence existing between different organizational subunits. Where a high degree of interdependence exists, for example, the coordination task is particularly difficult.

Three basic coordinating mechanisms used by management are the managerial hierarchy, objective setting and planning, and procedures and rules. The organization's managerial hierarchy with its chain of command, for example, establishes working and reporting relationships amongst its members. This facilitates information flow and the coordination of work between different parts of an enterprise. Objective setting and planning achieve coordination by enabling each subunit to work consciously towards the same broad targets. Where objectives are established in advance, it is easier for management to delegate authority for implementing tasks to various parts of the enterprise. Being aware of each other's objectives help subunits to act consistently with their own and corporate objectives.

Procedures and rules are managerial decisions made to handle routine events before they arise. Where organizational and departmental procedures and rules are regularly used by subordinates, the need to communicate with superiors about routine matters is reduced. This enables them to take action faster and leaves more time for managers to respond to new events. Where these basic coordinating mechanisms are inadequate, coordination can be supplemented by improving vertical information systems or by cutting across the chain of command with lateral relationships such as liaison groups or managerial subgroups.

The number of subordinates reporting to a manager is known as the 'span of control' or span of management. A span of control which is too wide or too narrow can impede coordination. Narrow spans result in tall organizations, with many levels of supervision, while wide spans produce flat structures with fewer supervisory levels. Structures which are too flat can result in lack of managerial control and in the inefficient use of managerial and supervisory time. Structures which are too tall can lead to oversupervision, delays in decision making and rising administrative costs. Early writers on management tried to define a single maximum span of control applicable to all organizations or to various levels of management. Recent writers advise spans of control which are appropriate to the contingencies of the enterprise.

5 Control

Control is the process through which managers ensure that actual activities performed within an organization or part of it conform to its planned activities and are contributing to corporate objectives. As shown in Figure 14 (p. 74), it involves four basic steps:

Figure 14
The control process

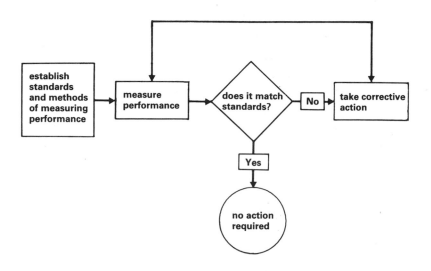

establishing standards and measure of performance; measuring performance; comparing performance against standards; and taking corrective action.

There are several factors necessitating managerial control within organizations: their changing environments; their complexity; the mistakes and errors made by subordinates; and the need to delegate authority. In establishing control mechanisms, managers normally try to find a balance between achieving appropriate organizational controls and maintaining the personal freedom and integrity of subordinate employees. With too little control, organizations become ineffective in achieving their objectives. With too much control, they become inhibiting and unsatisfactory places in which to work.

Control methods can be grouped into three basic categories: steering controls; screening controls; and postoperative controls. Steering controls detect below standard performance before a given operation is completed. They are particularly important, since they permit corrective action to be taken preventing failure or poor performance. Screening controls ensure that specific conditions are met before an operation proceeds further. Postoperative controls are those in which past experience is applied to future operations. In designing control systems, management decides on the types and number of measurements to be used, who sets the standards, how flexible the standards are, the frequency of measurement and the direction that feedback takes. For a control system to be effective, it needs to be accurate, economically realistic and focused on key result areas. As Drucker (1977) claims: 'work needs to be controlled in respect of its direction; its quality; the quantities turned out; its standard, and its economy'. But ultimately, 'control is a tool of the workers and must not be their master or an impediment to working'.[23] Obviously, it is difficult to achieve a balance between individual or personal control and managerial or systems control. In practice it is management which sets the limits within which control is structured and applied.

Management levels

Thomason (1981) amongst others points out that work roles in modern organizations are characterized by a high degree of specialization. This is as true of managerial roles as it is of subordinate ones. This organizational division of labour takes place both horizontally and vertically. Horizontally, job tasks and work roles are differentiated according to their operational, functional or departmental responsibilities, with managers heading organizational subunits. There is also a 'separation of decision taking from action taking so that vertical jobs are distinguished on the basis of the amount of discretion to decide', with management operating within its own structure and hierarchy of power and authority. Within a horizontal organizational structure 'into which both deciding and acting roles are slotted', therefore, there coexists a vertical structure within which managers are employed to decide and instruct and subordinates to act on managerial decisions.[24]

Chandler and Daems (1980) claim that by the mid 1970s one in every five industrial workers in Europe and the United States was employed by a company with a hierarchy of at least six vertical management levels. Large scale business enterprises, they claim, characterized by multiple operating units, varied activities 'and hierarchies of salaried managers are now at the center of the leading market economies'.[25] This extension of managerial hierarchies applies to public sector organizations too. In both cases, 'the visible hand of managerial direction' has now replaced 'the invisible hand of market mechanisms . . . in coordinating flows and allocating resources in major modern industries'.[26]

There are various ways in which managerial roles can be distinguished vertically. Chamberlain (1948) classifies them as corporate, administrative and executive, while Paterson (1972) describes them as policy making, programming and interpretive.[27] More simply, the terms corporate or senior management, middle or executive management and first line or supervisory management are commonly used. Senior management, who may or may not be board members or members of their governing bodies, comprises that small group of people responsible for the overall management of an enterprise. Its main task is to develop and review corporate objectives and its operating policies. It also has to evaluate the overall performance of the enterprise and its constituent parts. In undertaking its roles, senior management normally consults subordinate managers when objective setting and policy making.

Middle management implements corporate objectives and policies and manages subordinate managers. In fulfilling these tasks, it monitors departmental performance, consults subordinate managers and reports to senior management. Many middle managers are often technical specialists who have become managers. According to Torrington and Weightman (1982) the managerial component of their jobs comprises a 'combination of common sense, a moderate amount of flair for dealing with people, and knowledge of a few administrative routines'. If they allow their technical skills to wither and concentrate on management alone, however, they 'tend to accentuate and develop one or more of those elements to an extent which is counter-productive'.[28] First line management, by contrast, supervises the day to day activities of non-managerial subordinates and reports to middle management, with relatively low levels of job discretion.

Management functions

In addition to being organized vertically, managers are also grouped horizontally across enterprises by their specialist activities and tasks or management functions. The main management functions are production, marketing, finance and personnel, with research and development and administration sometimes regarded as additional functional activities. In many small organizations, there is relatively little differentiation of these functions and the horizontal division of managerial work is comparatively slight. Most of these managers undertake general management rather than specialist management duties. It is only as organizations grow in size that managers become functionally differentiated with the making, selling, financing and personnel aspects of management being staffed, directed and administered by management specialists. When this happens the general management function is largely a senior management responsibility. It is then the main job of senior management to direct and integrate the efforts of specialist functional managers towards stated corporate objectives.

1 Production

According to Lockyer (1983), 'of all the managerial tasks the production function is the least easy to define since it incorporates so many diverse tasks that are interdependent'. He analyses it under five headings: the product; the plant; the processes; the programmes; and the people. For Lockyer the product provides the interface between production and marketing which he believes should be closely integrated. 'And it is not sufficient that the consumer requires the product; the organization must be capable of producing it'.[29] The main elements in the product part of the production function are: design, quality, value control and variety control.

Product design translates production requirements into suitable forms for manufacture and use. It is separate from product research, which is the discovery of new techniques, ideas or systems, and product development, which is the improvement of existing ones. 'Quality is fitness for function', while 'reliability is the ability to continue to function to an accepted quality level'.[30] Value control looks at the basic design of products, rather than at improving the ways in which they are made. Variety control emphasizes the need to control costs and is carried out in three ways: by simplification; standardization; and specialization.

The plant, which accounts for the bulk of an organization's fixed assets, 'must match the needs of the product, of the market, of the operator and of the organization, and it must continue to do so for as long as the consumer need can be foreseen'.[31] When a plant is established, for example, its location, design, layout, equipment and maintenance all have to be determined. Such decisions need to take account of all those internal and external factors such as the financial, economic and social contexts affecting the plant as a sociotechnical system.

The processes of production include: types of production such as job, batch, flow and group technology; materials handling; estimating and planning; quality control; and costing. Job or one off production, for example, is where a single product is produced using a wide variety of machines and equipment, with a range of human skills. Batch production provides a number of products or components, each being completed before the next batch is begun. Flow production is continuous with little waiting time between operations. Group technology organizes small batch or multi-product production where specialist machines and their operators are grouped into 'cells'. Each cell contains various machines which perform all the operations on a 'family' of products.

The main programming activity is production control, though it also includes purchasing and storekeeping. Production control incorporates scheduling, loading, material control, despatching and progressing. Once a customer order is received, for example, a master schedule is prepared. This assesses the labour and material requirements which are notified to the appropriate departments. According to Lockyer, manufacture is then initiated by the despatch section. It 'collects all relevant documents, verifies the detailed availability of labour, materials, tools, equipment and product aids, and issues authorizing documents'.[32] Progressing ensures that the requirements of the master schedule are fulfilled and that the production process is successfully completed.

2 Marketing

Oliver (1990) defines the marketing function as 'a set of processes which stimulate and facilitate market exchanges for the mutual benefit of an organization and its consumers'.[33] The marketing function provides the interface between enterprises and their customers and assists selling and buying between them. As a management function, marketing incorporates product planning, product pricing, the promotion of goods and services and their distribution. Although marketing techniques have been used traditionally by profit and revenue oriented organizations, they are now being used by welfare and community oriented ones such as the public services, private charities and voluntary bodies. A useful framework for analysing the marketing function is provided by Oliver. He divides it into five main elements: buyer behaviour; segmenting; researching and forecasting markets; developing market strategy; and planning the marketing mix.

Buyer behaviour is concerned with the psychological, social and economic factors influencing the decisions of individuals, households and organizations as consumers. Market segmentation is 'the subdivision of a market into parts that are relatively homogeneous, so that separate and distinctive marketing plans can be prepared for each segment'.[34] It is a way of identifying target markets. The aim of marketing research is to collect, interpret and report information which is relevant to marketing decision making. According to Oliver the two central considerations here are: '(1) the need properly to define the specific problem and (2) the need to translate it into a form amenable to data collection'.[35] Forecasting markets anticipates customer requirements and provides a basis for marketing planning.

Developing strategy is a central part of marketing since it precedes the planning of the marketing mix. In the marketing mix what is offered in the market and its price are determined. Its basic elements include: product planning; test marketing; promotion planning; advertising and media planning; sales force planning; distribution planning; and price planning. The marketing mix, in short, consists of 'the composite plans made by an organization dealing with products, prices, promotion and distribution'. In appraising marketing operations, marketing managers normally consider the inputs and outputs of each marketing subsystem. In output budgeting attention is focused on appraising the outputs or 'missions' of an organization, in response to the increasing complexity of business operations.[36]

3 Finance

The survival of any organization depends ultimately on its economic viability and its ability to cover its operating costs. Hence the effective management of the finance function is crucial to success. A simple model of the main sources and flows of finance within private sector organizations is provided in Figure 15 on page 81, with those in the public sector and non-profit making bodies differing in detail rather than substance. The management and control of these financial inflows and outflows are the central activities of the finance function. The techniques used in doing this include financial methods, budgets and audits.

The main financial methods are financial statements, ratio analyses and break even analysis. Financial statements, for example, record the flow of goods and services to and from organizations. They show the general financial position of an organization, its profitability and its liquidity. Such statements are usually prepared historically and refer to a previous period in an organization's activities. The balance sheet, for example, shows the financial position of an organization at a particular time. Income statements, such as the profit and loss and trading accounts, summarize financial performance over an interval of time, normally a year. Sources and uses of funds statements show how new sources of finance become available and how they are used.[37]

Since financial performance is relative, ratio analysis compares information from one financial statement with another. Comparisons over a given period are made in one of two ways: first, comparison within the organization; or secondly, comparison with other similar organizations or with the industry as a whole. Ratio analyses serve several purposes. Essentially, they are measures of financial stocks and flows on a comparative basis. They enable financial planning and analysis to be done.

(i) They provide a means of showing interrelationships between groups of figures and can be used as a measure of efficiency.

Figure 15
The main sources and flows of finance within private sector organizations

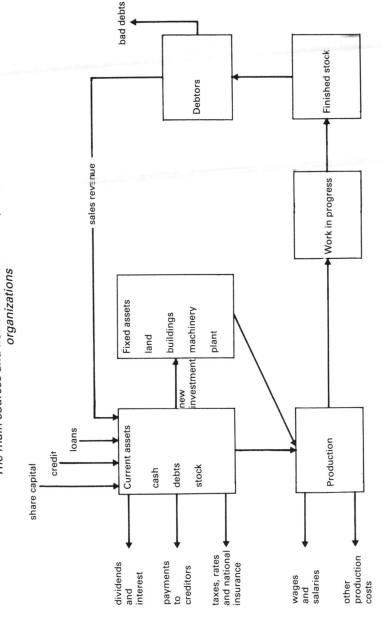

(ii) They enable a large volume of data to be conveniently summarized.
(iii) They can be used in forecasting and planning.
(iv) They can serve as an aid to communication . . . [and]
(v) They can be used to assess solvency, overtrading and profitability.[38]

The most commonly used ratios are liquidity, debt, sales, profitability, cost and return on investment ratios.

Break even analysis shows the relationship between costs, sales

Figure 16
A break even analysis chart

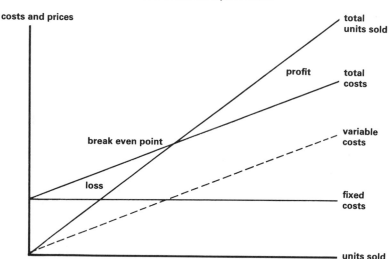

and profits (see Figure 16). It helps management in the following ways: to determine the break even point or the volume of sales at which neither profit nor loss occurs; to calculate the costs and revenues for all possible volumes of sales; and to calculate variable cost per unit. Although it is recognized that the information it provides may not always be strictly accurate, break even analysis is a useful tool aiding financial decision making.

Budgets are formal statements of the financial resources set aside for carrying out specific actions in an enterprise for a given period, normally a year. They are widely used for planning and controlling at every organizational level. In essence, a budget indicates the expenditure, revenues, investment or profits planned for some future date. The planned figures become the standard by which future performance is measured. The budgeting process begins when top management establishes its corporate objectives for a given period. The creation of the budget involves many levels of management, with a major role being played by the finance function.

There are two types of financial audit: external and internal. The external audit is largely confirmatory and involves the independent appraisal of an organization's financial accounts and statements by outsiders. The internal audit goes deeper. It inquires, for example, into the financial structure of an enterprise, appraising it not only for accuracy but also for operational efficiency. It also evaluates how adequately the organization's control mechanisms are working towards realizing corporate objectives.

4 Personnel

For Barber (1979) an effective personnel function is critical to the success of an enterprise. He claims that the fundamental problem underlying any organization, whether a factory, office, hospital or government department, is 'how the efforts of people who make up the enterprise can be so organized and developed in order to attain the highest levels of efficiency, adaptability and productivity'.[39] Ideally, he argues, personnel policy should be directed at the following: developing an effective organizational structure; staffing it with suitable people; and ensuring that its employees contribute to its efficiency and success. The sorts of activities coming within its scope include: corporate planning; organization and job design; manpower planning; pay and conditions; industrial relations; manpower development; and employee services such as welfare, counselling and health and safety at work. These aspects of the personnel function are explored in detail in Part II of this book.

Support services

There are a number of support services which are provided as aids to management, especially in larger organizations. Sometimes they are supplied centrally through a management services department, in other cases through specialist service units. Their basic task is to provide internal consultancy and advice to management. They include work study, organization and methods, operational research and electronic data processing systems, though this list is neither exclusive nor exhaustive.

The International Labour Office (ILO 1965) uses work study to describe 'the techniques of method study and work measurement which are employed in carrying out a specified activity'.[40] Work study is concerned with productivity and its techniques are used to increase output from given resources, without using additional labour or capital. Applying work study techniques has obvious implications for managing people and for this reason it is sometimes resisted by subordinates, unless the benefits are explained to them. From the managerial viewpoint, besides saving costs and making labour more efficient, work study procedures can reveal inefficiency, improve working methods and establish standard rates and times for certain jobs.

The purpose of method study is to reduce work content, while the purpose of work measurement is to reduce ineffective working time. Method study is the systematic recording, analysis and examination of existing and proposed ways of doing work. The aim is to develop and apply easier and more effective working methods, using appropriate analytical techniques. Work measurement is the application of particular techniques 'to establish the work content of a specified task by determining the time required for carrying it out at a defined standard of performance by a qualified worker'.[41] A related activity is predetermined motion time systems (PDMTS) which establish standard times for basic human motions. These are used to build up time allowances for various jobs at defined levels of performance.

Organization and methods (O and M) are the techniques used to investigate office systems and clerical and administrative tasks in order to improve working practices. In addition to applying standard work measurement methods such as PDMTS, activity sampling and timing, O and M practitioners use other techniques.

These include: method analysis to break down basic work procedures; flow charts to analyse operations; and string diagrams to determine work flows between individuals or groups. O and M specialists are also experts in form design and form control. Like work study practitioners, O and M specialists need to consult fully with those affected by their activities and to sell proposals for any new systems of working to the departments or individuals concerned.

Operational research (OR) was initially used as an aid to managerial decision making in the armed services during the second world war, when mathematical theory was applied to military problems. Now it has a wide range of managerial applications, particularly to improve organizational effectiveness by reducing decision making risks. Used in conjunction with the computer, OR is essentially the mathematical application of scientific method to the solution of organizational problems. The basic OR approach is to create a mathematical model, or a set of equations representing the problem, and to use it to solve the problem. The model is normally developed by an OR team, led by OR and computer specialists, including departmental managers. The specific techniques used to construct and solve OR models include: linear programming; queuing theory; and decision tree analysis. A major limitation of OR is that it cannot be used where problems are unquantifiable.

Electronic data processing (EDP) systems use electronic computers and related equipment for recording and analysing a variety of organizational and contextual information. Basically, raw material is fed in numeric form into the central processing unit of the computer, where the information is processed. It may be either stored or provided for immediate use. Processed data takes the form of punched cards, paper tape, line printers, graph plotters, graphical displays and so on. EDP systems are applied to a wide area of managerial decision making, planning and control, since they can process, store and provide information in virtually all areas of managerial activity.

In the production function, for example, EDP systems are used as an aid to job sequencing, machine loading, work scheduling and purchasing decisions. In marketing EDP systems are used in forecasting, stock or inventory control, distribution, scheduling and planning sales force allocation. EDP systems have important applications in the finance function too, not only in recording and storing routine accounting information but also in analysing and using it for managerial purposes. This includes budgetary control, costing and investment planning. Lastly, EDP systems are an aid to the personnel function in a number of areas, including manpower planning, personnel records and wage and salary administration.

With the development of microcomputers, personnel managers have an important aid for processing information and decision making. They can also interact and integrate with other managerial functions more effectively.

Conclusion

The managerial context within which the personnel function takes place is varied and complex. Basically, management is that body of people responsible for running enterprises in order to achieve corporate objectives. Collectively, managers are differentiated vertically by the level in which they are located in their organizational hierarchies and horizontally by their functional activities. Individually, they play a variety of interpersonal, informational, decisional and related roles which, although varying in detail, are common across organizations and within them. Collectively and individually managers are expected to plan, organize, direct, coordinate and control enterprise resources, including manpower, in order to meet corporate objectives. In practice, however, the realities of organizational life normally preclude such a rational and consistent approach to managerial decision making and executive action. As Hunt (1981) concludes: 'what the manager actually does is probably something between the traditional and interpersonal view' of the managerial role.[42]

References and footnotes

1   HUNT J. *Managing People at Work*. (London, Pan, 1981). p145.
2   HARBISON F *and* MYERS C A. *Management in the Industrial World* (NY, McGraw-Hill, 1959). p8.

3   MANT A. *The Rise and Fall of the British Manager.* (London, Macmillan, 1977). p13.

4   TRADES UNION CONGRESS. *Trade Unionism.* (London, TUC, 1966). p101.

5   See FAYOL H. *Industrial and General Administration.* (Trans. G Storrs. London, Pitman, 1949); URWICK L. *The Elements of Administration.* (London, Pitman, 1947); and BRECH E F L (ed). *The Principles and Practice of Management.* (London, Longman, 1975).

6   FALK R. *The Business of Management.* 3rd ed. (Harmondsworth, Penguin, 1963). p71.

7   DRUCKER P F. *Management.* (London, Pan, 1977). p20f.

8   STEWART R. *The Reality of Management.* Revised edition. (London, Pan, 1979). p69.

9   See CARLSON S. *Executive Behaviour.* (Stockholm, Strombergs, 1951); SAYLES L R. *Managerial Behavior.* (NY, McGraw-Hill, 1964); *and* STEWART R. *Managers and their Jobs.* (London, Macmillan, 1967). *Contrasts in Management.* (London, McGraw-Hill, 1976) and *Choices for the Manager.* (London, McGraw-Hill, 1982). MINTZBERG H. *The Nature of Managerial Work.* (NJ, Prentice-Hall, 1973) and 'The manager's job: folklore and fact'. *Harvard Business Review.* Vol. 53, No. 4, July–August 1975.

10 STEWART R. *Contrasts in Management.* (London, McGraw-Hill, 1976). p22f.

11 *ibid.* p47.

12 HUNT. *opcit.* p173.

13 These are sometimes called the 'functions' of management or the 'managerial functions'. In this text, the managerial activities described in this section are to be distinguished from management's organizational functions, such as production, marketing, finance and personnel, which are considered on pp77–83 above. 'Commanding' is usually taken to be 'direction'.

14 HUNT. *opcit.* p177.

15 For a more detailed analysis of these concepts see Chapter 2 above.

16 See pp48–54 above.

17 BARNARD C I. *The Functions of the Executive.* (Cambridge, Mass., Harvard University Press, 1968). p165f.

18 FRENCH J R P *and* RAVEN B. 'The social bases of power' in CARTWRIGHT D (ed). *Studies in Social Power.* (Ann Arbor, University of Michigan, 1959). pp150–67.

19 See LIKERT R. *New Patterns of Management.* (NY, McGraw-Hill, 1961) and PORTER L W *and others. Behavior in Organizations.* (NY, McGraw-Hill, 1975).

20 See FIEDLER F E *and* CHEMMERS M M. *Leadership and Effective Management.* (Glenview, Scott Foresman, 1974).

21 VROOM V H *and* YETTON P W. *Leadership and Decision Making.* (Pittsburgh, University of Pittsburgh Press, 1973).

22 See, for example, PORTER L W *and* LAWLER F E. *Managerial Attitudes and Performance.* (Homewood, Irwin, 1968).

23 DRUCKER P F. *Management*. (London, Pan, 1977). p219.
24 THOMASON G. *A Textbook of Personnel Management*. (London, IPM, 1981). p17.
25 CHANDLER A D *and* DAEMS H (eds). *Management Hierarchies*. (London, Harvard University Press, 1980). p1.
26 *ibid*. p9.
27 See CHAMBERLAIN N W. *The Union Challenge to Management Control*. (NY, Harper, 1948) and PATERSON T T. *Job Evaluation*. (London, Business Books, 1972).
28 TORRINGTON D *and* WEIGHTMAN J. 'Technical atrophy in middle management.' *Journal of General Management*. Vol. 7, no. 4, Summer 1982. p16.
29 LOCKYER K. *Production Management*. 4th ed. (London, Pitman, 1983). p4f.
30 *ibid*. p62f.
31 *ibid*. p5.
32 *ibid*. p280.
33 OLIVER G. *Marketing Today*. (London, Prentice-Hall, 1990). p331.
34 *ibid*.
35 *ibid*. p116.
36 *ibid*. pp331 and 308.
37 A special type of financial statement is human asset accounting (HAA). In HAA, an organization's personnel resources are regarded as an asset and the cost of training them becomes a contribution towards corporate objectives.
38 APPLEBY R C. *Modern Business Administration*. 3rd ed. (London, Pitman, 1981). p144.
39 BARBER D. *The Practice of Personnel Management*. 2nd ed. (London, IPM, 1979). p8.
40 INTERNATIONAL LABOUR OFFICE. *Introduction to Work Study*. (Geneva, ILO, 1965). p35.
41 *ibid*. p41.
42 HUNT J. *Managing People at Work*. (London, Pan, 1979). p177.

Part II
Modern personnel management

4

The personnel management function

The nature of the personnel function

There are many definitions of personnel management. In the British context, the IPM claims that personnel management forms part of every manager's job 'but it is the special concern of those employed as specialists in the management team'. As a managerial function, the IPM continues, personnel management seeks to develop into effective organizations those men and women who make up an enterprise, enabling each 'to make their best contribution to its success'.[1] For Lyons (1971) personnel management is 'that part of the function of management that arises out of the fact that an enterprise has to use people . . . [which] helps to show that the personnel function exists quite independently of whether specialists are employed or not'.[2] For Fowler (1980), all managerial jobs have common elements concerned with the management of people including selection, deployment, instruction, direction, consultation, advice and motivation. 'But a growth of awareness of the importance of the human aspects of management has led to the establishment of personnel management as a significant and distinct field of management studies'.[3]

Thomason (1981) writes that personnel management is found wherever management is and, therefore, wherever there are people in employment whose activities call for coordination and control. He goes on to say, however, that personnel management as a specialist function or specialist occupation is only found in larger enterprises, where there is a high degree of managerial division of labour. In his view, all managers are personnel managers insofar as they manage people as part of their general managerial duties. In the other sense of personnel management, 'the one which is usually in mind when "personnel managers" are being counted, only those who carry out duties specifically labelled "personnel" qualify for inclusion'.[4]

Torrington and Chapman (1983) view personnel management as an activity of managers as representatives of organizational interests and as makers of demands on employees. They define personnel as 'a series of activities enabling working man and his employing organisation to reach agreement about the nature and objectives of the employment relationship between them, and then to fulfil those agreements'.[5] They suggest that personnel work has three elements:

   (i) Determining the expectations that employees have of their organisations, and the expectations organisations have of their employees.
  (ii) Setting up a series of contracts or agreements between organisation and employee(s) that describe the mutual expectations.
 (iii) Servicing the contracts to ensure that the expectations are fulfilled.

They group personnel work into three categories of activity. The first relates to the individual within the organization and concerns the 'Contract for Work' and the 'Contract for Individual Control'. The second emphasizes the collective activities of personnel which they describe as the 'Contract for Collective Consent' and the 'Contract for Payment'. Thirdly, there is the 'Small Print of the Contracts' consisting of administrative methods and techniques which can be applied to a number of personnel areas.[6]

These and similar definitions of the personnel management function within organizations highlight it as a somewhat ambiguous and contradictory area of managerial activity. First, personnel management is seen to be not only the concern of those managerial specialists within organizations who are known as personnel managers. It also refers to the personnel activities and tasks of line managers in their dealings with subordinate employees as individuals and groups. There is, therefore, some degree of ambiguity about which aspects of personnel management should be left to line managers and which to personnel specialists. As Legge (1978) writes: 'ambiguities in definition generate confusion at the operational level about the nature and locus of personnel management responsibilities'. This in turn promotes lack of coherence in the allocation of personnel activities and tasks between line managers and personnel managers, which sometimes gives rise to critical assessments of the personnel role within enterprises,[7]

Secondly, even when the term personnel management is used to describe the work of personnel staff, it fails to distinguish between the activities of those personnel managers who are in charge of the personnel management function within enterprises and those of their supporting staff within the personnel department itself. Guest and Horwood (1980) describe the former group as 'generalists' or 'personnel managers' and the others as 'specialists' or 'personnel subordinates'. Personnel generalists normally undertake a large number of tasks across personnel activity, whilst specialist personnel staff, or personnel subordinates, do a narrower range of specific tasks directed by personnel managers.[8] The activities and tasks undertaken by personnel managers, in other words, vary between those who are in charge of the specialist personnel function in enterprises and those who are subordinates within it.

Thirdly, the essence of the personnel management function as provided in its definitions is to get the best out of the people or human resource element within organizations in order to carry out corporate policies and achieve corporate objectives. Yet the personnel function also seeks to provide opportunities for individuals and groups to receive equitable rewards for their efforts and some degree of self fulfilment at work. As Watson (1977) writes:

> The members of personnel departments are forced to pay attention to both the formally rational criteria of productivity, profit, effectiveness and the rest as well as the human needs, interests and aspirations of employees which, if not attended to, may lead to the formally rational means subverting the substantively rationally conceived ends of the ultimate controllers of the organisations.[9]

A potential conflict arises, in other words, between the efficiency objective of personnel management in achieving a successful enterprise, and the social objectives of the personnel function in providing justice and fairness to individual workers.

Furthermore, where one accepts the pluralistic model of business and service organizations, there is no reason to expect that the immediate work objectives of individuals and groups necessarily coincide with, or are consistently compatible with, the short and long term corporate objectives of their employing organizations.

As Legge argues, personnel management aims 'for the "optimum utilization of human resources in order to achieve the goals and objectives of the organization"'. Yet in a system of competing and incompatible interests and goals, 'both the definition and operationalization of "optimum" . . . must be problematic'.[10]

Turning to the specialist personnel function, Thomason (1975) argues that to understand the ambivalance so often associated with modern personnel management, it is necessary to recognize the diverse origins out of which it has grown. Of these, 'the one [is] paternalistically oriented towards the welfare of the employees and the other rationally derived from corporate needs to control'.[11] The welfare role of personnel management, for example, was the earliest form of personnel activity to develop in Britain. It emerged out of the altruistic concern for the welfare of employees, both within the factory and outside it, by a few paternalistic employers at the beginning of the century. It survives today in a limited form, predominantly in factories employing women. The management control role of personnel, according to Thomason, is the dominant emphasis within personnel management currently. It is rooted in managerial concern for efficiency at work and puts the management of people firmly into the mainstream of managerial work within the enterprise. While the management control role of personnel implies an executive function for personnel managers, it raises certain problems about the allocation of personnel activities and tasks between personnel managers and line managers respectively. 'In practice it means that personnel managers may become involved in an extremely wide range of activities, sometimes executive, sometimes advisory, but always as part of the management team'.[12]

Thomason also believes that there has been a revival in what is called the third party role of personnel management in recent years. This derives particularly from the need of employers to interpret and implement the mass of labour law which has been enacted by Parliament since the 1970s. By using this legislation as a basis for justifying certain personnel policies and practices, such as in the areas of discipline, health and safety at work, and equal opportunities for example, personnel managers necessarily adopt a third party or monitoring role in organizations. It is based on their expert knowledge of the law and of its implications for employers and personnel management practices. Such an approach implies, of course, that the law incorporates certain societal values and beliefs which override the self interest of any particular employers, thus providing some independence of the personnel specialist's role from that of management generally.

There is also the professional role of personnel management. This views the specialist personnel function as a profession and is particularly advanced by the IPM. It sees personnel managers not only as an important managerial resource, possessing key knowledge and specialist skills within the enterprise. It also sees them as having certain professional values and common standards of competence which exist beyond the particular employing organization where they work. The professional role of personnel management, though similar to the third party one, differs from it by being closely identified with the management function as a whole. It also emphasizes the transferability of the professional expertise and values of personnel managers across organizations, thus ensuring efficiency and fairness within them. However, as Guest and Horwood argue, 'the range of activities may be considerable, but they could become predominantly advisory rather than executive'.[13]

Some writers are more hostile towards the specialist personnel role. Drucker (1968), for example, sees personnel management as being a 'hodgepodge' of activities consisting of residual parts rather than having a holistic or coherent unity. For Drucker, personnel management

> is largely a collection of incidental techniques without much internal cohesion . . . it is partly a file clerk's job, partly a social worker's job and partly 'fire-fighting' to head off union trouble or to settle it. . . . They are most unpleasant chores. I doubt, though, that they should be put together in one department, for they are a hodgepodge, as one look at the organization chart of the typical personnel department . . . will show.[14]

This view of personnel management sees it as having a fairly limited range of relatively unimportant administrative activities and tasks within organizations, and largely ignores its executive and advisory ones. Such activities are not linked by skills, nor do they in Drucker's view provide a distinctive part of managerial work.

Perceptions of the personnel role

Perceptions of the personnel management role vary widely both within enterprises and between them. Some line managers have a clear view of the importance of effective personnel management in organizations and are highly supportive of the role and activities of personnel specialists. Others have less understanding of the general personnel management function and are more critical of personnel managers as a group. In the organizations studied by Legge (1978), for example, two major themes emerged. First, there was an absence of systematically formulated personnel policies. Secondly, the personnel management aspects of line management decision making tended to be neglected. She claims, for instance, that in these organizations senior management normally accepted the need for appropriate personnel policies, but was unable to think through and develop internally consistent personnel management strategies. She also found that line managers:

> while recognizing that much of their work was a form of personnel management tended to operate in the area in an *ad hoc* manner, without any clearly thought out and articulated framework to which to relate their activities. As a result, in company decision-making, the personnel management considerations involved in production, marketing and finance decisions were not so much overruled . . . as went by default.[15]

In practice, therefore, line managers often tend to underestimate the importance of the human resource element in organizational decision making.

Harvey-Jones (1982), chairman of Imperial Chemical Industries, claims not to have been generally impressed by the way in which people have been managed in the personnel departments of a number of organizations in which he has worked. Although personnel managers are the custodians of most of the theory of management, he writes, 'this all too often appears to be directed towards offering advice to others, rather than practising within their own house'. He does not believe that a long period of exposure in the personnel field provides an appropriate background for generating 'an all-round businessman with the particular qualities which are required for the highest positions in industry'.

Whilst accepting the case for putting line managers through a period of personnel work, he believes that personnel management should not be primarily a specialist activity but 'should be the responsibility of every line manager'.[16]

Manning (1983) is also critical of the specialist personnel role. He believes that as a managerial function personnel management began the 1970s with great promise but 'at the beginning of the 1980s that promise remains unfulfilled'. He argues that while the importance of getting the best out of human resources in enterprises has not changed, personnel management as a discipline has yet to meet that challenge and make the significant impact that he believes it should. For him, personnel management has the weakest conceptual base and the poorest technology among managerial specialisms. In his view, personnel departments too often show little unity of purpose which effectively excludes them from contributing to corporate decision making. He suggests that 'what is needed is the sort of analytic and creative thinking that has been demonstrated so successfully in disciplines like marketing and finance'. He adds that the widespread apathy of many line managers towards personnel may result from the confusion caused by its changing mixture of techniques. 'To the average manager, personnel all too often seems distant from the immediate problems of achieving his budget and from the wider business needs of the company'.[17]

Forte (1982), chief executive of the Trusthouse Group, is more supportive of personnel. Nevertheless, he too believes that its main purpose is to assist line managers in one of their prime responsibilities, the management of people. In his organization, the personnel function is decentralized, with prime responsibility for personnel matters falling on line management. He writes: 'even if we had a choice, I believe we would elect to put the prime responsibility for personnel on line management rather than on specialists'. He does not believe that this diminishes the importance of the contribution made by personnel specialists, for in his organization, all units with 50 or more staff have a personnel specialist in the managerial team. In the Trusthouse Group, the nature of the work requires active participation by line management in the day to day operations of the business. This means that line managers have a very close working relationship with and understanding of their subordinates. Equally, staff need to know that line management has the authority and responsibility for taking decisions which vitally affect them in their immediate working environment. For Rocco Forte, therefore, the link between line managers and staff must be a direct one. It is the role of the personnel function to assist line managers in this responsibility.[18]

George Turnbull, chairman and managing director of the Talbot Motor Company, sees 'the personnel and IR function' as critical in achieving greater productivity in both his company and the motor industry generally. For him, the essential role of the personnel department is to act as a catalyst in bringing about changes in attitude amongst employees and management. In his opinion, it is the role of the personnel department to devise and administer effective training programmes which not only help employees perform their tasks more efficiently, but also enable them to accept organizational change, and the need for it, more readily. He argues that personnel 'must formulate pay and remuneration policies which are logical, economically defensible and fair'. The personnel department must also play a key role in selecting managers and in developing managerial skills within the enterprise. In this writer's view, the personnel function in the motor industry was for too long forced to play a fire fighting role. 'There is strong evidence now that those problems are diminishing and that the personnel function is adopting a far more creative and constructive role'.[19]

Alex Jarratt (1982), chairman of Reed International, has no doubt about the role of personnel managers and personnel directors. He views them as 'managers with special knowledge and skills about what is the most important asset of our business – the people we employ'. He believes that three main issues vitally affect employee relations and the success of every business. These are: collective bargaining and pay determination; employee involvement; and career development and the remuneration of managers. In any company or group of companies, he argues, these are all matters on which the business must establish clear policies and strategies. It is here that the personnel department with its special knowledge and skills has a major contribution to make. Nonetheless, Jarratt believes that individual managers in their own departments must carry out the prime responsibility for industrial relations and the outcome of pay bargaining. Turning to employee involvement, he argues that personnel professionals should help develop and implement appropriate policies. 'At the heart of it, both industrial relations and [employee] involvement are matters of good management in which personnel has a vital part to play'.[20]

In the public sector, the former chairman of the National Coal Board (NCB), Derek Ezra, believes that the main role of the professional personnel function is to create an 'environment in which a contented, healthy, skilled and committed workforce can operate, with the prospect of increased rewards through increased efficiency'. This requires, Ezra (1982) claims, very close interaction between line managers and personnel departments, with personnel specialists needing to be positive and outgoing in their activities and tasks. All four elements within the personnel function (contentment, health, involvement and skill) come together, he believes, in management development. This means not only getting the right people into the right jobs at the right time. It also means providing opportunities for people to develop their own aspirations 'whether this will take them to the top or no further than achieving maximum satisfaction in the job they are doing'. In the NCB, he points out, management development is largely carried out on the job by rotation, experience exchanges, coaching and career counselling.[21]

Looking optimistically to the future, Ezra concludes that skills involving a very high order of professionalism, such as those which the IPM seeks to foster, are increasingly required of the personnel specialist. These personnel skills touch every point of a business, he argues, and he sees personnel managers being drawn more and more into the general management of the business.[22]

Another former chairman of a nationalized industry, Peter Parker of the British Railways Board, also has a progressive view of the personnel function. He sees the personnel role as being the special agent of change within the enterprise. Parker (1983) looks to personnel management to help not only managers but also the unions to understand what he calls the 'different cultures of enterprise and of the community'. It is the paramount 'new role' of the personnel manager 'to be the co-ordinator of two cultures' and to emphasize the mutuality of the social and industrial purposes of work. In Parker's view, the personnel department's major responsibility is to sustain the effectiveness of human resources corporately, whilst extending every individual's sense of scope at work. 'To succeed, therefore,' he says, 'I see personnel increasingly involved in the effort to clarify the social policy of an enterprise.' The central point for Parker is that 'industry cannot separate its own working relationships and values from those of the community in which it operates and serves'.[23]

Parker also claims to be 'an ardent advocate of professionalism in personnel management'. There must be, for example, a core of disciplined expertise especially in such areas as: pay policies and welfare; negotiations; manpower planning and development; organizational planning; communications; and research. Although there is a danger that professional personnel management might become insulated from the rest of corporate life, Parker argues, he believes that there are three ways of countering this. First, personnel managers should be moved around the managerial functions, even if they return finally to the personnel role. Secondly, line managers should also get a feel for specialist personnel work by experiencing it for themselves. Thirdly, the personnel function needs to be fully integrated into the organization 'by being absolutely clear about it as supportive of line management'. In negotiations with trade unions, for example, both nationally and locally, Parker regards line managers as the initiators, with personnel specialists playing an important but supporting role.[24]

Summing up, Parker excepts three things from personnel managers. One of these is professionalism. Another is the need to be outward looking and in touch with other industries and society generally. The third is the need to operate on two time scales. In Parker's own words:

> Personnel must develop long-term policies and strategies and it must also be in there pitching when day-to-day problems arise, when tough negotiations are being faced, when the line managers need their skill and experience to the full. In a sense, there is the creative philosophical role, the preventive role and the day to day role.[25]

The job is not, in Parker's view, purely fire fighting, but it has to be recognized that even with the best long term strategies, personnel 'fires' need to be put out.[26]

From the relatively limited evidence which is available, trade union perceptions of the personnel role, it seems, are not always supportive of personnel specialists. Jenkins (1973), for example, criticizes the lack of power that some personnel managers have to authorize pay settlements. The impression of some union negotiators, he says, is 'that all too often, personnel managers have no real authority to reach settlement . . . [which] imparts an air of unreality to negotiations'. He also claims that 'brighter managers steer clear of the personnel function because of its lack of status'. Consequently, the personnel function often remains in low regard because of its relative lack of talent. He concludes that the best managers go into those departments most directly concerned with profit, such as production, marketing and finance.[27] Poole (1973 and 1976) comes to similar conclusions. He suggests that managers, shop stewards and other workplace representatives rarely sought the advice of personnel staff on industrial relations in the plants which he studied.[28]

Line managers and the personnel function

From what has been said so far, it is evident that the nature of the personnel management function in organizations is problematic. This is especially the case in determining the operational relationship between the personnel responsibilities of line managers, on the one side, and those of personnel specialists on the other. As outlined above, in some organizations line managers have full executive authority for all personnel matters in their departments, with the personnel department acting only as an adviser to line management. In others, by contrast, full executive authority, as in certain aspects of industrial relations and training for example, is given to a senior personnel manager or personnel executive. In these cases, such persons have both the authority and the responsibility to instruct line managers in appropriate courses of action in particular personnel matters. As the Commission on Industrial Relations (CIR 1973) comments, however, 'a simple distinction between executive and advisory functions of personnel managers, while useful for analytical purposes, obviously needs to be qualified and is likely to become blurred in practice'.[29]

Line managers are mainly concerned to see that organizational policies are executed and that target outputs and performance standards are achieved in their areas of responsibility. Personnel matters constitute a vital part of these overall responsibilities. There are clear advantages in ensuring that decisions on day to day personnel issues, such as handling grievances, determining promotions, or participating in disciplinary matters, are dealt with by the line managers directly concerned. Since the job of line managers is to manage their subunits efficiently and effectively, their managerial authority is undermined if basic personnel decisions are referred to other managers in the organization. Similarly, production and personnel problems at the operational level are too bound up together to be separated managerially. Line managers are also in the best position to communicate and consult with their subordinates on everyday personnel issues, thus demonstrating their awareness of personnel management as an integral part of their job.

On the other side, line managers are often so submerged in target dates, production schedules, working within budgets and other day to day matters that they find it difficult to give full attention to all the personnel aspects of their managerial role. In these cases, they may make hasty decisions which harm relationships with their subordinates. Seeking appropriate advice and assistance from the personnel department helps to ensure equity and consistency in the application of corporate personnel policies at line level. This is particularly so where the respective roles of line management and personnel management in human resource matters are clarified and agreed in advance, with the means of resolving any conflicts which may emerge between them being clearly laid out.

The CIR argues that senior and middle line managers need to give special attention to the role of supervisors in personnel management. They are advised to keep supervisors fully informed about corporate policies and managerial plans affecting work groups and subordinate employees. In this way, supervisors can communicate information both up and down the line. Although the task of ensuring that supervisory managers communicate regularly and effectively with their subordinates is a prime responsibility of line managers, personnel managers can aid the process. The essential feature of the supervisory role is that it provides management's immediate contact with subordinate employees. Supervisors are directly responsible for organizing and monitoring the day to day job tasks and activities of their work groups. They can also usefully contribute to the development of personnel policy and, with their first hand knowledge of work operations, can help promote the orderly conduct of personnel management practices at operational level.

The contribution which experienced personnel managers make towards the personnel function within their enterprises derives from two sources: first, their capacity to take an overall view of personnel issues and secondly their specific knowledge and skills. These include their problem solving, negotiating and interviewing skills and their specialist knowledge and expertise in employment law and health and safety at work. Further, most personnel managers provide basic personnel services such as maintaining personnel records, administering recruitment procedures and inducting new employees into their jobs. Personnel specialists can also ensure that: appropriate personnel systems and procedures are set up and maintained; industrial relations activities are coordinated; and personnel policies are consistently applied by line management throughout the organization.

Ultimately, however, line managers judge personnel managers 'on the extent to which their advice is found to be constructive and helpful in solving problems or preventing their occurrence'.[30] Advice takes several forms including: advice to top management on the formulation of personnel policies and plans on organizational structures; advice to top and middle management on the implementation of policy and plans; and advice to all levels of management on everyday personnel management practices. Ideally, personnel managers should be an integral part of the management team and should be consulted on all policy decisions having human resource implications. As the CIR argues, their 'fundamental role is to make line managers more effective without diminishing their authority'.[31]

The efficient and effective use of manpower plays a significant part in the personnel function. Policies and practices in this area aim to promote efficiency and productivity, to increase employee satisfaction and rewards from work, and to encourage stable employment, thus providing a sound basis for managing people and for maintaining organizational operations generally. The areas requiring particular attention normally include manpower planning, recruitment and selection, training and development and job security. In all these areas it is possible to identify a variety of activities and tasks which are best carried out by personnel specialists rather than by line managers. This is either because such activities require specialist knowledge and skills which it would be wasteful to develop in all managers, or because they involve a measure of coordination or policing in the organization as a whole.

Manpower planning, for example, is a complex process. Future manpower needs have to be estimated from corporate plans, future availability of particular skills determined from analyses of labour market trends, and the two brought together to produce manpower projections. Recruitment requires a knowledge of the sources of labour supply and of the most effective means of advertising job vacancies. Devising satisfactory appraisal schemes needs specialist personnel knowledge, whilst interviewing and training necessitate high standards of specialist skill.

Some specialist personnel skills are also needed by line managers. Line managers need interviewing skills, for example, in selecting employees, in handling grievances and in dealing with disciplinary matters. They need negotiating skills when bargaining with trade unions and their representatives. They also have the responsibility for appraising employees, recommending employees for promotion and ensuring that individuals are doing the sort of work best suited to their abilities and motivations. In performing all these activities, line managers can be made more effective not only by developing the appropriate skills but also by using the specialist services and advice provided by personnel managers.

In industrial relations, there are a variety of practices involved in the leadership, composition and authority of management negotiating teams. In some cases, the lead is taken by line managers with personnel managers providing advice when required. In other cases, personnel managers lead negotiations, with line managers providing advice where technical factors and changes in working practices are involved. Negotiations may even be conducted exclusively by line managers or personnel managers alone. There is no best method of negotiating with trade unions since so much depends on the circumstances and the skills required in each case. The practical need for a combination of knowledge and skills is normally met by ensuring that both line managers and personnel managers are represented in management–union negotiations.

The power and authority of personnel managers

According to Legge (1978), there are a number of factors affecting a manager's power in exercising the personnel function and implementing the policies believed to be appropriate in the personnel area. These include:

(1) The organization's dominant ideology. ⎱

(2) The areas of contextual uncertainty it defines as being of crucial importance to resolve. ⎬ Organizational factors

(3) How it defines, measures and evaluates success. ⎰

(4) The manager's own level of expertise in the areas of activity he undertakes whether specifically personnel management or not.

(5) His right of access to those he needs to influence and from whom he requires information in order to design and implement policy. ⎬ Individual factors

(6) His ability to establish credibility with those individuals he seeks to influence and from whom he seeks support.

(7) The resource power his position commands.[32]

The degree of authority or legitimate power which a managerial function has within an organization, for example, is likely to be directly related to the extent to which its activities and tasks are seen to contribute to the achievement of corporate objectives and enterprise success. Some managerial functions find it easier to claim a more direct relationship between their activities and enterprise success than do others. It is likely, for example, that a positive relationship between managerial activity and corporate success could be defended in the following cases: between a production manager achieving greater quality and output on the production line and a growth in corporate profit; between a marketing manager's increased sales results and enterprise growth; or between entrepreneurial activity in the research and development department and product success. The personnel department, however, is not normally in this position. As Legge and Exley (1975) write:

> Personnel has difficulty in defining what it should be doing because of the difficulty of relating potential 'personnel' activities directly to the achievement of organisational ends, yet the lack of definition by encouraging the undirected collection of a hodgepodge of miscellaneous activities further confuses the question of contribution to organisational success.[33]

They go on to suggest that personnel managers often abandon the attempt to demonstrate a direct relationship between particular corporate objectives and their own departmental goals. A disparity may also develop between their own goals and the activities in which they are chiefly engaged.[34]

The difficulty of relating the personnel department's role to organizational success, claim Legge and Exley, is partly because personnel managers are more concerned 'with means rather than ends and inputs rather than outputs, and in situations where there is difficulty in determining the relationship between the two'.[35] Personnel managers in other words are largely concerned with obtaining, maintaining and discharging an enterprise resource, people or manpower, through which corporate objectives are achieved rather than with the objectives themselves. Further, personnel managers deal with people as complex individuals who cannot normally be manipulated and deployed like inanimate objects, such as technology, finance or other material resources. The relationship between the effort and ability of personnel managers in achieving both their own objectives and corporate objectives is far less apparent than it is for the production manager, marketing manager or finance manager.

Also, since the specialist personnel function is largely concerned with providing efficient human inputs for use within other parts of the organization, such as production, marketing and finance, the outputs or outcomes which these resources generate are usually seen to be the achievement of other parts of the enterprise rather than of the personnel department itself. The root of the problem is that if employee effort to achieve required enterprise outcomes is even indirectly a result of sound personnel management practices, such as effective recruitment, well designed training programmes or good pay and conditions of employment, the personnel department seldom gets the credit. Indeed the specific contribution of effective personnel management to organizational success is normally difficult 'to measure and isolate from effects of market and other organizational factors'.[36]

Another source of confusion in examining the personnel role in achieving organizational success is the widespread nature of its function. This gives rise, as we have seen, not only to difficulties in defining the boundaries between personnel management and other managerial activities. There is also the problem of arriving at realistic definitions of what the personnel department's unique contribution within an organization is. Since every managerial activity has personnel elements, personnel managers and the personnel department cannot claim that it is their contributions alone which facilitate organizational success. They cannot even do so when personnel outputs are quantifiable and measurable. Thus low labour turnover, low absenteeism and strike free industrial relations, for example, can be measured and might be considered as indicative of the personnel function's positive contribution towards achieving corporate objectives.

Such behaviour, however, need not necessarily be attributed to the activities of the personnel department and personnel managers. Indeed, where managing human resources produces few organizational problems, line managers might even claim that it is they who deserve the credit for good personnel management and not the personnel department. Alternatively, they might blame the personnel department when things go badly. Either way, the diffusion of the personnel function into line management activities sometimes leads line managers to question whether the personnel function needs a specialist presence within an organization at all.

In some cases, too, the involvement of line managers in personnel activities and tasks can undermine the status of the personnel specialist. This is largely because personnel work does not then appear to be a specialist activity, requiring particular knowledge, skills and expertise. Personnel specialists have a further difficulty which arises in most line and staff relationships. It is this: while the personnel department may be responsible for designing particular personnel systems, such as pay structures, methods of staff appraisal and job evaluation schemes, it does not usually implement them. Implementation takes place within different managerial functions and is largely the responsibility of functional or line managers. In other words, success or failure in a given personnel activity is removed from the direct control and influence of personnel specialists when it is managed by line managers, rather than by the personnel department.

Lyons (1971) claims, for example, that recruitment is the main work by which personnel departments are judged by other managers.

> This usually seems to them to be unfair because they cannot manufacture people, and they frequently feel that their failure to recruit is due more to management's refusal to accept their advice on personnel policy than their own incompetence at recruiting.
> . . . Few aspects of the personnel function show up fundamental weaknesses more clearly than does the problem of recruitment.[37]

Given such problems, it is difficult for personnel specialists to demonstrate a direct relationship between their organizational contribution and the achievement of corporate objectives. Moreover, as Legge and Exley point out, personnel staff are often 'unable to claim that the activities they undertake are successful even in their own terms, irrespective of any indirect contribution to organisational success'.[38]

Because of these factors, personnel departments are frequently considered by other managerial functions to have a low status within the enterprise and to be able only to attract individuals of low ability and low personal drive. Also, without relevant information and without firm political support for the personnel department to assume a more positive role, any new activities which it undertakes are likely to be unsuccessful. In this way 'a vicious circle of information denial, lack of support and credibility is set up'.[39] Faced with the problem of demonstrating both functional and organizational success, the authority of the personnel department and of the specialists within it can be constantly undermined. In these circumstances it is hardly surprising, as Legge indicates, that in many organizations:

(1) Line management tend to have a confused, hazy and/or stereotyped perception of the potential nature and scope of a personnel department's activities.
(2) Middle and junior line management in particular tend to consider that personnel departments are 'out of touch' with the kind of problems and constraints which face them.[40]

The basic strategies by which it is suggested that personnel specialists can attempt to 'break out of the vicious circle of lack of authority, denial of information and support, low levels of expertise and credibility, inability to demonstrate success, [and] diminished authority'[41] are considered in the following chapter. But essentially, in their quest for organizational authority and for recognition and acceptance by line management, personnel specialists normally need to improve their functional position through collective effort and departmental professionalism, rather than through individual flair or personal charisma.

Conclusion

A central problem of personnel management is its ambiguity in the management function. On the one side, managing people is part of every manager's job and of all managerial work. On the other hand, particular aspects of personnel work are the special concern of personnel specialists working in personnel departments. This gives rise to three basic issues relating to personnel management within organizations. First, there is the question of how personnel activities and tasks should be divided between line managers and personnel specialists. Secondly, there is the extent to which the work of personnel specialists has staff or line authority. Thirdly, there is the problem of coordinating personnel management across an enterprise. There is no general agreement on the answers to these issues. Practices differ between organizations and depend on the organizational and managerial contexts in which personnel management takes place.

Given the inherent ambiguities and uncertainties of the personnel function within enterprises, it is not surprising that personnel specialists often feel that it is difficult to demonstrate their department's vital contribution to the enterprise's efficiency and success. In this, they are constantly trying to increase the power and authority of the personnel department within the organizational and managerial hierarchy.

References and footnotes

1　INSTITUTE OF PERSONNEL MANAGEMENT. *The Institute of Personnel Management.* (London, IPM, 1980). p1.
2　LYONS T P. *The Personnel Function in a Changing Environment.* (London, Pitman, 1971). p1f.
3　FOWLER A. *Personnel Management in Local Government.* 2nd ed. (London, IPM, 1980). p18.
4　THOMASON G. *A Textbook of Personnel Management.* 4th ed. (London, IPM, 1981). p6.
5　TORRINGTON D *and* CHAPMAN J. *Personnel Management.* 2nd ed. (London, Prentice-Hall, 1983). p12.
6　*ibid.* pp4–8.
7　LEGGE K. *Power, Innovation and Problem Solving in Personnel Management.* (London, McGraw-Hill, 1978). p26.
8　GUEST D *and* HORWOOD R. *The Role and Effectiveness of Personnel Managers: A Preliminary Report.* (London, LSE, 1980). p30.
9　WATSON T J. *The Personnel Managers.* (London, Routledge and Kegan Paul, 1977). p63.
10　LEGGE. *opcit.* p5.
11　THOMASON G. *A Textbook of Personnel Management.* 1st ed. (London, IPM, 1975). p26.
12　GUEST *and* HORWOOD. *opcit.* p11.
13　*ibid.*
14　DRUCKER P F. *The Practice of Management.* (London, Pan, 1968). p332.
15　LEGGE. *opcit.* p37.
16　HARVEY-JONES J. 'How I see the personnel function'. *Personnel Management.* Vol. 14, No. 9, September 1982. p26f.
17　MANNING K. 'The rise and fall of personnel'. *Management Today.* March 1983. p74ff.
18　FORTE R. 'How I see the personnel function'. *Personnel Management.* Vol. 14, No. 8, August 1982. p32ff.
19　TURNBULL G. 'How I see the personnel function'. *Personnel Management.* Vol. 14, No. 5, May 1982. p40.
20　JARRATT A. 'How I see the personnel function'. *Personnel Management.* Vol. 14, No. 6, June 1982. pp32–35.
21　EZRA D. 'How I see the personnel function'. *Personnel Management.* Vol. 14, No. 7, July 1982. p31f.
22　*ibid.* p32.
23　PARKER P. 'How I see the personnel function'. *Personnel Management.* Vol. 15, No. 1, January 1983. p17f.
24　*ibid.*
25　*ibid.* p19.
26　*ibid.*
27　JENKINS C. 'Is personnel still underpowered?'. *Personnel Management.* Vol. 5, No. 6, June 1973. p34f.

28 POOLE M. 'A back seat for personnel'. *Personnel Management.*
    Vol. 5, No. 5, May 1973 and 'A power analysis of workplace labour
    relations'. *Industrial Relations Journal.* Vol. 7, No. 3, Autumn 1976.
29 COMMISSION ON INDUSTRIAL RELATIONS. *Report no. 34.*
    The Role of Management in Industrial Relations. (London, HMSO,
    1973). p16.
30 *ibid.* p19.
31 *ibid.* p20.
32 LEGGE. *opcit.* p34.
33 LEGGE K *and* EXLEY M. 'Authority, ambiguity and adaptation:
    the personnel specialist's dilemma'. *Industrial Relations Journal.* Vol.
    6, No. 5, 1975. p54.
34 *ibid.* p55.
35 *ibid.*
36 *ibid.*
37 LYONS. *opcit.* p37.
38 LEGGE *and* EXLEY. *opcit.* p57.
39 *ibid.*
40 LEGGE. *opcit.* p52.
41 *ibid.* p67.

5

Personnel work and personnel policy

Activities and tasks

There are a variety of ways of classifying the work activities of personnel staff. The IPM (1980), for example, distinguishes between the activities of a typical personnel manager in a small organization and those done by a team of personnel managers in larger enterprises. In the first case, it suggests that a personnel manager might carry out all or some of the following activities: recruitment and selection; training; maintaining personnel records; providing employment statistics; negotiating with trade unions; administering collective agreements; and administering employee services such as canteens, pensions and so on. In larger organizations, the IPM says, it is common to find a team of personnel managers dealing with each of the following specialist activities within the personnel department: employment, especially recruitment and selection; training and development; industrial relations; salary policy and salary administration, including job grading, job appraisal and merit rating; employee services such as health, safety and welfare; and organization and manpower planning.[1] Similar classifications of the main activities of personnel staff and the personnel department are provided in Armstrong (1983), Barber (1979), Grant and Smith (1977) and in an earlier study of training for human resources management by the Department of Employment (1972).[2]

An empirical survey on the structures, roles and tasks of personnel managers in two large organizations by Guest and Horwood (1980) provides a useful insight into the activities which personnel managers actually do in larger enterprises. One organization was a manufacturing firm employing 31,000 people in 40 manufacturing units with 175 personnel staff. The other was a regional health authority (RHA) in which there were 61,500 employees in 315 operational units with 106 personnel staff. From their survey, Guest and Horwood identified 85 different personnel tasks which they grouped into 12 activities. They also classified these 85 personnel tasks into five vertical categories of job autonomy, varying with the degree of freedom of action implicit in each task.[3]

The 12 activities and the main personnel tasks within each of them are summarized for both the manufacturing organization and the RHA in Table 14. The percentages in each case indicate the proportion of personnel staff engaged in each task, not the frequency with which they did it. One feature of the breakdown of these activities and tasks was the degree of commonality which existed between personnel work in each organization. Of the 31 main tasks listed, 15 were performed by more than 50 per cent of personnel staff in both organizations. The most common activity was recruitment and selection followed by industrial relations. A greater proportion of the personnel staff in the RHA were involved in personnel planning and research, and in the development of personnel policy, than were their counterparts in the manufacturing organization. By contrast a lower percentage of the RHA personnel staff were engaged in day to day activities, such as employee communications and health safety and welfare, than were the personnel staff in the manufacturing organization.

Guest and Horwood also distinguish between the activities and tasks of 'generalist' personnel managers and 'specialist' personnel managers. They define personnel generalists as those in charge of personnel activity in their own organizational units reporting to senior line managers. Personnel specialists are personnel subordinates, doing a more limited range of personnel work than generalists, who report to someone within the personnel department.[4] The researchers then compared the involvement of personnel managers and personnel subordinates in the 12 activity classifications within the company and the RHA. They did this by taking the performance of more than half the tasks making up an activity as being a significant degree of specialization in that activity. Their findings are summarized in Table 15 on page 115.

A number of points arise from these findings. First, personnel managers in both organizations seemed to be involved in a much wider range of activities than were their subordinates. Secondly, they were also more likely to be involved in industrial relations

Personnel in Context

Table 14
Activities and main tasks of personnel managers in two organizations

Activity	Task	Per cent doing task Company	RHA
Recruitment and selection	Determining methods	59	43
	Defining requirements	64	48
	Advertising	53	54
	Processing applications	74	71
	Interviewing	85	70
	Taking part in decisions	78	71
	Organizing programmes	52	57
	Offering jobs	66	65
	Taking up references	56	56
Industrial relations	Attending meetings	51	24
	Applying agreements	55	63
	Acting as specialist	55	57
	Advising on law	69	65
	Participating in procedures	65	49
Direction and policy determination	Developing policy	33	52
	Managing staff	71	70
	External relations	62	44
Health safety and welfare	Counselling	55	44
	Occupational health	52	60
	Pension advice	53	38
Payment administration	Initiating transactions	53	51
	Dealing with complaints	39	59
Manpower planning and control	Maintaining records	41	63
	Controlling numbers	31	56
Training and development	Identifying needs	70	56
	Instructing	57	54
Employee communications	Planning	56	33
	Operating	52	32
Personnel planning and research	Participation in planning	29	51
Organization design and development	Producing job descriptions	41	73
Personnel information and records	Determining requirements	56	44
Pay and benefits determination	(Not available)	N/A	N/A

Source: GUEST D and HORWOOD R, *The role and effectiveness of personnel managers,* LSE 1980

Table 15

Specialization among personnel managers in two organizations

Activity	Per cent doing more than half of tasks per activity			
	Company		RHA	
	Generalists	Specialists	Generalists	Specialists
Direction and policy determination	28	11	59	27
Personnel planning and research	35	18	50	8
Industrial relations	90	35	73	15
Pay and benefits determination	48	14	–	4
Payment administration	48	47	27	27
Organization design and development	24	11	32	8
Manpower planning and control	34	25	41	4
Personnel information and records	38	51	32	19
Training and development	24	41	18	19
Recruitment and selection	53	75	77	58
Employee communications	72	47	50	35
Health safety and welfare	45	37	41	15

Source: GUEST D and HORWOOD R, *The role and effectiveness of personnel managers,* LSE 1980

than were their subordinates. Thirdly, there appeared to be wide variations between the manufacturing organization and the RHA in the levels of involvement in particular activities by personnel subordinates. Fourthly, there was a relatively high degree of involvement by both personnel managers and personnel subordinates in recruitment and selection in the two organizations, with subordinates in the manufacturing enterprise being more highly involved than were their managers. Finally, compared with the RHA, subordinate involvement in the manufacturing firm in training and development, and in personnel information and records, was much higher than it was for personnel managers.

Further evidence of the range of the generalist personnel role was shown by comparisons between the tasks performed by personnel generalists and personnel subordinates in the two organizations. Of the 85 tasks on Guest and Horwood's checklist, 41 were done by over 50 per cent of the generalists but only 19 were done by over 50 per cent of the subordinates. Again, generalists tended to concentrate on industrial relations and subordinates on recruitment and selection. In the manufacturing organization the generalists undertook an average of 42.30 tasks, compared with 38.88 in the RHA. By contrast, personnel subordinates averaged only 28.09 tasks in the manufacturing organization and 31.89 in the RHA. As Guest and Horwood conclude: 'the contrast between generalist and specialist appears well founded'.[5]

Turning to the most important tasks which were rated 'highly important' by over 75 per cent of those doing them, Guest and Horwood make the following points. Taking the manufacturing organization first, they identified industrial relations tasks as being very prominent among the personnel managers, with very little overlap between personnel managers and personnel subordinates. Further, 'for subordinates the important tasks are those in their specialist area which managers regard as less significant and are therefore prepared to delegate'.[6] This applied particularly to recruitment and selection. There were also a limited number of activity classifications into which the most important tasks fell. Personnel managers, for example, concentrated on direction and policy determination, industrial relations and, surprisingly, training and development. For personnel subordinates, recruitment and selection and training and development figured most prominently.

A similar pattern emerged in the RHA, where a high importance was attached by personnel managers to industrial relations and certain aspects of recruitment and selection such as testing and selection administration. Again, there was little overlap between personnel managers and personnel subordinates, 'confirming the difference in criteria used to judge the importance of tasks'. The RHA personnel staff identified tasks from eight of the 12 activity classifications as 'highly important'. Among the generalists, the emphasis once more was on direction and policy determination, industrial relations and, in contrast to the manufacturing organization, recruitment and selection. The distribution of tasks among the personnel subordinates was spread more widely with 'the main concentration . . . in Pay Determination and Administration, Training and Development and Recruitment and Selection'.[7]

The organization of personnel work

In larger enterprises the activities of personnel specialists are differentiated both horizontally and vertically. The horizontal division of work among personnel practitioners defines their specialist activities across the personnel department, as outlined above. The vertical division of work among personnel staff distinguishes personnel managers from their subordinates by delimiting their levels of responsibility and types of activity within the personnel department. Barber (1979), for example, basing his analysis on a survey of personnel managers by the IPM, suggests that there are four vertical levels at which the personnel manager's role is carried out. These are:

(1) Operational personnel officer, including those who are primarily concerned with the day to day personnel function carrying out policies determined by others.
(2) Senior personnel officer, including those who not only carry out an operational role but also advise others on the implementation of broad policy outlines, and possibly contribute to the evolution of policy.
(3) Personnel manager, including those whose role is primarily advisory and carries responsibility for subordinate personnel officers.
(4) Senior personnel manager, including those who are primarily responsible for the creation of company personnel policy for approval by the board of directors, and for the direction/co-ordination of personnel activities throughout the organization.

Barber adds, however, that personnel job titles do not always indicate the level at which the specialist personnel function is carried out.[8]

Guest and Horwood provide a similar classification of personnel work based on what is claimed to be a conventional structure of the personnel hierarchy in large organizations. These are: the personnel assistant; the personnel manager; the corporate specialist dealing with personnel planning and coordination; and the personnel director concerned with policy development and policy determination. Their research findings show, however, that this traditional organizational structure of personnel responsibilities did not exist in the two organizations which they studied, though the manufacturing company came closer to it. They prefer to cluster personnel tasks into five vertical 'autonomy classifications', depending on the nature of each task and its degree of job discretion. They define the five autonomy classifications as follows:

(1) *'Strategic'*   Tasks involving overall direction and leadership of the function.

(2) *'Analytical/ Conceptual'*   Tasks involving research into and development of concepts and policy proposals necessary to support performance of 'strategic' tasks.

(3) *'Advisory/ Responsive'*   Tasks involving provision of specialist expertise or professional services in support of line management.

(4) *'Instrumental- Active'*   Tasks involving implementation of policy within broadly prescribed limits, but with scope and need for creative input and judgment.

(5) *'Instrumental- Passive'*   Tasks involving implementation of administration systems providing little scope for independent judgment.[9]

The contrast of autonomy classifications between the two organizations studied by Guest and Horwood was considerable (Table

Table 16

Personnel tasks at different organizational levels

Autonomy activity	Per cent of personnel staff engaged in over half the tasks in each autonomy activity			
	Manufacturing organization		RHA	
	Corporate level	Division/ factories	Region	Lower tiers
Strategic	21	1	22	26
Analytic	21	28	22	13
Advisory	0	29	11	20
Instrumental-active	0	47	11	35
Instrumental-passive	0	19	11	20

Source: GUEST D and HORWOOD R, *The role and effectiveness of personnel managers*, LSE 1980

16). In the manufacturing organization, for example, only corporate staff were engaged in strategic personnel activities, with none of them being involved in day to day short term activities such as instrumental tasks and providing specialist advice. By contrast, in the RHA, involvement in the strategic personnel activities was just as heavy below regional level as it was at regional level. Similarly, personnel staff below corporate level in the manufacturing organization tended to be involved in a fairly wide range of non-strategic personnel activities, including advisory services and routine implementation of personnel procedures. There also appeared to be a wider range of personnel activities undertaken by personnel staff in the health service region and its lower tiers, compared with their counterparts in the manufacturing company. Legge (1978) argues that the structure and nature of the roles in the personnel department should match the organizational context in which the department operates. Turning first to the development of particular organizational cultures, and their resulting behavioural patterns, she identifies six key factors influencing these. They are: the history and ownership of an organization; its size; technology; goals and objectives; employees; and environment. The latter includes the organization's product market, labour market, the state of scientific knowledge and any political, social and legal factors affecting the organization.[10]

Following Handy (1976), Legge suggests that the patterns of managerial activity in organizations, resulting from the interaction of the six factors cited above, may be characterized under four headings. These are: steady state activities; innovative developmental activities; breakdown/crises activities; and policy/direction activities. According to Handy, steady state activities are routine, can be programmed and have a 'role' culture characterized by hierarchy and bureaucratic organizational structures. Innovation/development activities are directed towards changing the things which are done in organizations or the ways in which they are done. They operate within a 'task' culture which is project oriented. Breakdown/crises activities deal with the unexpected and, like policy/direction activities, have a 'power' culture focused on a central power source with little bureaucracy. Policy/direction activities are concerned with the setting of priorities, the establishment of standards, the direction and allocation of resources, and the initiation of action.[11]

Legge concludes that organizations, and departments within them, become differentiated or develop different patterns of activities and different cultures, according to the environmental factors facing them. Further, 'this differentiation is necessary for their achievement of high performance'. She suggests that those activities which comprise the organization's specialist personnel work 'may be differentiated according to whether they can be classified under a steady-state, innovative/developmental, breakdown/crises, policy and direction label'. When a personnel department is designed, she argues, personnel roles need to be structured taking into account the organizational context.[12]

Specialist roles within the personnel function can be designed and allocated on a matrix basis, as shown in Figure 17 on page 121. These depend on the 'substantive' expertise and the 'activity based' expertise which is required in each case. An organization characterized by a role culture, for example, might require a personnel department supplying a comprehensive range of substantive expertise principally directed towards steady state personnel activities. These might include well administered, regularly monitored and fairly formalized personnel systems. Alternatively, an organization characterized by breakdown and crises might require a personnel department skilled in experimental organization design. According to Legge:

> the precise design of any personnel department must take account of three major factors: the dominant culture of the organization in which it is to operate (which will influence the style of the operation), the model of the factors which determine this organizational context (which will suggest in which directions the personnel department may, in the future, have to change and develop), and the extent to which both suggest that the organization is more or less differentiated.[13]

Legge is arguing, in other words, that the structure and nature of the roles in the personnel department should match the organizational context and contingencies within which they operate.

Personnel roles

Fowler (1980) says that there is no agreed prescription for the work of the personnel manager. 'The extent of his duties varies in

Figure 17
A matrix for designing personnel departments

	Steady state (role culture)	Innovation development (task culture)	Breakdown crises (power culture)	Policy direction (power culture)
Recruitment and selection				
Industrial relations				
Health, safety and welfare				
Payment administration				
Payment benefits				
Manpower planning				
Training and development				
Planning and research				
Employee communications				
Organization design				
Personnel information				

SUBSTANTIVE EXPERTISE

ACTIVITY BASED EXPERTISE

practice from one employer to another and depends on several factors'. The nature of personnel work, he argues, falls broadly into three categories: executive action, advisory action and administrative action. But the simplified view of the personnel manager as merely an adviser, or as someone who does other managers' work for them, is 'misleading and inaccurate'.[14] The executive role of personnel managers, for example, requires them to take full responsibility for particular elements of personnel work and to make decisions and take action accordingly. The advisory role of the personnel manager provides line managers with specialized knowledge and information about personnel matters, and appropriate guidelines for managerial decisions. The administrative role of personnel management involves maintaining personnel procedures and personnel systems. It is closely related to what Handy categorizes as the 'auditing', 'coordinating' and 'servicing' roles of personnel specialists which are, in effect, refinements within the administrative role.[15]

Most of the activities in which personnel managers are involved contain elements of the executive, advisory and administrative roles to varying degrees (Figure 18). This is particularly the case with manpower planning, recruitment and selection, industrial relations, training and development, and health safety and welfare. In manpower planning, for example, personnel managers typically have the executive authority to make manpower forecasts based on information provided to them by line management. But they also advise on the means of controlling manpower levels within their organizations, while maintaining manpower records. The executive role of the personnel manager in recruitment and selection is largely concerned with such tasks as determining selection methods, job advertising, processing job applications and interviewing candidates, with advice being given to line management when they make selection decisions. The administrative tasks undertaken by personnel staff in selecting employees include organizing selection programmes, taking up references and making offers of employment.

In industrial relations, personnel staff often act as negotiators on behalf of the employer, exercising the executive authority to determine collective agreements with the trade unions. They also participate in disciplinary, grievance and disputes procedures in both executive and advisory capacities. Additionally, they provide

Figure 18
The executive, advisory and administrative roles of personnel managers

Personnel activity	Executive role	Advisory role	Administrative role
Manpower planning	√	√	√
Organization design and development	–	√	–
Recruitment and selection	√	√	√
Pay and benefits determination	√	√	–
Payment administration	–	–	√
Industrial relations	√	√	√
Employee communications	–	√	√
Personnel information	–	–	√
Training and development	√	√	√
Health safety and welfare	√	√	√

advice to line managers on such matters as the interpretation and implications of labour law. It is usually the responsibility of the personnel department to administer the collective agreements covering the terms and conditions of employment for various bargaining units. Personnel also has to ensure that collective bargaining procedures are properly and consistently applied and that they are audited and reviewed regularly.

In training and development, the personnel manager acts primarily in an advisory role, although s/he has an executive responsibility when personnel staff are instructing or lecturing employees within particular training programmes. Thus, for example, the personnel department helps line managers to identify the training needs of their staff and to design training programmes to meet these needs. The personnel department also provides the administrative services necessary for maintaining training programmes and for coordinating them within the enterprise. The executive role of the personnel department in health safety and welfare provides employee counselling and welfare services to employees, both individually and collectively. It also advises on pensions and health and safety matters. It is normally the personnel department's responsibility to act as the administrative link between the employer and external medical and social services.

In organization design and development, the personnel manager has mainly an advisory role, although when this activity is a major part of managerial planning, the personnel department has an executive role too. In Britain, however, organization design and development are not widespread practices. In this area of personnel work, the personnel role is usually confined to the limited administrative one of producing job descriptions for line managers and their staff. In pay and benefits determination, the personnel role is largely advisory but it sometimes contains executive elements. Payment administration, by contrast, is largely administrative with the personnel department organizing payments for employees and dealing with individual pay complaints and related matters. In employee communications, the personnel manager provides advice in the planning of communications and normally administers communication procedures. In personnel information, the personnel role is normally limited to administering and maintaining manpower records and statistics.

Personnel policy

According to Anthony (1977), 'policies are generally understood to be limitations or constraints which management imposes on its own freedom of action'. Some are self imposed constraints representing 'what is sometimes rather grandiloquently called the philosophy of management'. These include, for example, the statutory duty placed on some public sector employers to negotiate and consult with representative trade unions. Others, such as where a company has a high wage policy in order to recruit and retain scarce labour, are imposed 'in a recognition (real or imagined) of the limitations of the circumstances in which the enterprise finds itself'.[16]

It was the Royal Commission on Trade Unions and Employers' Associations, chaired by Lord Donovan between 1965 and 1968, which first drew attention to the lack of positive personnel policies in large sections of British industry at that time. While conceding that the scope of personnel work had expanded considerably since the appointment of the first women welfare officers during the first world war, the Commission continued: 'if companies have their own personnel specialists why have they not introduced effective personnel policies to control methods of negotiation and pay structures in their firms?' The Commission concluded that although personnel officers were responsible for activities like staff record keeping, selection, training, welfare and negotiations, 'many firms have no [personnel] policy, and perhaps no conception of it'.[17]

The Commission was concerned mainly with promoting the orderly and effective regulation of industrial relations between employers and unions within companies and factories. It recommended that the boards of companies should review industrial relations policies within their undertakings with a view to developing, together with trade union representatives, comprehensive and authoritative collective bargaining machinery to settle the terms and conditions of employment between them. But, it went on, in order to pursue such objectives, companies 'will need to develop positive management policies on such matters as recruitment, promotion, training and retraining', as well as collecting systematic information on which to base action in these matters.[18]

After the Donovan Commission had reported, the need for establishing properly formulated personnel policies began slowly to be accepted by many sections of British industry. Currently, in larger enterprises at least, defined personnel policies often form an integral part of the overall strategy by which senior management seeks to pursue its corporate and business objectives. Such policies normally define courses of action to be taken by managers towards particular personnel issues, including recruitment, selection, training, discipline and so on. They also provide links with other policy areas, such as production, marketing and finance. The major pressures acting on employers to formulate such policies have been external rather than internal. These include government, legislation, the European Community and trade union power.

In its inquiry into the role of boards of directors in determining the industrial relations and employment policies of their companies, the Commission on Industrial Relations (CIR 1973) concludes that companies differ widely in the scope of their personnel policies and in the extent to which they actually think them out and define them. At one extreme, there are those enterprises which have written policy statements covering a wide range of subjects. At the other there are those with only a rudimentary policy on basic terms and conditions of employment, backed by observance of the minimum legal obligations placed on them as employers. In other cases, some employers have well defined policies in certain areas but limited ones in others.[19]

There are a number of arguments favouring the setting out formally of clearly defined personnel policies. The first is that defined policies promote consistency in managerial action towards employees. They also enable employees to know where they stand in relation to the personnel objectives of their employers. Secondly, the processes involved in producing written policy documents are invaluable in focusing managerial attention on the purposes and details of particular employment policies. As the CIR writes: 'they clarify intentions and eliminate uncertainties when reliance is placed on custom and practice or when policy is a matter of surmise'. Thirdly, written policies provide a convenient reference point in the communication of policy to managers, employees and their representatives. Fourthly, by making policies explicit, written policy documents can be reviewed and adapted as circumstances require, thus providing a basis for policy and organizational changes from time to time.[20]

Not all managements view personnel policy in this positive and proactive way. Many managements would feel highly threatened by committing themselves to written policies of this kind. They adopt an implicit and covert approach to personnel policy, preferring to retain flexibility and adaptability within a relatively negative and reactive policy framework. Anthony argues that the notion of advocating written policies probably stems from the idea of management being a kind of governmental, open and democratic function in society. In his view:

> the idea itself is probably mistaken and our recent experience may in any case have discredited the belief that even governments are necessarily open and consistent in their processes of decision making.[21]

Given a proactive approach, a necessary condition for formulating a set of explicit personnel policies is for senior management and its governing body to give full attention to the task. It is they who have the final responsibility for such policies and it is they who exert the major influence on their form and content. They can also ensure the integration of personnel policy with other corporate and operational policies in the enterprise. Policy formulation is normally a time consuming process, especially in the personnel area, since personnel policies cannot be expected to succeed without the agreement and acceptance of those who implement them and of those whom they directly affect. In practice, this requires that line managers and employees are kept fully informed about what is happening in the personnel policy making process and that they are able to influence policy determination from the outset.

Although top management is responsible for ensuring that personnel policies are defined, implemented and regularly reviewed, effective policy formulation requires the active guidance and coordination which senior personnel practitioners are able to provide. The contribution of personnel practitioners is based on their specific functional responsibilities, their ability to give the necessary time to the task, and the specialist knowledge and skills within the personnel department. The personnel manager, for example, is in a position: to make an overall study of enterprise needs; to consult and involve the people who have to implement policy at various levels; to produce policy proposals; and to secure agreement to the policies prior to their authorization.

The communication of personnel policies to managers and employees is an obvious requirement, if the purposes of having explicit policies are to be realized. As the CIR says, 'one advantage of written policy documents is as an aid to communication but their value depends of course on the use made of them'.[22] This necessitates developing positive attitudes towards keeping everyone fully informed about personnel and other policies, together with effective means of communicating them to those directly affected by them. In these circumstances, overall responsibility for personnel matters needs to be assigned to a senior manager or personnel director, with the authority for ensuring that personnel policies are effectively communicated to all managers, subordinates and employee representatives.

The Department of Employment (DoE 1972) in its code of practice on industrial relations provides some useful guidelines for managements when establishing employment and industrial relations policies in their enterprises. It interprets industrial relations in the widest sense, as being concerned with both collective matters and with those issues directly affecting individual employees in their jobs. The code states that since it is the principal aim of management to conduct the business of an undertaking successfully, one of its major objectives should be to develop effective personnel policies commanding the confidence of all employees. Managers at the highest levels, continues the code, 'should give, and show that they give, just as much attention to industrial relations as to such functions as finance, marketing, production or administration'.[23] Turning to employment issues, the code states that clear and comprehensive policies are essential in establishing good relations between management and employees. 'They help management to make the most effective use of its manpower resources and give each employee opportunity to develop his potential'.

The code goes on to suggest that while management should initiate and accept primary responsibility for these policies, they need to be developed in consultation and negotiation with employee representatives. It also states that management should develop effective policies for promoting equal opportunity in employment, thus ensuring that its employment policies do not discriminate against individuals on the grounds of their age, sex, ethnic origin or other personal attributes. The areas where managements are recommended to develop such policies include: the planning and use of manpower; recruitment and selection; training; payment systems; the status and security of employees; and working conditions.[24] The DoE code also provides guidelines on the collective aspects of personnel policy, including employee communications, joint consultation, collective bargaining and employee representation.

The guidance in the DoE code on disciplinary policy has now been superseded by that provided in the Advisory Conciliation and Arbitration Service code of practice (ACAS 1977a). ACAS states that 'disciplinary rules and procedures are necessary for promoting fairness and order in the treatment of individuals and in the conduct of industrial relations'. It goes on to say that they should be designed to emphasize and encourage improvements in individual conduct, rather than as a means of imposing sanctions on individuals. In ACAS's view it is management's responsibility to maintain discipline within the enterprise and to ensure that adequate disciplinary rules and procedures exist. 'However, if they are to be fully effective the rules and procedures need to be accepted as reasonable both by those who are covered by them and by those who operate them'.[25]

Personnel strategies

Legge suggests that in their search for professional credibility and functional authority within organizations, personnel specialists have to adapt themselves to the contexts and situations facing them. Given that the personnel department wishes to gain power and influence in corporate decision making, and that personnel specialists wish to win support and contribute to corporate effectiveness, she argues that personnel managers derive their authority from any of three paths. She calls these 'conformist innovation', 'deviant innovation' and that of the personnel 'problem solver'.[26]

Conformist innovation is defined by Legge and Exley (1975) as attempts by the personnel specialist 'to demonstrate a closer relationship between his activities (means) and organizational success criteria (ends)'. In using this approach, personnel managers accept the dominant utilitarian values and bureaucratic structures of their organizations and try to show the importance of their specialist activities within this framework. Using this mode of action, personnel specialists try to highlight their departmental role in indirectly facilitating organizational success, by tackling potentially costly obstacles to it. They might, for example, seek to reduce labour turnover or design a career structure to alleviate management succession problems. Personnel's contribution to organizational success 'becomes less important than its role in anticipating, preventing, or rectifying a range of organizational malfunctions'.[27]

As conformist innovators, personnel managers tend to emphasize what Sayles (1964) describes as their 'auditing' and 'stabilization' relationships with management, rather than their advisory ones.[28] Auditing relationships involve finding out whether various managerial activities conform with organizational policies and rules. Stabilization relationships involve granting prior approval to certain managerial decisions, on the basis of specialist expertise, that takes organizational needs into account in the area concerned. They are aimed at coping bureaucratically with problems of control and coordination by scrutinizing managerial decisions before, when and after they are taken. Both sorts of relationship require personnel specialists to minimize the costs of potentially inconsistent and inappropriate personnel decisions by line managers.

According to Legge and Exley, the conformist innovation approach 'develops an appreciation on the part of personnel specialists that their contribution will appear more tangible if presented in financial terms'.[29] Because of this, conformist innovators are likely to attempt various cost benefit analyses of personnel work. These include costing labour turnover, evaluating training programmes, estimating the benefits of introducing new payment systems and so on. They are also likely to encourage human asset accounting and the use of the computer in personnel work. As conformist innovators, personnel managers accept line management's prior definition of how organizational activities should be determined and evaluated and what their priorities should be.

Legge and Exley further argue that the conformist innovation strategy of personnel managers derives from the 'trait' model of professionalism. They list the most frequently mentioned professional traits as:

   (i) skill based on theoretical knowledge.
  (ii) the provision of education and training.
 (iii) competence evaluated by fellow professionals.
 (iv) organization, that is, a professional culture is sustained by formal professional associations, which have the power to regulate entry to (and, sometimes, promotion within) the profession.
  (v) adherence to a professional code of conduct.
 (vi) altruistic service.

In these circumstances, becoming a personnel professional largely involves acquiring expertise and skills from the appropriate education and training. The expertise required is that 'which can be demonstrated as relevant in performing the personnel function in the manner described above'.[30]

A second way of describing professionalism is, according to Johnson (1972), as a special 'type of occupational control rather than an expression of the inherent nature of particular occupations. A profession is not then an occupation, but a means of controlling an occupation'.[31] By this approach, professionalism exists where personnel professionals are able to define the needs of their managerial and employee clients and the ways in which these needs are to be met. Legge and Exley call the personnel strategy derived from this model of professionalism 'deviant innovation'.

Whereas conformist innovators accept their ends and adjust their means in the personnel role:

> the deviant innovator, rather than making his activities conform to the dominant values about what constitutes success, attempts to change this means/end relationship by gaining acceptance for a different set of criteria for the evaluation of organizational success and his contribution to it.[32]

In the role of deviant innovator, then, the personnel specialist seeks to gain acceptance of human resource policies and procedures based on altruistic as well as utilitarian values within the enterprise. The personnel manager may contend, for example, that work should satisfy individual social needs as well as instrumental organizational ones. In doing this, s/he is introducing an external reference group into the enterprise to evaluate recognized personnel and corporate activities. Legge suggests that the personnel specialist might even act as 'interpreter and advocate' of society to the enterprise, showing that its dominant values are not necessarily the same as those of society as a whole.[33]

Using the deviant innovation approach, personnel specialists base their role, their internal relationships and their authority less on a managerial than on a more independent professional footing. It is personnel managers, in other words, who define the personnel needs of line managers and then decide how these needs should be met. They do this in accordance with their own professional expertise and values and with what they see to be appropriate in given organizational circumstances. Their managerial clients, in turn, are expected to accept the personnel specialist's definition of what activities should be provided to them rather than asserting their own right to do so. Further, line managers normally evaluate personnel's authority in this initiating role on the basis of its reputation amongst its peers. They may even judge personnel's performance, and the validity of its activities, not on their own criteria, but on more neutral professional grounds.

In practice, few personnel specialists are in a position to

change dominant organizational values so fundamentally. Nor are they normally able to exert this high level of control over other managerial groups in their organizations. Nevertheless, movement towards this occurs when personnel specialists take on the role of internal consultants. A good example of this is where legislation places certain restrictions on an enterprise's freedom to achieve its desired objectives. In these cases, personnel specialists can use their role as legal experts to advise management on certain courses of action. This advice is backed by the full authority of the law and it compels the attention of line managers as personnel's clients.

It is claimed, however, that 'neither of these attempts to gain "professional" authority is fully viable'. Although conformist innovators try to use their professional expertise to show person-nel's contribution to organizational success in financial terms, many personnel activities are difficult to quantify and to evaluate in this way. Similarly, attempts by deviant innovators to get new organizational ends accepted, which are not evaluated financially, are likely to provoke resistance among those who accept existing dominant organizational values. In practice, claim Legge and Exley, 'personnel specialists tend to oscillate between these two paths to "professional" authority'. In deflationary situations, for example, the strategy of conformist innovation is likely to be more acceptable, whilst in periods of boom 'the climate for experimentation of all kinds is likely to be more favourable than at other times'. The strategy of deviant innovation generally requires such an economic context in which to develop.[34]

Legge argues that although conformist innovation and deviant innovation may be seen as distinct and separate personnel strategies, they may also be regarded as two different styles of performing the role of the personnel manager as a problem solver. It is in the role of problem solver, she suggests, whether directed towards conformist or deviant innovatory solutions, that the personnel manager's approach to effective personnel policy and practice perhaps may be best found. She concludes that diagnostic problem solving requires a contingent approach to personnel management where the design and implementation of personnel policy matches or is contingent upon specific organizational circum-stances and requirements. A contingent approach to personnel problem solving, she claims, 'brings with it the combined advantages of flexibility . . . with a sensitivity to the political dimensions of organizational life' [35]

Conclusion

Personnel work varies in its scope, activities and tasks between organizations. It also varies between personnel managers and personnel subordinates within the same organization. Personnel managers, for example, tend to do a wide range of general tasks, with personnel subordinates doing a narrower range of specialist ones. This has implications for how personnel roles are perceived in enterprises and how personnel departments are organized within them. There is no agreement as to how the executive, advisory and administrative duties of personnel work should be distinguished and differentiated. Much depends on the organizational and managerial contexts within which the personnel specialist operates.

Given the importance of personnel policy within organizations, personnel managers have a vital part to play in its development, application and monitoring. In developing appropriate personnel strategies, and in seeking to achieve professional recognition internally, personnel managers have a choice of approaches. They may be conformist innovators, deviant innovators or diagnostic problem solvers. In adopting a contingent approach to personnel problem solving, as argued by Legge, personnel specialists are in the best position to develop relevant policies and practices. In this way, they not only contribute to organizational effectiveness but also strengthen the authority of the specialist personnel function with line managers. This is important since without organizational power and the support of line managers, the specialist personnel role is severely constrained.

References and footnotes

1   INSTITUTE OF PERSONNEL MANAGEMENT. *The Institute of Personnel Management.* (London, IPM, 1980). p11.

2   See ARMSTRONG M. *A Handbook of Personnel Management Practice*. 2nd ed. (London, Kogan Page, 1983); BARBER D. *The Practice of Personnel Management*. 2nd ed. (London, IPM, 1979); GRANT J V *and* SMITH G. *Personnel Administration and Industrial Relations*. 2nd ed. (London, Longman, 1977); and DEPARTMENT OF EMPLOYMENT. *Training for the Management of Human Resources*. (London, HMSO, 1972).

3   GUEST D *and* HORWOOD R. *The Role and Effectiveness of Personnel Managers: A Preliminary Report*. (London, LSE, 1980). pp18, 20 and 22.

4   *ibid*. p28.

5   *ibid*. p32f.

6   *ibid*. p34.

7   *ibid*. p35ff.

8   BARBER. *opcit*. p10f.

9   GUEST *and* HORWOOD. *opcit*. pp20 and 38f.

10 LEGGE K. *Power, Innovation and Problem Solving in Personnel Management*. (London, McGraw-Hill, 1978). p118ff.

11 HANDY C B. *Understanding Organizations*. (Harmondsworth, Penguin, 1976). pp178–84.

12 LEGGE. *opcit*. pp124–9.

13 *ibid*. p130.

14 FOWLER A. *Personnel Management in Local Government*. 2nd ed. (London, IPM, 1980). p25.

15 HANDY. *opcit*. p273.

16 ANTHONY P D. *The Conduct of Industrial Relations*. (London, IPM, 1977). p18.

17 ROYAL COMMISSION ON TRADE UNIONS AND EMPLOY-ERS' ASSOCIATIONS 1965–1968. Chairman: The Right Hon. Lord Donovan. *Report*. (London, HMSO, 1968). p25.

18 *ibid*. p45.

19 COMMISSION ON INDUSTRIAL RELATIONS. *Report no. 34. The Role of Management in Industrial Relations*. (London, HMSO, 1973). p5.

20 *ibid*. p6.

21 ANTHONY. *opcit*. p21.

22 COMMISSION ON INDUSTRIAL RELATIONS. *opcit*. p14.

23 DEPARTMENT OF EMPLOYMENT. *Industrial Relations Draft Code of Practice*. (London, HMSO, 1972). p4.

24 *ibid*. pp9–13.

25 ADVISORY CONCILIATION AND ARBITRATION SERVICE. *Code of Practice. 1. Disciplinary Practice and Procedures*. (London, HMSO, 1977a). p1f.

26 LEGGE. *opcit*. Especially pp69–116.

27 LEGGE K *and* EXLEY M. 'Authority, ambiguity and adaptation: the personnel specialist's dilemma'. *Industrial Relations Journal*. Vol. 6, No. 3, 1975. p59f.

28 SAYLES L R. *Managerial Behavior*. (NY, McGraw-Hill, 1964).

29   LEGGE *and* EXLEY. *opcit.* p60.
30   *ibid.* p59ff.
31   JOHNSON T J. *Professions and Power* (London, Macmillan, 1972). p45.
32   LEGGE *and* EXLEY. *opcit.* p61.
33   LEGGE. *opcit.* p85f.
34   LEGGE *and* EXLEY. *opcit.* p62f.
35   LEGGE. *opcit.* p115.

6

Personnel management as an occupation

Managers as a social group

Managers are a heterogeneous and a growing occupational group. In 1961, for example, it is estimated that there were 1.3 million managers in Britain, comprising 5.4 per cent of the occupied population. By 1971, this had risen to 1.7 million or 6.7 per cent of the occupied population. The 1981 Census estimated there to be some 2.5 million managers in Britain representing over 10 per cent of the occupied population at that time.[1]

There are a number of studies of British managers, such as those of the Acton Society Trust (1956), Clements (1958), Clark (1966) and Melrose-Woodman (1978).[2] A survey of some 1,000 members of the British Institute of Management (BIM) in the early 1980s by Mansfield and his colleagues (1981) provides a useful profile of the 'typical' British manager in 1980. It also contains valuable information about their social backgrounds, education, careers and political attitudes. According to the BIM study:

> the 'typical manager' in Britain in 1980 is male, married and between 36 and 45 years of age. He is likely to work in the private sector, be employed in a British-owned manufacturing industry, be involved in general management at senior levels and earn between £10,000–£15,000 a year. He probably works for an organization with between 1,000–10,000 employees but on a site with less than 100 employees.[3]

In this sample 36 per cent of the respondents were in manufacturing, 34 per cent in commerce and service industry, 17 per cent in public administration and education, with the rest in private practice and the armed services.

Turning to the social origins of British managers, the BIM study cites over a quarter of its sample having fathers who worked in senior managerial or professional occupations and some two thirds with fathers in white collar employment. A majority of the sample was educated at either grammar or technical schools. This was especially the case among private sector board members, with almost a third of these being educated privately. Ninety-seven per cent of the sample had some full time or part time post school education, and about a third had been to university.[4] The educational qualifications of the managers in the BIM sample are

Table 17

Educational qualifications of British managers in BIM survey 1980

	Private sector		Public sector	Total
	Board members per cent	All managers per cent	per cent	per cent
'O' and 'A'levels	74.0	74.5	80.9	76.4
Technical qualifications	31.5	38.4	39.7	38.8
Science degrees	13.6	13.0	10.6	11.7
Technical degrees	9.8	7.4	10.0	8.4
Other degrees	14.9	14.5	20.3	16.1
Professional qualifications	58.5	61.9	80.0	67.3

Source: MANSFIELD R and others, *The British manager in profile*, BIM 1981

summarized in Table 17. This shows that over a third of the sample had a degree and some two thirds claimed a professional qualification. It also suggests that public sector managers tend generally to be better qualified than their private sector counterparts.

The BIM survey shows that there is a high degree of professional consciousness among modern managers. 'Whatever the tensions between professional and organizational control, professional status is overwhelmingly claimed'.[5] A majority of the sample, for example, was in favour of a code of ethics for managers. Although the survey was conducted only among BIM members, the respondents were also members of other professional and managerial associations. Generally, they belonged to over two associations each but they were not particularly active within them, only participating in one organization regularly. Most considered, however:

that the knowledge base of modern management practice should be fostered; that commitment to professional norms should be independent of income and employing organisation; and that professional bodies should increasingly represent their interests in dealing with the state and government.[6]

They were, in other words, highly supportive of the professional aims of the BIM, as the body representative of managerial occupational interests.

To find out managerial attitudes towards trade unions, the sample was asked to indicate agreement or disagreement with a number of statements about union power and activities. The replies revealed that 87 per cent of the respondents believed that the trade unions do not act in the country's national economic interests and that 82 per cent thought that trade unions have too much power. Indeed, 53 per cent of the sample believed that the unions have more power than management. Further, 89 per cent thought that union membership should be voluntary, with some 79 per cent believing that trade unions should not use industrial action to achieve their bargaining objectives. Public sector managers in the sample tended to be slightly less hostile to the trade unions than did those in the private sector. For example, 'while 86 per cent of private sector managers consider that unions have too much power today, this figure is reduced to 73 per cent for managers in the public sector'.[7]

The BIM survey also shows, somewhat paradoxically, that there has been a rise in managerial unionism in recent years. Whilst only a minority of enterprises in which the respondents were employed recognized managerial unions or staff associations for collective bargaining purposes, 23 per cent reported that their organizations had managerial unions, nine per cent had staff associations and nine per cent had both. In the private sector, 78 per cent of the managers had no opportunity for collective representation for themselves. In the public sector, on the other hand, only 10 per cent of the managers did not have the opportunity for some form of collective representation: 49 per cent had managerial unions, 13 per cent staff associations and 20 per cent both.[8] The researchers conclude: 'managers are still opposed to trade unions, although a minority are now themselves trade unionists and in the public sector this is actually a majority'.[9]

Table 18
Managerial experience of collective bargaining by job category

Job category	Formal collective bargaining	Informal meetings with union represen- tatives	Handling grievances brought by union represen- tatives
		per cent of respondents	
Personnel	36.3	56.1	56.3
Production	28.7	66.7	65.5
General management	27.5	46.3	52.6
Engineering and maintenance	20.0	66.1	66.1
Administration	13.2	50.0	55.9
Finance and accounting	11.5	23.9	29.2
Other	9.1	30.9	48.2
Research and development	6.7	21.7	38.3
Sales and marketing	5.9	25.2	25.2

Source: MANSFIELD R and others, *The British manager in profile*, BIM 1981

According to the BIM survey, as can be seen in Table 18, managers in personnel, production, general management, and engineering and maintenance are the managerial groups most likely to be involved in formal collective bargaining arrangements with union representatives. These groups together with administrative managers are also more likely to be involved in informal meetings with trade union representatives. When it comes to handling grievances brought by union representatives, most managerial groups appear to have had some experience here, apart from those in research and development, finance and accounting, and sales and marketing. This is probably accounted for by the generally low levels of union activity in these parts of organizations, especially in the private sector.

More than a third of the BIM sample reported that they were involved in some kind of joint consultation or employee involvement in their enterprises. Not surprisingly, joint consultation was greater in the public sector than it was in the private sector, with almost half of the public sector managers being involved, compared with only a third in the private sector. The respondents were not very supportive of employee participation, with marked agreement on this between private and public sector managers. Generally, the survey's findings suggest 'that statutory forms of employee participation designed to encourage strategic power sharing [with employees] are still likely to be opposed by Britain's managers'.[10]

Another part of the BIM survey was aimed at finding out managerial attitudes towards governmental intervention in the economy and industrial affairs. The general tenor of managerial responses was very much 'non interventionist'. According to Mansfield and his colleagues, the central findings to emerge from this part of their inquiries were that:

- Managers tend to endorse state intervention only on certain specific industrial relations issues (notably in the form of legislation on strikes and compulsory arbitration).
- There is some support for the control of foreign enterprises in Britain and particularly for the state assuming responsibility for setting up strategic stocks of essential raw materials.
- Managers in Britain are generally against the statutory control of prices, wages and salaries.
- Only a minority wish to see extensive import controls and the subsidising of exports.
- There is marked opposition to increasing the industrial powers of ministers and to the principle of state monopolies.[11]

Public sector managers were more likely to endorse interventionist policies than were those in the private sector.[12]

A survey of the heads of personnel in 428 companies, and of the chief executives in a further 110 companies, by Urwick Group consultants at the end of 1982, provides a useful complement to some of the findings of the BIM study. According to this study, 47 per cent of the sample considered that trade unions were a hindrance to productivity improvement, with chief executives being more inclined than personnel specialists to see the unions as a threat. Forty-two per cent of the respondents thought that further legislation was necessary to curb the power of the unions, although the chief executives were notably more in favour of legislation than were the heads of personnel. There were also emphatic objections to worker directors in companies which was one of the major options proposed by the EEC draft fifth directive. Finally, only 30 per cent of the respondents saw the need for a national incomes policy 'when recession lifts', with 59 per cent opposing it.[13] Managers appear, then, to be supportive of state intervention in union affairs and industrial relations but not in corporate matters.

Personnel specialists as an occupational group

There are over 50,000 personnel specialists in Britain, of whom about 35,500 were members of the IPM in June 1989.[14] Nichols (1969) claims that 'if one must talk of professionalism at all, those in personnel management probably approximate most closely to the notion of the "professional manager"'.[15] Personnel specialists however, like many professional employees such as other managers, teachers, scientific workers, accountants and engineers, are not a homogeneous occupational group. Although personnel specialists undertake a range of common activities and tasks, the ways in which they carry them out vary according to the type of organization and the contexts in which they take place. Some work in large organizations, whilst others are employed in small ones. Some are employed in private firms, others in public enterprises. Some are graduates with IPM qualifications and others are non-graduates with or without IPM membership. These and the other personal characteristics of personnel specialists, and their organizational circumstances, reflect their diversity as an occupational group.

Tyson (1979) argues that personnel management varies organizationally. He suggests that the power, authority and status of personnel managers are basically dependent on their organizational position and on the ways in which they conduct their work. In his view, personnel managers are not there to further the social responsibilities of business. Nor is it their role to humanize industrial capitalist enterprises. They are experts in managing the employment relationship between employers and employees. As such, Tyson concludes, personnel managers have primarily an organizational rather than an occupational orientation. They need to be studied in the context of their work and different organizational cultures, not of their wider professional roles in society.[16]

Watson (1977) in his study of personnel managers concludes that, as an occupation, personnel management contributes to the socialization process integrating subordinate employees into industrial capitalism. Personnel management does this, he says, by acting 'as a social institution contributing to the maintenance of a given social order'. If managements were to fail to achieve their corporate objectives by not coping with the unintended consequences of their policies with which the personnel function is expected to deal, he argues, 'then each organisation would disintegrate, so leading to the collapse of the societal mode of integration'.[17]

This view is reinforced by Watson's finding that the background of personnel managers is predominantly middle class. In conducting interviews with 100 personnel managers, Watson identifies four modes of entry into the occupation. He describes these as 'initial choosers', 'employee-initiated career change (positive)', 'employee-initiated career change (negative)' and 'organisation-initiated career change'. Twenty-four of his sample were initial choosers, 20 had initiated positive career changes, 20 had initiated negative career changes, and 27 had experienced organizationally initiated career changes. In analysing his sample by social class, Watson found that only 24 per cent were from working class homes. He also shows that the 24 per cent of 'initial choosers' who entered personnel management as a first career were 'predominantly the younger, better-qualified people from homes of higher status'.[18]

Watson also provides useful evidence on the appeal and dislikes of personnel work amongst its practitioners. His main finding is that there appears to be a significant shift in orientation in terms of what personnel work means to individual personnel specialists between entering the occupation and practising it afterwards. Their pre-entry impressions were strongly oriented towards 'dealing with people' and the welfare aspects of the personnel role. In their current employment situations, by contrast, the personnel managers showed a 'clear positive orientation towards what might be seen as the more managerial content of their work'. Watson concludes that it is personnel's dual orientation to people as people and to people as organizational resources which provides personnel as an occupation with its essential difficulties and problems. It 'also provides some of the basic reward for being in the work'.[19]

When it came to their dislikes of personnel work, Watson's respondents put these into two main categories. First, there were those routine personnel activities such as personnel administration and personnel record keeping which, whilst essential and vital to the personnel role, were regarded as mundane and repetitions by its participants. Secondly, there were those issues relating personnel work to the organization and to management generally. The respondents' dislikes included, for example:

'We're not seen as part of the management by the management'.

'We're only used to fire-fight'.

'The lack of clear personnel policy in the company'.

'Our lack of status and people knowing what to do'.

'Everybody thinks he's a good personnel manager'.

'Being a service department: not being seen as contributing to the organisation'.[20]

Lack of credibility, low status and non-recognition of their role were those aspects of a personnel specialist's work which were seen as the most frustrating.

Research by Guest and Horwood (1981) into personnel management careers identifies five types of career path. They designate these: 'the mobile professional'; 'the late professional'; 'the local specialist'; 'the general manager'; and the 'part-time personnel manager'. Mobile professionals, for example, spend their whole working lives in personnel management. They tend to be employed in a number of organizations and have transferable skills across them. They are normally IPM members. Late professionals move into personnel management from other jobs and careers and often have IPM qualifications. Local specialists spend their whole career in personnel management but only work for one organization. They may or may not be IPM members. General managers are usually passing through personnel management, are not normally IPM members and are not particularly committed to personnel work as a career. Part time personnel managers can be found in 'quite sizeable organizations with no formal personnel function where the role is a part-time one covered by someone in administration or finance'.[21]

Guest and Horwood conclude that different types of personnel specialists seem to have greater chances of career success in different organizations. In the manufacturing organization which they studied, for example, the authors suggest that career success is more likely to be associated with the professional ethos of the mobile professional or late professional manager. In the health service regional health authority which they studied, it seems that the knowledge and experience associated with the local specialist personnel manager are just as important to career success. In summarizing their results, Guest and Horwood suggest that for success in personnel management, 'you should be a graduate, be male, change jobs regularly in your organisation, report to someone outside the personnel function and be a member of the IPM'. But their data also highlights the range of career types of personnel management as an occupation.[22]

Watson in his study of personnel managers asked his respondents if they detected anything generally different or distinctive about people who work in personnel management and whether they could be categorized in any way. According to his findings, three types of personnel manager were reported:

> There's the older 'soft-option' type interested in welfare or who has just been 'shunted in'. Then there are those who have worked up from manual or lower-clerical jobs and, thirdly, there are the young professional types who choose Personnel as a career.[23]

Of these the third category, the qualified professional, was seen to be growing in size. He also points out that when recruiting to personnel departments, senior managers seem to be poorly disposed towards personnel applicants with 'religious attachments, an interest in social work or, very importantly, who are women'. He believes that this is related to the personnel department's problems of credibility with line management and the need to kill the 'welfare image' of personnel management as a managerial specialism.[24]

Professionalism and personnel management

For Thomason (1981), whether personnel management qualifies as a profession is a question 'which will continue to be debated within the more general discussion of whether any managerial occupation could qualify given the usual template applied'.[25] Guest and Horwood believe that the different backgrounds and fields of operation of personnel managers 'raise doubts about the value of the professional model and of any attempt to view personnel problems as amenable to solution through a primary focus on professionalisation'.[26] Lupton (1978), by contrast, concludes that 'we ought to be looking to the future development of personnel management as a profession, and not merely for ways of improving present practice'. For him, personnel management must involve the application of the behavioural sciences to the structure and functioning of industrial and commercial organizations.[27]

Whether personnel management is or is not a profession is obviously controversial, though notions of professionalism and professionalization are highly significant for those speaking for occupational groups such as personnel managers and similar professional workers. We have seen in Chapter 4 how professionalism can be defined in terms of either a 'trait' model or as a means of occupational control. Friedson (1973) argues, for example, that:

> Professionalisation might be defined as a process by which an organised occupation . . . obtains the exclusive right to perform a particular kind of work, control, training for and access to it, and control the right of determining and evaluating the way work is performed.[28]

In the classical sense of having full occupational autonomy and of providing exclusive personal services to individual fee paying clients, personnel management is not a profession. If, however, professionalism occurs where a given occupational group makes a claim for power and authority in specified areas of occupational performance, then personnel management can be regarded as a professionalized activity.

This concept of professionalism has two essential elements. The first is that there are common occupational interests amongst its practitioners, even when the professional group itself is heterogeneous. The second is that its practitioners both claim and demonstrate high standards of professional competence and expertise. The first point is made by Watson. He claims that there is a common consciousness among personnel specialists, whether or not they are IPM members, especially in their need to gain status with senior management in their organizations. He writes:

There is, in fact, a coherence within the occupation which is far greater than I expected when I set out to investigate areas of employment some of which were, until then, unfamiliar to me. To find personnel officers and managers in banks, engineering companies, co-operative societies, council offices and so on, speaking in such similar ways on aspects of their jobs was a considerable surprise to me.[29]

There are, then, strong empirical grounds for viewing personnel managers as members of a coherent occupational group, even though their roles differ between organizations.

To be seen as professionally competent and expert in their organizational roles is important to personnel managers in claiming professional status. In providing high levels of expertise, knowledge and skills within their organizations, for example, personnel specialists increase their credibility and authority with line managers. They also provide management with tangible evidence that personnel managers are contributing to the effectiveness and success of the enterprise. Being professional in this sense means being professionally competent in one's job as a personnel specialist. It does not necessarily mean being a member of a generally recognized professional body, with its underlying assumptions of specialist education and training and high occupational status and prestige. This is underlined by the fact that many personnel professionals do not bother obtaining IPM qualifications. But it does mean that professional management practices are closely linked with providing specialist competence and expertise in managing organizations, especially in managing the employment relationship between employers and employees.

It is interesting to note that over three quarters of Watson's sample, when asked whether they saw personnel management as a profession, felt that a professional image was appropriate for it. Only 48 per cent of his respondents were IPM members, however, including only 14 per cent who had obtained entry to the Institute by examination. Belonging to the IPM was seen largely in instrumental terms, even for those with IPM membership. Some saw it instrumentally advantageous in terms of getting a qualification or in advancing their careers. Others saw it as instrumental in terms of making useful contacts within the personnel occupation, or of obtaining information, publications or access to IPM services. Even the majority of non-IPM members was not against the idea of IPM membership. Of the 52 non-members whom he questioned only nine, according to Watson, expressed 'hostility either to the IPM or to professional bodies in general'.[30]

With the development and expansion of personnel management as an occupation, we see growing aspirations among personnel specialists for acceptance by line management and for membership of the managerial team. In this sense, there is a strong identification by personnel managers with organizational needs and corporate objectives rather than with those of employees and the wider society. As Watson concludes: 'what the notion of professionalism symbolises for the contemporary personnel specialist is . . . competence in the meeting of general managerial goals'.[31] Criteria of service do not seem to be particularly important in the personnel practitioner's definition of professionalism. To be professional is seen largely as contributing to the effective management of the enterprise. Success here can lead to personal career advancement, with membership of the IPM being instrumental to this end.

The Institute of Personnel Management

The IPM was founded in 1913 and claims to be the professional personnel management organization in Britain. Its major purpose is to develop and advance professional knowledge and competence in personnel management. As a professional body, the IPM has five main aims. First, it promotes the professional standing of its members through the widest possible exchange of knowledge and experience in personnel management. Secondly, it develops an evolving body of professional personnel management knowledge and expertise in response to changing demands and conditions. Thirdly, it seeks to develop and maintain professional standards of competence among personnel practitioners. Fourthly, it encourages investigation and research into personnel management problems and subjects related to personnel management. Fifthly, it presents a national viewpoint on personnel management to interested parties and establishes links with other national and international bodies concerned with personnel work.

Membership of the IPM is on an individual basis. In June 1985, the IPM had 25,096 members including 1,764 who were admitted in the preceding 12 months.[32] Its membership distribution by grade

Personnel in Context

Table 19
IPM membership mid 1985 and mid 1989

Membership grade	Number of members	
	(1985)	(1989)
Companions	190	208
Fellows	1,839	2,802
Members	6,159	9,819
Associates	5,182	–
Graduates	2,368	7,506
Students	5,881	11,120
Affiliates	3,477	4,093
Total	25,096	35,548

Source: *Annual report of the IPM,* IPM 1985 and IPM 1989

of membership in 1985 and 1989 is shown in Table 19. Although membership is open to all those working in personnel management, or in one of its related specialist functions, corporate membership of the IPM is limited to those obtaining it by examination and experience, although some members are admitted by 'management entry'. Corporate members are Companions, Fellows or Members. Non-corporate members are Graduates, Students and Affiliates. To become a Member of the Institute, an applicant must: be a Graduate who has passed the Institute's professional examinations; hold a responsible post in personnel management as a practitioner; and have performed executive and/or advisory duties in personnel management for at least three years. Student members are required to be at least 20 years old, hold academic qualifications acceptable to the Institute and be following an approved course of study in personnel management. Affiliates must have successfully completed a foundation course in personnel management practice approved by the Institute and hold a post in personnel management.[33] On joining the IPM, all members are allocated to one of its 43 local branches which hold professional meetings and social activities regularly.

Basically the IPM carries out three main functions: it acts as a qualifying association for those wishing to become professionally qualified personnel managers; it provides a range of specialist services to its members including some which are also available to non-members; and it acts as a pressure group for personnel specialists to outside bodies such as employers, employers' associations, government and other public agencies. In its role as a qualifying association, for example, the IPM supervises and administers a two stage examination scheme leading to Membership of the Institute.[34]

The services provided by the IPM to its members include: information on personnel and related matters; courses and conferences; an appointments and communication service; and personnel management publications. The information services of the IPM fall into two categories: inquiries and advisory services; and library services. In 1988, for example, the IPM handled almost 20,000 inquiries, many of them dealing with legal advice on such matters as unfair dismissal, contracts of employment, employee redundancy and disciplinary issues. The information service also undertakes special projects and research work and writes guides for managers on particular personnel practices. The library has a loan service for readers and is open to visitors wishing to consult its wide range of specialist books, articles or surveys in the personnel field.

The short courses provided by the IPM, which are open to both members and non-members of the Institute, are closely monitored to keep pace with the developing needs of personnel managers and employing organizations. In addition to its basic five day course on the work of the personnel department, the IPM also runs courses on salary administration, negotiating skills, personnel statistics and practical manpower planning.

The IPM's annual conference is held at Harrogate in October, with between 1,000 and 2,000 delegates. It lasts two days, culminating in the induction of the incoming President and the Presidential Address to delegates and visitors.

The IPM also has an appointments service. This is provided in its professional journal and *Personnel Management Plus* (*PM Plus*). *PM Plus* is the IPM's main means of regularly communicating its activities and events to members, including the promotion of branch and regional meetings. *PM Plus* also publishes summary reports on the IPM's contributions to public debate on topical personnel issues.[35] *Personnel Management* is the IPM's official professional journal, providing articles of current interest to personnel practitioners. The IPM is also a major publisher, with a list of over 100 publications, covering a wide range of personnel topics.[36]

As a pressure group for professional personnel practitioners and for effective personnel management practices, the IPM maintains regular contact, both through individuals and institutionally, with a wide range of people and external bodies. These include: government ministers; Members of Parliament; departments of state; overseas personnel practitioners and their professional organizations; employers' associations; trade unions; educational institutions; and other relevant bodies.

The IPM undertakes a number of major internal projects aimed at developing effective personnel management practices in industry and the public services. These are carried out by its seven National Committees and its two Standing Committees. It is the task of the Personnel Management Policy Committee (PMPC) to coordinate the progress of the Institute's programme of major projects. The PMPC consists of the IPM's President, Past President, President Elect, eight Vice-Presidents, Treasurer and Director, with the Assistant Director (Development) acting as its Secretary. The PMPC is charged with the development of personnel practice. In meeting this role the various committees represented on PMPC each put together a comprehensive programme covering specific responsibilities which is subject to scrutiny by the full policy committee. In this way, gaps in the programme are identified and ideas for research and further work are exchanged.[37]

As a representative and democratic body of personnel managers, the IPM has a National Council comprising the President, and other honorary Officers of the Institute, together with branch representatives and regional nominees. The Director General of the Institute, as its chief executive, is an *ex officio* member of Council and of all its subcommittees. In addition to the PMPC, the Finance and General Purposes Committee and the Advisory Committee on Nominations, the IPM has seven other representative committees and two standing ones. Its seven National Committees are: Education; Employee Relations; International; Membership; Organization and Human Resource Planning; Pay and Employment Conditions; and Training and Development. The IPM's two other committees are its Standing Committees on the Public Sector and Equal Opportunities.[38]

Other managerial associations

In addition to the IPM, there are two other major managerial associations in Britain: the British Institute of Management (BIM) and the Institute of Directors (IOD).[39] The BIM was established in 1947 with the aim of becoming the central institute of professional management in the UK. In 1958, it absorbed the Institute of Industrial Administration into membership, whilst in 1978 the Institute of Industrial Management became affiliated with it. Until October 1976, the BIM was registered as a charity. It then deregistered, becoming a company limited by guarantee, so that it could represent individual members of the Institute which it was precluded from doing under its charitable status. At the same time, the BIM Foundation was established as a charitable trust. This enabled the BIM to carry on its professional and related activities in the management field. It was these two bodies which constituted the BIM as a unified professional management institute in Britain, until its reorganization during the mid 1980s.

The BIM claims to be the largest institute of its kind in the world. Its primary objectives are:

(i) the development of the highest standards of management by individual members and by corporate bodies.
(ii) the continuance of the Institute's representational role in association with the formulation of economic and social policy of importance to management and managers.

It has four subsidiary objectives which are:

(i) the achievement of a continuing increase in the number of individual members and their increased involvement in Institute affairs.
(ii) the seeking and development of continued financial support from the corporate sector through collective subscribers and sponsorship.
(iii) the development of affiliation/integration with other management bodies.
(iv) the continued development of a national role to give full support to aims and activities of all members at home together with a limited adoption of an international role with a special reference to the interests of members overseas initially allied to the development of representation in the European Community.[40]

Personnel in Context

Membership of the BIM is on both an individual and a corporate basis. In March 1989, the BIM's register of individual members totalled about 71,000 compared with over 76,000 at the end of the financial period 1984–85. Its membership distribution by grade of individual members in 1982, 1985 and 1989 is summarized in Table

Table 20
BIM individual membership 1982, 1985 and 1989

Membership grade	Number of members		
	1982	1985	1989
Companions	1,250	1,372	1,571
Fellows	13,696	14,866	12,895
Members	50,677	52,976	50,212
Graduates	32	(discontinued)	(discontinued)
Associates	7,195	7,231	5,887
Others	49	–	192
Total	72,899	76,445	70,757

Source: *Annual reports*, BIM 1982, 1985 and 1989

20. There was a net loss in individual membership over the previous year of some 2,000 members. The BIM's register of collective subscribers or corporate members at the end of March 1989 consisted of 924 principal organizations and a further 2,644 subsidiaries. During the same year, 'the number of overseas members dropped by 1,187'.[41]

As the BIM's governing body, its Council sets and reviews the Institute's strategies, policies, priorities and objectives. Supervisory and monitoring work is delegated to its standing committees and various boards. To preserve charitable status, the Council and its subordinate committees separate business at their meetings into 'charity' and 'non-charity' sections. Council has a majority of nationally elected members and representatives from its branch area committees. The Chairman's Committee has a wide role and is responsible for supervising and coordinating the work of the BIM's other committees and boards. These are grouped into specific areas of activity including Economic and Social Affairs, Membership, Audit, Information and Advisory Services, National Branch Policy, Public Affairs, Management Development Services, and Professional Standards.

The activities of the BIM are wide. They include providing conferences, seminars, management development, in company training and other practical help for individual members, corporate members and other organizations. The BIM also has specialist advisory services covering, amongst other things, management training, employee relations and career development. The BIM has a good library and also publishes a variety of books, management checklists, information sheets, information notes and occasional papers. These cover a broad spectrum of managerial subjects including company surveys, labour turnover, employee handbooks, office efficiency, performance appraisal and company pension policy. The Institute also supplies members with a monthly journal, *Management Today*, which examines topical managerial issues and matters of economic and social concern to management.

The Institute of Directors (IOD), which is organized into 23 home branches and 10 overseas ones, claims to represent '33,000 directors, sole proprietors and senior partners in professional practice'.[42] It was founded in 1903 and became incorporated by Royal Charter in 1906. It claims to be a non-party political body, though it declares itself to be 'dedicated to preserving free enterprise through [industrial] capitalism as the bedrock of individual freedom and the system of parliamentary democracy upon which it depends'.[43] It believes that the best way of maintaining free enterprise is to raise professional standards in boardrooms and to minimize governmental interference in private businesses. Its two primary objectives are:

(1) Providing an effective voice for members both inside and outside parliament.
(2) Providing the help and encouragement [its] members need to improve their own competence as business leaders.[44]

In representing company directors as individuals, the IOD claims, it cannot stay outside politics. It is prepared to fight, therefore, for those policies and principles in which it and its members believe.

The main services which the IOD provides to its members are: an information and advisory service; a non-executive directors' appointments service; and courses and seminars dealing with the legal and professional responsibilities of directors. The business information service covers a range of subjects including: service contracts; salary surveys; industrial relations; company law; taxation; and exporting. Information staff and advisers work from the Institute's library where there is a select collection of books, journals and pamphlets. The non-executive directors' appointments service provides help for company chairmen who are considering recruiting non-executive board members in order to improve board effectiveness. The IOD also maintains links with overseas business leaders through its European Association, its overseas branches and other bodies.

The governing body of the IOD is its Council. It has a large membership comprising the honorary Officers of the Institute, including its President, two past Presidents and three Vice-Presidents, branch chairmen and elected members. Its committees consist of the following: Policy and Executive; Taxation; Membership; Employment; Education; Company Affairs; and House. Its full time staff is headed by a Director-General and six other Directors covering External Relations, Education, Executive, Marketing, Public Relations and Recruitment. As its chief executive, the Director-General is responsible for national and internal organization and for Institute development.[45]

Conclusion

British managers are a diverse social and occupational group, playing a key role in all kinds of business, public service and other organizations. They are an expanding group, comprising about 10 per cent of the work population. Judged by the recent evidence of the BIM survey, British managers are a well qualified, socially conservative and professionally conscious group. Personnel managers, by contrast, are a relatively small occupational group among managers generally and, according to Watson, are generally more liberal in their social and political attitudes.[46]

There is a wide variety of career types in personnel management ranging from the 'mobile professional' through to the 'part-time personnel manager'. Personnel managers tend to be organization-ally and managerially oriented, rather than externally and socially directed. It also seems that there is a considerable degree of common occupational interest among personnel specialists, even though they do not all belong to the IPM. In claiming professional status, personnel managers need to demonstrate high standards of practitioner competence within organizations, rather than showing the attributes and characteristics of classical professional groups. In this context, the IPM often fulfils an instrumental function for many personnel professionals. This partially explains the relatively low levels of membership participation within it.

As the professional management institute representing personnel specialists, the IPM is a well organized and nationally recognized body with a wide range of external contacts. Compared with the BIM and the IOD, it has a much higher level of membership density, though the two other managerial bodies have larger memberships. Of the three managerial institutions, the IOD is by far the most politically assertive, with the IPM and BIM playing lower key and more sensitive organizational roles.

References and footnotes

1   OFFICE OF POPULATION CENSUSES AND SURVEYS. *Census 1981. National Report. Great Britain. Part 2.* (London, HMSO, 1983b). p6.
2   See ACTON SOCIETY TRUST. *Management Succession.* (London, Acton Society Trust, 1956); CLEMENTS R V. *Managers: A Study of their Careers in Industry.* (London, Allen and Unwin, 1958); CLARK D G. *The Industrial Manager: his Background and Career Pattern.* (London, Business Publications, 1966); and MELROSE-WOODMAN J. *Profile of the British Manager.* (London, BIM, 1978).
3   MANSFIELD R *and others. The British Manager in Profile.* (London, BIM, 1981). p3.
4   *ibid.* p7.
5   *ibid.* p19.
6   *ibid.* p18.
7   *ibid.* p21.
8   *ibid.* p22.
9   *ibid.* p23.
10 *ibid.* p26f.
11 *ibid.* p28.
12 *ibid.* p29.
13 URWICK GROUP. *Employee Relations Survey 1982/83.* (London, Urwick, 1982). Appendix two.
14 INSTITUTE OF PERSONNEL MANAGEMENT. *Sixty-ninth Annual Report.* (London, IPM, 1989). p16.

15 NICHOLS T. *Ownership, Control and Ideology.* (London, Allen and Unwin, 1969). p198.
16 See TYSON S J T. Specialists in ambiguity: personnel management as an occupation. Unpublished Ph.D. thesis. University of London 1979.
17 WATSON T J. *The Personnel Managers.* (London, Routledge and Kegan Paul, 1977). p203.
18 *ibid.* pp72 and 81.
19 *ibid.* p90.
20 *ibid.* p93f.
21 GUEST D *and* HORWOOD R. 'Characteristics of the successful personnel manager'. *Personnel Management.* Vol. 13, No. 5, May 1981. p20.
22 *ibid.* p23.
23 WATSON. *opcit.* p113.
24 *ibid.* p114.
25 THOMASON G. *A Textbook of Personnel Management.* 4th ed. (London, IPM, 1981). p55.
26 GUEST *and* HORWOOD. *opcit.* p23.
27 LUPTON T. *Industrial Behaviour and Personnel Management.* (London, IPM, 1978). p(i).
28 FRIEDSON E. 'Professions and the occupational principle' in FRIEDSON E (ed). *The Professions and their Prospects.* (London, Sage, 1973). p22.
29 WATSON. *opcit.* p50.
30 *ibid.* pp131, 134 and 136.
31 *ibid.* p198.
32 IPM (1983) *opcit.* p6.
33 INSTITUTE OF PERSONNEL MANAGEMENT. *The Institute of Personnel Management.* (London, IPM, 1980). p7f.
34 For further details see IPM (1985). *opcit.* p12f.
35 The IPM also publishes regular policy statements on a range of personnel management, industrial relations and training issues.
36 See IPM (1989), p24.
37 INSTITUTE OF PERSONNEL MANAGEMENT. *69th Annual Report.* (London, IPM, 1989). p13.
38 *ibid.* p25f.
39 It is not known how many IPM members are also members of the BIM and IOD.
40 BRITISH INSTITUTE OF MANAGEMENT. *Summary of Recommendations of the Constitution and Structure Working Party.* (London, BIM, 1983a).
41 BRITISH INSTITUTE OF MANAGEMENT. *Annual Report 1989.* (London, BIM 1989). p21.
42 INSTITUTE OF DIRECTORS. *Institute of Directors.* (London, IOD, 1983). p1.
43 *ibid.*
44 *ibid.*

45 *ibid.*

46 When asked whether there were any 'religious, political or moral influences' relevant to their work, only three of Watson's respondents mentioned 'conservative allegiances', while 22 gave accounts which he labelled 'left'. This was 'either because of a mention of "socialist" views or because of a stated political interest in "increasing equality", "changing the way the staff are treated – they're usually overlooked or ignored", "being sympathetic to the unions" and so on'. WATSON. *opcit.* p109.

Part III
The external contexts

7

The political context

Politics begins whenever there are disagreements or conflicts of interest between people and groups and, to achieve peace and stability, constitutional means have to be devised to resolve them. If political disputes are not settled, physical violence or social disorder can result. Contrary to much popular opinion, therefore, politics is not the cause of conflicts within societies or between them. It merely reflects the differences of policy interests between organized groups. The political process, or the machinery of politics, is the means by which such conflicts are identified and channelled in order to contain and settle them peacefully, if only temporarily.

Politics takes place at different levels including families, social clubs, trade unions and work organizations. This is usually called 'micropolitics'. It also takes place between nations, which is called international politics or international relations. Most commonly, politics is concerned with national government and with affairs of state. This is called 'macropolitics'. It is mainly the macropolitical context and some aspects of the international context, especially the role of the European Community, which provide the basis for this chapter. Following Crick (1964), macropolitics is defined as 'the activity by which differing interests within a given unit of rule are conciliated by giving them a share in power'. It is 'a way of ruling divided societies without undue violence – and most societies are divided, though some think that this is the very trouble'.[1]

Liberal democracy

Many students of politics describe the UK as a liberal democracy. Carter and Herz (1969) believe that the characteristic feature of liberal democracy, in contrast with totalitarianism, is that constitutional limitations are placed on governmental action and political power within the state. One means by which liberal democracies maintain the basic constitutional rights of their citizens is by 'the regular, periodic and peaceful change of their [political] leaders, and by organs of effective popular representation'.[2] To be effective, liberal democracy requires not only appropriate political institutions. It also requires liberal political attitudes. This means that individuals and groups normally need to be tolerant of political views and opinions different from their own, and to respect minority and individual rights within the liberal state.

Ball (1988) lists the main features of liberal democracy. First, more than one political party competes for political power and the competition for power is open rather than secretive. Secondly, there are periodic elections based on a universal franchise, with recruitment to political office being relatively open. Thirdly, pressure groups are able to organize and to influence governmental policy decisions, with voluntary bodies, such as employers' organizations, trade unions and professional associations, being independent of governmental control. Fourthly, certain basic civil liberties, such as freedom of association, freedom of speech and freedom from arbitrary arrest, are recognized and protected within the constitution. Lastly, there is a separation of political powers within government so that 'a representative assembly has some form of control over the executive and the judiciary is independent of both executive and legislature'.[3]

Elections play a key role in liberal democracy. They not only legitimize political power but also provide the means for removing unrepresentative governments and officeholders. Elections also provide the opportunity, for those qualified to do so, to participate in the political process. Democracy in the UK is normally indirect. This means that the electorate votes for candidates who, when elected, become 'representatives' of their constituencies or electoral divisions. This is an important feature of liberal democracy. For although winning candidates are normally representatives of the major political parties, liberal democracy requires each of them 'as in the UK Parliament, in the UK local authorities and the European Parliament, to be accountable to the whole constituency which they represent, not just to part of it'.[4]

Elections also provide voters with the right to pass political judgment on their elected representatives at the end of their term of office. Under liberal democracy and representative government, it is the ballot box which provides the ultimate freedom of choice for the electorate, so protecting it against unrepresentative officeholders and unpopular governments. At election time, either those in political office are confirmed in power for a fresh term, 'or they are replaced and a constitutional change of government, or of local government, is effected'.[5] In this way the popular sovereignty of the electorate is expressed.

Given that the political role of the judiciary is constitutionally limited,[6] the two most important arms of government are the legislature and the executive. If popular sovereignty rests with the electorate in the UK, then its legal sovereignty rests with the Monarch-in-Parliament. It is Parliament which enacts laws, determines the structures and powers of the public authorities, and regulates the conduct of citizens and private organizations within the state. Laws are enacted, usually on the proposal of the government, after they have been approved by the House of Commons and the House of Lords and have received the Royal Assent, given on the advice of the Cabinet. Though it is part of the legislature, the Lords is politically subordinate to the Commons and its constitutional powers are strictly limited. In theory, the doctrine of Parliamentary supremacy implies that Parliament has the legal right to make, amend or repeal any laws which it chooses. In practice, since the UK is now a member of the EC, it is 'very unlikely that the absolute doctrine of legislative supremacy in the UK can any longer be upheld'.[7]

The political executive in the UK consists of government ministers and the administrative machinery which supports them. Its functions include: initiating legislation; maintaining civil order; promoting social and economic welfare; administering the public services; and conducting external relations. The executive function thus ranges from policy formation, on the one side, to the detailed management of specific public services on the other. Now that the UK is a member of the EC, the Council of Ministers and the European Commission also exercise certain executive functions. Other than elections, the immense complexity of modern government places practical limitations on its executive powers. Parliament only normally exercises its legislative powers, for example, after the major interests affected by proposed legislation, such as employers or trade unions, have been consulted by the relevant minister.

This model of liberal democracy provides a useful description of formal political power in a liberal state. In practice, however, power in a liberal democracy like that of the UK also exists outside the established political institutions of government and the state. Large companies, the trade unions, and the churches, for example, as well as other major interests such as the banks, the Stock Exchange and the mass media, have considerable economic and social power. To govern effectively, government requires the cooperation and political consent of the powerful corporate interests outside Parliament. When political, economic and social power is fragmented in this way, it is described as a 'pluralist' political democracy. In a pluralist democracy, power is diffused and competition for political control takes place largely amongst elite power groups. This does not mean that all individuals and all groups have equal power. Nor does it mean that all persons are members of organized power groups. But it does imply, as Clegg (1975) says, that 'within any political system there are groups with their own interests and beliefs, and [that] the government itself . . . depends on their consent and cooperation'.[8]

The pluralist analysis of politics is not without its critics. Marxists argue, for example, that pluralist societies are class dominated. They assert that certain policy issues within pluralist democracies, such as the distribution of wealth and the case for even greater power sharing, rarely get on the political agenda. They also argue that public debate within pluralist states like the UK is largely limited to those marginal areas of political activity which do not threaten the positions of those with entrenched political, economic and social power. As Miliband (1973) puts it: 'the pluralist-democratic view of society . . . is in all essentials wrong . . . this view, far from providing a guide to reality, constitutes a profound obfuscation of it'.[9]

Political behaviour

Figure 19 on page 165 provides a simple model of the UK political system. It is a systems model based on the work of David Easton, an American student of politics.[10] It provides a useful basis for identifying and analysing the 'inputs', 'processes' and 'outputs' of the UK macropolitical system. The inputs to the political system

Figure 19
A simple model of the UK political system

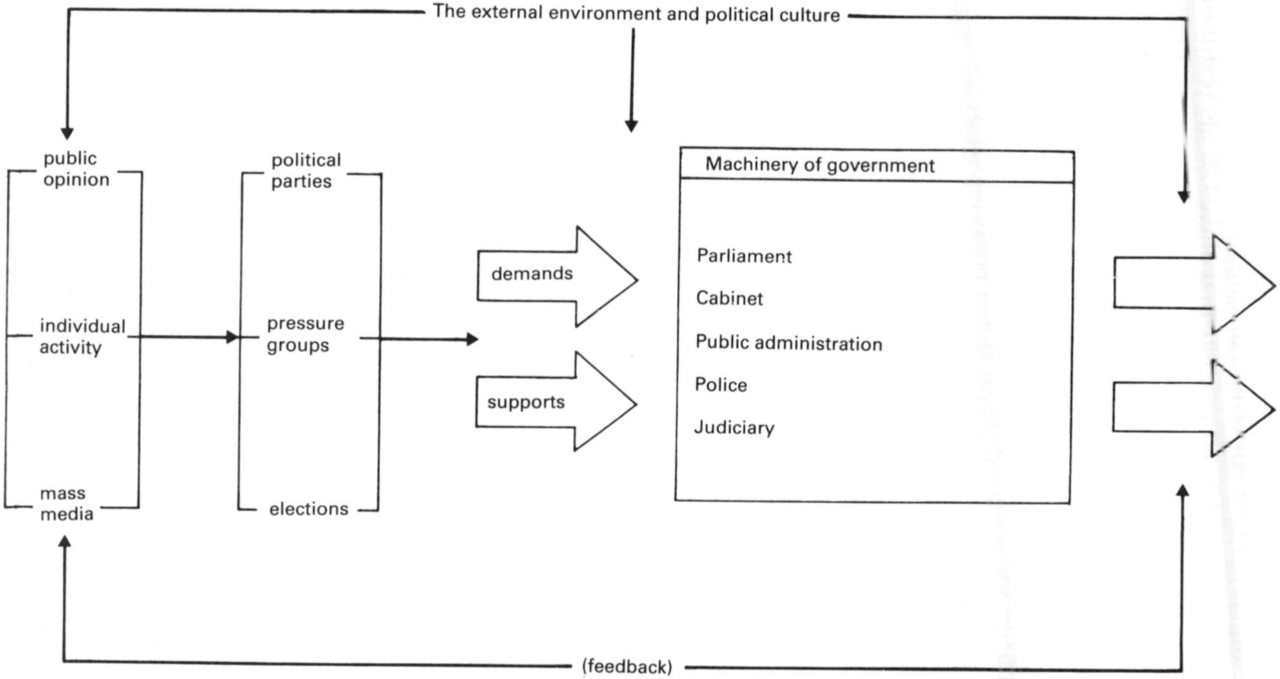

The external environment and political culture

Machinery of government

Parliament

Cabinet

Public administration

Police

Judiciary

demands

supports

political parties

pressure groups

elections

public opinion

individual activity

mass media

(feedback)

Source: FARNHAM D and McVICAR M, *Public administration in the UK*, Cassell 1982

are its 'demands' and 'supports'. Its demands are what individuals and groups want from the political system, whilst its supports include the resources required to achieve them. Politics begins with individual political activity. This is influenced by such things as public opinion and the mass media and is collectively channelled through elections, political parties and pressure groups into political demands and supports. Some of these are injected into the machinery of government, whilst others are rejected by it. The policies and decisions of government are the outputs of the political system. These feed back into it, helping to generate further demands and supports by individuals and organized groups.

To understand British politics and its political processes, it is necessary, first, to look at its political culture, since this helps to shape the political behaviour of its participants. Rush and Althoff (1971) define political culture 'as the politically relevant values and attitudes of a society'.[11] There is, for example, a general consensus in Britain about its central political values and a wide acceptance of its established political institutions such as Parliament, the Civil Service and the Monarchy. Thus most Britons believe in: parliamentary democracy and government by consent; peaceful and non-violent political protest; political and social reform; the importance of individual rights and personal liberty; the tolerance of opposing political viewpoints. This procedural consensus, however, coexists with severe disagreements about the major substantive issues of contemporary politics. Britain's wider political culture, therefore, incorporates a number of competing political subcultures which are represented and institutionalized within different political parties.

Ball considers that British political culture is a mixture of 'tradition' and 'modernity'. He thinks that an aristocratic political structure has become adapted to an urban and industrial society without any major discontinuities. He argues that most people do not feel alienated from the political system and, with the emergence of mass political parties and universal suffrage, that political participation has become democratized. He also suggests that while there is trust in an elite political leadership, producing a relatively harmonious conservative society, 'the concept of an egalitarian society does battle with the notion of deference'. There is, in short, 'a political culture of hierarchical traditional values interspersed with more recent liberal democratic and collectivist [ones]'.[12]

Politics starts with the individual. It is individuals who vote, become members of political parties or pressure groups, become active in political affairs, and seek political office. It is through individuals, too, that 'the politically relevant values and attitudes of a society'[13] are transmitted from generation to generation. This takes place through a series of personal socialization experiences in the family, at school and at work. It is the process of political socialization which 'differentiates persons into Conservative and Labour supporters, and into a small minority actively involved in politics or a large group of . . . intermittently active citizens'.[14] According to Rose (1989), more than two thirds of the explained variation in party preference can be accounted for by early childhood influences. Thus 'father's class and, independent of class, parents' party preference are of substantial importance, together accounting for more than half the total variance explained'.[15]

Table 21
Involvement in UK national politics

	Estimated number of people	Estimated per cent of adult population
MPs, senior civil servants	4,000	0.1
Individual party members	1,500,000	3
Protest demonstrators	2,500,000	6
Very interested in politics	2,500,000	6
Political activists	2,800,000	7
Political officeholders	5,500,000	14
Members of pressure groups	26,000,000	61
Voters	32,500,000	75
Eligible electorate	43,000,000	98

Source: ROSE R, *Politics in England,* Faber 1989

Individual political involvement in UK macropolitics (Table 21) is low. It can be classified into three main categories of behaviour. First, there is the very small group of individuals holding political office or positions of political power, such as MPs or senior civil servants. Secondly, there is a larger group of political activists. They either seek political office or are participating members of political parties or pressure groups. Thirdly, there is the rest of the adult population which is on the political periphery. According to this evidence, the eligible electorate comprises 98 per cent of the adult population of whom some 50 per cent are in receipt of some form of state cash benefit and some 60 per cent are members of pressure groups including trade unions but only about 20 per cent are interested in politics and only three quarters bother to vote in general elections. This amounted to 76 per cent of the electorate in 1979, 73 per cent in 1983 and 75 per cent in 1987.

Political parties provide the vital link between the electorate and the representative machinery of government. They are heterogeneous organizations, each being a coalition of political subgroups. They have four main functions. First, they recruit individuals indirectly for public office by providing the machinery for selecting and nominating candidates in local, Parliamentary and European elections. Secondly, they act as channels of political communication by providing the means through which the political demands of the electorate are transmitted to the political authorities. Thirdly, they act as overt agents of political socialization and political education by making known their policy programmes and party ideologies to the public. Fourthly, 'by channelling competition for political power through legitimate organizations, parties help to sustain the political system'.[16]

Despite the claims of the Liberal Democrats and the nationalist parties in Wales, Scotland and Northern Ireland, 'Britain still has a two-party system'.[17] The two main parties are the Conservatives and the Labour Party. In modern times, it is these two parties which have alternated in office and have competed for political power at Westminster. The party which wins a general election is normally able to obtain a majority of seats over all other parties in the House of Commons and to govern alone. Table 22 summarizes General Elections in the UK for the period 1945–87. This shows that the two major political parties have generally dominated these Elections, though minor parties have managed to win an increasing number of seats since the mid 1960s.

Following Ball (1987), modern, one nation 'Conservatives generally have a pessimistic view of man's nature . . . Man is evil unless curbed by authority . . . [and] the enforcement of order is one of the prime duties of the state'.[18] The fundamental goal of modern Conservatism is to maintain existing political and social institutions and the economic and social *status quo*. Social reforms must be controlled and should be remedies for specific ills if social stability

Table 22

Number of UK parliamentary seats won by political parties at general elections 1945–87

						Election Year				(Feb)	(Oct)			
	1945	1950	1951	1955	1959	1964	1966	1970	1974	1974	1979	1983	1987
Conservative	213	298	321	344	365	304	253	330	297	277	339	397	376
Labour	393	315	295	277	258	317	363	287	301	319	269	209	229
Liberal	12	9	6	6	6	9	12	6	14	13	11	17	17
Social Democrat	*	*	*	*	*	*	*	*	*	*	*	6	5
Communist	2	–	–	–	–	–	–	–	*	–	–	–	–
Plaid Cymru	*	*	*	*	–	–	–	–	2	3	2	2	3
Scottish Nationalist	*	*	*	*	*	*	*	1	7	11	2	2	3
National Front	*	*	*	*	*	*	*	*	–	–	–	–	–
Others (GB)	20	3	3	3	1	–	2	6	2	–	–	–	–
Others (NI)	*	*	*	*	*	*	*	*	12	12	12	17	17
Total	640	625	625	630	630	630	630	630	635	635	635	650	650

* no seats contested by these parties in these elections

Sources: BUTLER D and SLOMAN A, *British Political Facts 1900–1979*, Macmillan 1980 and FRASER R (ed), *Keesing's contemporary archives*, Longman 1983 and 1987

and national unity are to be maintained. For one nation Conservatives, society has a life of its own, existing beyond the sum of the
individuals who comprise it. As Heater (1974) argues, belief in
the country as an organic whole, the cherishing of traditions
and the rejection of the idea of a class struggle lead modern
Conservatives 'to a heightened sense of patriotism and national
self-consciousness'.[19] Conservatives of this persuasion generally
wish the state to be used paternally rather than fraternally,
believing that society must be structured hierarchically, with
distinctions being drawn between the rulers and the ruled and the
successful and less successful.

The main traditional economic policies of the Conservative Party
are to encourage incentive, profit and the acquisition of private
property. People must have the incentive to work hard, Conservatives argue, and there are constant attempts by Conservative
governments to reduce taxation as an inducement to individual
effort. 'Free enterprise and the profit motive are economic principles dear to the Conservatives, providing a system within which
incentive can have free play'.[20] Conservative economic policy also
seeks to reduce the role of the state in economic affairs. This means
that Conservatives generally prefer the creation and distribution of
private wealth to be given a higher economic priority than the
creation and distribution of public services. There is also hostility
by some Conservatives to the trade unions which, they believe,
'should be weakened so they do not operate as a monopolistic
brake on free economic forces'.[21]

There is another set of ideas and policies which have emerged
in the Conservative Party during the late 1970s and 1980s. These
are associated with the 'New Right' in the Party. They re-emerged
when the Party was in opposition after 1974 and reflected a new
dominant right-wing orthodoxy. Their underlying aims were to
make the economy competitive, to facilitate growth and to combat
the so-called 'welfare dependency culture' of post-war Britain. This
new orthodoxy claims that the major economic policy objectives
of government must be to squeeze inflation out of the economy
and to change the balance of the mixed economy by reducing the
role of the public sector within it. Central to these policies have
been attempts to control the money supply, to reduce and
eventually eliminate the public sector borrowing requirement and
to use interest rates as the major tool of economic management.

This approach has been described as one supporting a 'free economy' and a 'strong state'. Gamble (1988) sees ambiguities in this position which derive from the fact that the New Right has two elements within it. One is a liberal tendency which argues for a freer, more open, competitive economy, the other is a conservative tendency which is more interested in restoring social and political authority in society. The liberal tendency embraces the ideas of monetarists, supply side economists and supporters of privatization. Their economic preferences include: restricting money supply; using fluctuating exchange rates; limiting government spending; reducing income tax; and denationalizing public industries.

The Conservative tendency in the New Right argues that the state must be strong. This is necessary, it is argued, to unwind the social democratic consensus, to police the market order, to make the economy productive and to maintain political authority. By this view, public spending must be cut, taxes lowered and public assets privatized to restore a free economy. It is also asserted that a strong state facilitates economic efficiency, advances industrial modernization and reforms the remaining public services.

Another feature of the New Right within the Conservative Party is its social authoritarianism which is basically anti-libertarian. This strand holds that personal discipline, duty and responsibility and social stability are higher order social values than is unrestrained individual freedom. It is the role of the state – a strong state – to impose that order and prevent social anarchy. This social authoritarian strand in Conservatism is, surprisingly perhaps, collectivist rather than individualist and it emphasizes patriotism, nationalism, political allegiance and the concept of the family. Society exists through authority which requires allegiance to a bond which is not contractual but transcendental.

There are also tensions in the Labour Party between those supporting class conflict theories of socialism and those supporting social democracy. The central tenet of 'old' Labour Party thinking is that politics is about social class. Because economic and social power are unequally distributed, its supporters argue, the Labour Party's role is to rectify these imbalances through the political and parliamentary system. For this reason, the old Labour Party was committed to a fundamental shift in the balance of economic and social power within Britain away from the controllers of private capital and big business towards its workers, 'by hand or by brain'. The main Labour Party goal, by this view, is greater equality. As Gaitskell (1958) said: 'by this I do not mean identical incomes or uniform habits and tastes. But I do mean a classless society . . . one in which people develop differently, [where] there is equal opportunity for all to develop'.[22] For many Labour Party sup-porters, industrial capitalism represents an economic system based upon the socially unacceptable principle of business competition, which in their view is neither free nor fair. They want it replaced by an alternative form of industrialism motivated by social goals and humanitarian values, rather than by private profit and purely commercial criteria.

The traditional economic policies of the Labour Party have been government intervention in the economy, the extension of public ownership, cooperation with the trade unions, and expansion of the welfare state. The means used by Labour Governments to achieve their goals have included: high levels of public spending; demand management of the economy; nationalization of major industries; prices and incomes policies; and the extension of the public services. These policies have invariably run into economic difficulties, such as 'balance of payment crises, low growth, increasing unemployment, high taxation levels, large public-sector borrowing requirements, and rising prices'.[23] Further, relations between Labour Cabinets and the trade unions have often broken down on issues such as incomes policy and cuts in public expendi-ture. Nevertheless, as Heater argues, 'most radicals still support the Labour Party as the most likely vehicle for social reform . . . even if in economic terms it is merely trying to create capitalism with a human face'.[24]

It is the social democratic strand of Labour Party ideology which once more came to the fore in the late 1980s. This was buttressed by the surprising break-up of orthodox Marxism in eastern European states at that time. The central idea of social democracy, or democratic socialism, is equality. The aim is to create equality of wealth, income and opportunity, equality of esteem and equality of political rights and political power. Social democracy insists on the use of political persuasion within a parliamentary system and the repudiation of violence. Social democrats are committed not only to representative democracy but also to the mixed economy.

The overall aim of the 'new' Labour Party is 'the creation of a genuinely free society, in which the fundamental objective of government is the protection and extension of individual liberty irrespective of class, sex, age, race, colour or creed'. The principal aim of Labourite socialism is creating 'for all people, material ability to make the choices that a free society provides'. It is also necessary to create a more equal distribution of power as well as of wealth. This means that all men and women should have the right to determine the decisions influencing their daily lives by a major extension of democratic control. Further, for socialists, 'the state is an instrument for sustaining and enhancing the liberties of the whole community'. In the Party's view, democratic government should be the guarantor of fundamental citizenship freedoms.[25]

Turning to the economy, the Labour Party insists that in the modern world, with its fierce competition for resources, trade and wealth, and the pressures put on the environment, such demands must be balanced by a collective approach to common economic problems. To promote economic success and efficiency, large investment in research, development, schooling, further and higher education, and in training depend on a positive lead from government. Support of the mixed economy is endorsed, since there are many areas where market allocation and market competition are essential to serving the consumer and promoting efficiency. On the other hand, common social ownership is to be encouraged in other cases, not only because of greater efficiency but also because of social justice and individual fulfilment. Labour's strategy for 'supply side' socialism argues that the economic role of government is to help make the market system work more efficiently. This means establishing a new partnership with business and enabling companies to produce quality commodities, with government investing in education, training and science, and creating incentives for success.

The Liberal Democrats see themselves as a classless centrist party, bridging the political gap between Labour Party moderates and reformist Conservatives. They draw support from across the classes, and must do this if they are to fulfil their objective of breaking the class antagonisms that the two old parties have fostered. Liberal Democrat supporters believe in such principles as: individual freedom; social and constitutional reform; the mixed economy; and supranationalism. The policies which the Liberal Democrats advocate include: a bill of individual rights; proportional representation; trade union reform; a balance between private and public ownership of industry; a variety of methods to manage the economy; and committed membership of the EC. They also condemn the short termism of economic decision making in Britain. Three critical areas demand public interventionism: environmental protection, long-term investment and urban regeneration.

Pressure groups are also part of the political process within pluralist democracies. Like the political parties, they make political demands through the UK's policy making machinery. But unlike political parties, they do not seek to win political control directly. They want to influence those holding political office and political power in their own interests. Unlike political parties, pressure groups such as the Campaign for Nuclear Disarmament or Friends of the Earth pursue much narrower organizational objectives.

Parliament and government

Constitutionally Parliament is the supreme legislative authority within the UK. It consists of the Monarch-in-Parliament, the House of Commons and the House of Lords. Each of its elements is outwardly separate and is based on different constitutional principles. Both Houses meet at the Palace of Westminster but they do so separately and only come together on ceremonial occasions such as the State Opening of Parliament. This is when the Queen summons the Commons to the House of Lords to hear the 'Queen's Speech'. This sets out the government's intentions during the forthcoming Parliamentary session. A parliament can sit for up to five years, though it is often dissolved on the Prime Minister's initiative within the five year period.

The Commons is the dominant chamber within Parliament. It is a representative assembly, elected by universal adult suffrage. For electoral purposes, the UK is divided into 650 electoral constituencies, each of which returns one Member of Parliament (MP) to the Commons. At the June 1987 General Election, England returned 523 MPs, Wales 38, Scotland 72 and Northern Ireland 17. The party system is central to the role of Parliament. At every general election, each party lays its policies before the electorate in its manifesto and puts up candidates for election. It is the party which wins the majority of seats within the Commons, not necessarily with a majority of all the votes cast, that forms the government. The distribution of seats within the Commons by political parties after the 1987 General Election is shown in Table 23.

Table 23
Distribution of seats within the House of Commons and percentage of votes cast, by political party, 1987

	Number of seats	Votes	Percentage of votes cast
Conservative	376	13,763,134	42.3
Labour	229	10,003,633	30.8
Liberal-SDP Alliance	22	7,339,912	22.6
Plaid Cymru	3	123,589	0.4
Scottish Nationalist	3	416,873	1.3
Others	17	857,516	2.6
Total	650	32,504,657	100.0

Source: BUTLER D and KAVANAGH D. *The British general election of 1987*, Macmillan 1987

By convention, the leader of the majority party within the Commons is appointed Prime Minister (PM) by the Monarch. Some 100 of its members in both Houses, but mainly in the Commons, are selected as ministers of the Crown. They form the government or political executive. Party control of the government and opposition members in both Houses is maintained by the party 'whips'. Their task is to keep MPs and peers in touch with parliamentary business and to maintain party voting strength during debates. They also keep party leaderships informed of backbench parliamentary opinion.

The formal powers of the House of Lords are strictly limited. Whilst it has the right to amend bills, especially those subject to closure or shortened debate within the Commons, it has no power to veto or delay money bills. But it can impose a temporary veto of one year on other bills. Most bills originate in the Commons but governments sometimes raise uncontroversial bills in the House of Lords first. The most striking feature of the House of Lords is that its members are not elected. As Rose points out: it 'is unique among the upper chambers of modern Western Parliaments because it is primarily a hereditary institution'.[26]

Parliament has four main functions. First, it legislates by passing acts or statutes which regulate those aspects of political, economic and social life regarded as being within the sphere of politics and government. Secondly, it votes taxation and public funds for carrying out governmental policy decisions. Thirdly, it holds the government and public administration accountable by scrutinizing their activities through a number of parliamentary devices. These include parliamentary questions, House of Commons debates and select committees which bring the relevant facts to the notice of the public and thereby influence public opinion. Fourthly, Parliament acts as a channel of representation and as a major channel of political communication between the electorate and the government.

This formal model of the role of Parliament, especially that of the House of Commons, needs to be modified in practice. Although the Commons is technically the supreme legislative authority in the UK and could effectively control government and hold the administration accountable, in practice it rarely does so. This is because the Commons is divided on party lines and the forces keeping the parliamentary parties apart are much stronger than those drawing them together. Over 90 per cent of the bills proceeding through Parliament are sponsored by the government which consistently wins votes in the House of Commons because of party loyalties. As Rose concludes: 'the government represents the majority party in the Commons, and the MPs in the majority party are expected to support Cabinet measures . . . in order to maintain their party in control of government'; not many majority party MPs vote against the government on important issues.[27] The role of the Commons is best understood, therefore, not primarily as a check on the executive, but as one of the institutions through which the government governs.

The opposition parties in the House of Commons are effectively excluded from policy making. Nevertheless, the presence of an official opposition party and a shadow cabinet is a major feature of British liberal democracy. First, opposition criticism of governmental policy can induce marginal shifts in its direction and emphasis. Secondly, criticism of the government by the major opposition party contributes to the process of public political education. Thirdly, periods in opposition, away from the responsibilities of government, enable an opposition party to reassess its own political thinking and policy programmes in preparation for the next general election.

The government consists of some 100 members appointed to executive positions by the PM. About 20 of these hold Cabinet posts, the rest are junior ministers. The main function of the Cabinet is to decide governmental policy on matters submitted to Parliament, such as proposed legislation or public expenditure plans. It also coordinates governmental administration and arbitrates between ministers who fail to agree between themselves. As long as ministers hold office, they share the collective responsibility of all ministers. This means that they must neither criticize nor dissociate themselves publicly from governmental decisions, though they can have their views recorded in the private minutes of the Cabinet. Collective responsibility reinforces party unity in Parliament and maintains governmental control over legislation and public spending. It also reinforces the confidentiality of cabinet decision making.

The role of the PM, who is also First Lord of the Treasury and minister for the civil service, is of central importance in British government. S/he is normally leader of the majority party in the Commons and has to have the command not only of majority party MPs but also of the House of Commons generally. Although the PM appoints senior civil servants and bishops of the Church of England, the real power of the office derives from the influence which s/he exercises over the cabinet. S/he appoints the Cabinet, presides over its meetings and controls decision making within it. The PM also effectively controls the machinery of central government. This is done partly by approving senior ministerial appointments and partly by deciding how the tasks of government should be distributed among different departments. Above all, it is the PM who has the constitutional right to recommend to the Monarch that Parliament should be dissolved and a general election held.

It is largely the PM who presents and defends major governmental policies to Parliament and to the public. S/he regularly attends the Commons for question time and strongly influences communications to the media about Cabinet business and public affairs generally. The PM normally takes a special interest in economic affairs, defence policy and foreign relations. Some intervene personally in major trade disputes. To maintain an authoritative government and party unity, the PM has to carry senior Cabinet colleagues along with government policy and retain the support of most of the majority party's backbench MPs. Clearly, the prime ministerial role in government is both a powerful and a crucial one. Mackintosh (1977) sums it up as follows:

> These then are the sources of the Prime Minister's strength – party loyalty, patronage, the support of colleagues and of the machinery of government and the capacity, under most circumstances, to set the terminal date for the government and, throughout its period of office to command public attention.[28]

The European Community

The first common market treaty set up the European Coal and Steel Community in 1951. This was followed in 1957 by the Treaties creating the European Economic Community (EEC) and the European Atomic Energy Community. Six countries became full members of the EEC in 1957: Belgium, France, Germany, Italy, Luxembourg and the Netherlands. Denmark, Ireland and the UK joined in 1973, Greece in 1981, Spain and Portugal in 1986. An aim of the EEC was to lay the foundations of a European union which would prevent conflict emerging between its member states. A second aim was to provide economic recovery in Europe after the second world war, and to expand the European economy through the creation of a 'common market' for the goods and services of its member states.

The last three decades have seen growing interdependence among the EEC countries. First, free movement of people enables workers, traders and industrialists to work in the countries of their choice. Secondly, free movement of goods and services has been largely accomplished, with customs duties being abolished for the six founding countries in 1968 and for the others in 1977. Thirdly, a European agricultural policy is now established, based on common prices and on Community price support. Lastly, a common external customs tariff now operates, while measures guarding against uncontrolled competition from third world countries are also within the Community's powers. Today, some would argue, the EEC is 'the most powerful grouping in the world since it accounts for 21 per cent of world trade',[29] exclusive of that within the Community itself.

Within the framework of its three treaties, the European Community is managed by three main institutions. These are the European Commission (EC), the Council of Ministers (CM) and the European Parliament (EP). The links between them are summarized in Figure 20 below.

Figure 20
The political institutions of the European Community

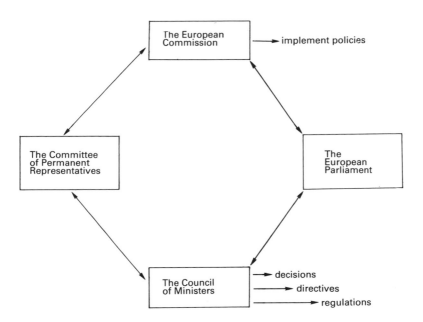

The EC, which is appointed for four years by its member governments, is the Community's executive arm and the initiator of Community policy. Its members act only in the interests of the EEC and may not receive instructions from national governments. The EC's tasks are, first, to ensure that EEC rules and the principles of the Common Market are respected; secondly, to implement Community policies based on the decision of the CM or on the provisions of its Treaties; and thirdly, to propose measures to the CM likely to advance Community goals.

The CM consists of ministers from each member state and it decides the Community's principal policies. The CM is assisted by a Committee of Permanent Representatives which coordinates the preparatory work leading to Community actions. It issues three types of legislative acts: decisions, directives and regulations. Decisions are binding only on those member states, corporations or individuals to whom they are addressed; directives set down compulsory policy objectives but leave it to the discretion of member states to implement them through their own national legislation; while regulations supersede national laws and apply directly as Community laws.[30]

The third direct elections to the EP were held in June 1989. In that year, 434 members of the European Parliament were elected; 81 from each of the four largest countries; 25 from the Netherlands; 24 from Belgium and Greece; 16 from Denmark; 15 from Ireland and six from Luxembourg.[31] There are no national groupings in the EP, only political groupings. The seven political groups are: European People's Parties; European Democrats; European Right; Liberal Democrats and Reformists; Socialists; Rainbow; and Communists and Allies. The EP does not have the same legislative powers as the Westminster Parliament, since it is the EC which takes initiatives and the CM which passes most Community laws. The tasks of the EP include the following: power to remove the EC, though it requires a two thirds majority to do so; supervising the EC and the CM; and providing opinions on EC proposals before the CM makes any decisions. It also has budgetary powers requiring all major expenditure from the Community budget to be submitted for its approval. It is effectively the EP, therefore, which accepts or rejects the budget proposals of the EC following consultations with the CM.

The Single European Act 1987 brings about major amendments to the Treaties of Rome. It changes the way in which decisions are made at the CM; it increases the powers of the EP; and it calls for a comprehensive reform of the structural funds of the European Community. The Act also formally adopts 31 December 1992 as the deadline for the creation of a 'Single European' internal market. This will result in a European Community without frontiers or barriers to the free movement of people, goods and services within member states. The implications of the Single European Act are considerable. It marks a major step in the direction of economic union and the beginnings of a process leading to greater political union also.

The implications for personnel management

The political context of personnel management is very complex because modern government is an intricate and powerful machine. Governmental decisions now impinge on a variety of personnel policies and activities including recruitment and selection, pay determination, redundancy and dismissals, training and so on. Employer autonomy in dealing with employees both individually and collectively is constrained by both parliamentary and EEC requirements. In order to influence public policy making and its implementation in their own interests, employers and managers now have to put collective pressure on MPs, ministers, governments and the EEC through their own business and professional organizations. Pressure group lobbying of this kind is now as much an activity of employer and managerial groups as it is of trade unions and employee associations.

More unsettling from the personnel management point of view is the volatile nature of British politics and the recent instability in the British political system. At the end of the second world war, British liberal democracy was based on a broad political, economic and social consensus between the two major political parties and their supporters. Since 1964, but especially from the mid 1970s, the postwar consensus evaporated. The policy differences between the Conservative and Labour Parties became accentuated and the minor parties began winning a larger proportion of seats in the House of Commons. Given the existing plurality voting system and electoral voting patterns, the majority party in the Commons now receives a declining proportion of the votes cast in general elections. This not only weakens the legitimacy of government, but also can lead to wide swings in public policy where one government reverses what its predecessor has established, especially in the areas of labour law and labour market policy. Both personnel management planning and its operational activities are affected, as employers and managers have to respond periodically to radical shifts in governmental policy.

A volatile political context is also likely to politicize personnel management, especially in the public sector. Financial and manpower cutbacks in the public services since the late 1970s, for example, and unpopular governmental decisions, adversely affected relations between employers and employees in some public industries, where traditionally they had been good. Throughout the 1980s, for instance, there were bitter and protracted industrial disputes in many parts of the public sector including school teaching, the local authorities, civil service, fire service, steel industry, water industry, coalfields and National Health Service. Industrial conflict of this sort obviously has political repercussions and sometimes results in political campaigns being conducted by the unions concerned in order to reverse governmental decisions. Such conflicts often become very emotionally charged and, even after they have been resolved, can leave a legacy of resentment and bitterness between employers and employees which takes a long time to dissipate.

Observations also suggests that the political scene in Britain during the 1980s was highly contentious. As Mackintosh puts it: 'there [were] remnants of old beliefs, a new hedonism, an interest largely in the outcome of government, an impatience with authority, a dislike of elite assumptions, all mixed together'. Public opinion was very volatile and traditional party loyalties were challenged. There was also a drift towards centralized executive power and a weakening of representative government. 'The public as citizen, taxpayer and consumer will probably continue to feel bemused, neglected and somewhat alienated'.[32] The uncertainties and ambiguities of the wider political system provide a difficult environment for personnel specialists to operate in, especially in those public sector organizations which are subject ultimately to political control and direction.

References and footnotes

1   CRICK B. *In Defence of Politics*. 2nd ed. (Harmondsworth, Penguin, 1964). pp21 and 33.
2   CARTER G M *and* HERZ J H. *Government and Politics in the Twentieth Century*. (London, Thames and Hudson, 1969). p16.
3   BALL A R. *Modern Politics and Government*. 4th ed. (London,

Macmillan, 1988). p42f. The theory of the 'separation of powers' states, first, that the same persons should not be part of more than one element of government; secondly, that one part of government should not interfere with the work of another; and thirdly, that any one part of government should not exercise the functions of another. In the UK, there is some overlap between the legislative and executive functions of government, with the judiciary largely independent of them both.

4 FARNHAM D *and* McVICAR M. *Public Administration in the UK.* (London, Cassell, 1982). p16.

5 *ibid.* p17.

6 Not all writers would agree with this view. As Miliband (1973) puts it: 'judges are by no means, and cannot be, independent of the multitude of influences, notably of class origin, education, class situation and professional tendency, which contribute as much to the formation of their view of the world as they do in the case of other men'. See MILIBAND R. *The State in Capitalist Society.* (London, Quartet Books, 1973). p124.

7 FARNHAM *and* McVICAR, *opcit.* p22.

8 CLEGG H A. 'Pluralism in industrial relations'. *British Journal of Industrial Relations.* Vol. XIII, No. 3, 1975. p309.

9 MILIBAND R. *The State in Capitalist Society.* (London, Quartet Books, 1973). p6.

10 EASTON D. *A Framework for Political Analysis.* (NJ, Prentice-Hall, 1965) and *A Systems Analysis of Political Life.* (NY, Wiley, 1965).

11 RUSH R *and* ALTHOFF P. *An Introduction to Political Sociology.* (London, Nelson, 1971). p68f.

12 BALL. *opcit.* p54.

13 RUSH *and* ALTHOFF. *opcit.* p68f.

14 ROSE R. *Politics in England.* 5th ed. (London, Faber, 1989). p143.

15 *ibid.* p166f.

16 FARNHAM *and* McVICAR. *opcit.* p43.

17 BALL A R. *British Political Parties.* 2nd ed. (London, Macmillan, 1987). p262.

18 *ibid.* p207.

19 HEATER D. *Contemporary Political Ideas.* (London, Longman, 1974). p18.

20 *ibid.* p20.

21 BALL (1987). *opcit.* p208.

22 GAITSKELL H. 'Public ownership and equality'. *Socialist Commentary.* June 1958.

23 FARNHAM *and* McVICAR. *opcit.* p47.

24 HEATER. *opcit.* p14.

25 LABOUR PARTY. *Democratic Socialist Aims and Values.* (London, Labour Party, 1988). pp3–6.

26 ROSE. *opcit.* p100.

27 *ibid.* p88. Some Conservative MPs did so after 1983.

28   MACKINTOSH J P. *The Government and Politics of Britain*. 4th
     ed. (London, Hutchinson, 1977). p74.
29   COMMISSION OF THE EUROPEAN COMMUNITIES. *A Euro-
     pean Community – Why?* (Brussels, EEC, 1979). p4.
30   The EEC also has a Court of Justice based at Luxembourg. Its
     functions are, first, to pass judgment at the request of national courts
     on the interpretation or validity of Community law. Its second
     function is to annul any measures taken by the European institutions
     or by national governments which are incompatible with the EEC
     treaties.
31   The first elections were held in June 1979.
32   MACKINTOSH. *opcit.* p213f.

8

The economic context

The prevailing economic climate strongly influences personnel management practices and the standing of personnel management generally. What happens in the national and international economies, for example, crucially affects output, aggregate demand and levels of economic activity in the UK, on the one side, and income, expenditure and living standards on the other. In general, when the economy is expanding, employer demand for labour is high and the personnel function plays a key role in organizational decision making. Thus when labour supply is relatively scarce, the personnel department helps to recruit employees, retain them, motivate them, reward them and train them to high standards of job performance and task effectiveness. It also defends employer and managerial interests in industrial relations, with trade union power at its strongest.

During economic recession, by contrast, the personnel role in organizations is weakened and changed, as employers shed labour by natural wastage, early retirements and employee redundancies, with trade union power much reduced. In this chapter, attention is focused on the nature and problems of the UK economy and the impact of macroeconomic policy and changes in labour markets on personnel management policies and activities.

Scarcity, choice and the market economy

The central economic problem facing any society is that people's economic wants exceed the output of the scarce resources which are required to produce them. Since the factors of production (land, capital and labour[1]) are limited in supply, there are physical limits to what any society can produce and consume at any one time. Conscious choices have to be made therefore, by society's economic decision makers, about how to allocate scarce economic resources to alternative uses. Producing more consumer goods or services, for example, can only normally be achieved in the short term at the economic cost of not producing more capital or investment goods and *vice versa*. Similarly, increasing the stock of corporate or personal wealth is usually possible only in the short term at the economic cost of not increasing the stock of public or communal wealth and *vice versa*.[2]

In outline all economies, or more specifically those individuals and groups with economic power within them, attempt to solve five basic economic problems. These are: what goods and services to produce and in what quantities; how to produce them in the most efficient way; how to distribute them among consumers; how to induce economic growth; and how to ensure that society's economic resources are fully utilized. In the advanced economies of Europe and North America, resource allocation, the adjustment of production and consumption, income distribution, economic growth and economic efficiency are achieved by either the 'market mechanism' or the 'command principle'. According to Grossman (1967), the market mechanism operates in the following conditions:

(1) The individual economic units [firms and households] by and large decide themselves what, how, where and when they produce and consume.

(2) They do so largely with reference to the terms on which alternatives are available to them – ie, with reference to *prices* in the broadest sense of the word.

(3) Prices respond, more or less, to the forces of demand and supply for the individual goods or factors [of production].[3]

With equilibrium reached in all markets through the price system, innumerable economic activities are coordinated and a given allocation of resources determined. Under the command principle, by contrast, the central authorities instruct firms and households what, when, where, how and how much to produce and consume, so that the economy as a whole moves towards planned economic goals and targets.[4]

The main features of a free market economy operating through the price mechanism are, first, that economic decisions are decentralized and, secondly, that no single producer or consumer significantly influences the working of the system as a whole. The allocation of economic resources between different possible uses is the combined result of millions of separate economic decisions by firms and households in the market place. Firms make production plans in response to demands in the product market; consumers spend their incomes according to personal choice in the product market; and households earn incomes by selling their labour or other services in the factor market. In a free market economy, the role of government as an economic decision maker is minimal. Its activities are limited to maintaining law and order, providing national defence, ensuring the enforcement of contracts and protecting the civic and economic freedoms of individuals.

In practice, free market economies are subject to a number of economic and social limitations. First, they can result in extreme inequalities in the distribution of income and wealth. In this way, they do not maximize economic satisfactions in the use of scarce and costly resources. Secondly, when operating at less than their full employment level, they fail to make full use of the limited economic resources at their disposal. Thirdly, certain markets tend to be dominated by one or a few large firms, thus ceasing to be economically competitive. Fourthly, the real costs of production are hidden, because the social and ecological costs of producing certain goods and services are not incorporated in the financial calculations of firms. Lastly, changes in resource allocation between alternative uses can result in painful socioeconomic disruptions and dislocations during the adjustment process.

For these reasons, the performance of a free market economy may fall below that necessary to maximize economic satisfactions. This has led to governments taking a more positive and interventionist role in the western economies in the postwar period, with economic *laissez faire*[5] giving way slowly to the mixed market economy. This combines private and public enterprise, on the one side, with government economic stabilization policies on the other. The major determining forces within the mixed market economy remain demand and supply and the price mechanism. But the less acceptable socioeconomic consequences of the unregulated free market, including the worst features of income inequality, restrictions on competition, unemployed resources, differences between private and social costs and economic dislocation, though never totally removed, are partly mitigated by government economic intervention.

Government microeconomic policy in the mixed market economy, for example, is largely aimed at achieving greater efficiency in the use of business and manpower resources and more equity in the distribution of personal incomes and private wealth in the economy. The government's major areas of microeconomic intervention can include: pay determination; tax policy; industrial training; labour productivity; regional planning; the location of industry; pricing policy; the regulation of monopolies and encouragement of business competition; corporate investment and capital formation; intervention and support in particular markets such as agriculture; subsidies to industry and so on.

Mesoeconomic policy is mainly directed towards the efficient provision and control of key public industries and public services. These include the nationalized industries, other public corporations and the personal and social services such as education and health care. Many of these goods and services are not supplied according to market demand but social demand, with the enterprises providing them being financed largely from taxation and public borrowing, not by private capital. Some public industries however, such as railways and the Post Office, are revenue earning, selling their products in the market to individual and corporate consumers.[6]

Macroeconomic policy, or government management of the overall economy, is aimed at achieving a reasonably high rate of economic growth coupled, until recently, 'with low unemployment and an acceptable degree of stability in the general level of prices, which implies a minimum amount of inflation'.[7] The policy instruments used by governments in pursuit of these economic goals are fiscal policy, monetary policy, prices and incomes policy and exchange rate policy. Britain was a prime example of the mixed market economy between 1945 and 1979. After 1979, Britain moved towards a more *laissez faire*, market based model where monetarist approaches dominated and where large sections of publicly owned industries were privatized.

National income

As we have seen, an enormous number of economic transactions involving firms, households, government and the financial institutions take place within the UK economy at any one time. Goods and services are bought and sold, wages and salaries and other income are earned and spent, imports and exports are paid for, taxes are collected and used, and money is saved and invested. Figure 21 shows the circular flow of income which occurs within the UK economy resulting from the production and sale of domestic goods and services. Gross revenue received by the firm sector, for example, comes from a number of sources. These are: income from other firms buying intermediate goods and services for production purposes; household or consumption expenditure; investment or capital expenditure *via* the financial institutions; government or public expenditure on public goods and services; and revenue received from overseas by export sales.

Payments made by the firm sector include the following: to other firms selling intermediate goods and services used in the production process; to the household sector as wages and salaries for employment services, rent on property and interest on loans; and to overseas firms in payment for foreign imports. Anything else which is paid out by firms is by definition pretax profit, part of which goes in dividends to households, part in taxation to government and the rest is retained earnings or undistributed profit. Household income in turn goes in savings, income tax or consumption expenditure, some of which includes indirect taxes on certain goods and services, such as customs and excise duties and value added tax. The nontax element of household income is spent on either other domestically produced goods or services or imports. 'Thus all the funds paid out have either "leaked" into saving, taxation, or imports, or have come back again to the productive sector'.[8]

Table 24 shows the national expenditure and national income accounts of the UK for 1988. These accounts attempt to measure in money terms the total expenditure of consumers, investors, government and net exporters within the national economy for a given period, normally a year, and the total income received by firms, households and public enterprises in return for contributing towards industrial and service production.[9] Total domestic expenditure on home produced goods and services, total factor income and total value added production are alternative ways of measuring the value of productive output in the UK economy or its gross domestic product (GDP) over a year. Total output comprises GDP plus UK residents' net property income from abroad. This is

Figure 21
The circular flow of income in the UK

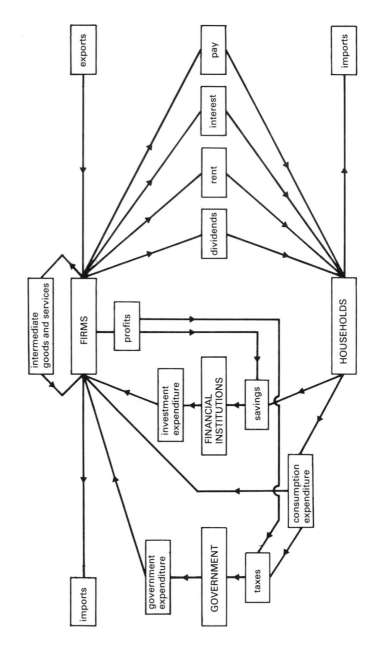

Table 24
UK national expenditure and income accounts 1988

Expenditure		Income	
	£000,000s	at factor cost	
Consumer expenditure	241,873	Income from employment	249,775
Government expenditure	86,061	Income from self-employment	42,617
Investment expenditure	86,125	Gross trading profits	70,242
Exports	103,866	Gross trading surpluses of public enterprises	7,210
Total final expenditure	517,925		
Less imports	−125,194	Rent	27,464
		Imputed charges for	
Gross domestic product	392,731	consumption of non-	
Net property income from		trading capital	3,408
abroad	5,619	Less stock appreciation	−6,116
Gross national product	398,350	Residual error	−1,875
			392,731
		Net property income from abroad	5,619
		Gross national product	398,350

Source: Central Statistical Office, *United Kingdom national accounts*, HMSO
1989

known as the UK's gross national product (GNP), gross national expenditure or gross national income. More generally, GNP is described simply as national income and it provides the focal point for macroeconomic analysis. The UK's national income is important for two main reasons. First, it provides a general measure of personal living standards, though it does not take distribution of income into account so it must be used with caution. Secondly, it is the main determinant of employment levels in the macroeconomy.

Macroeconomic policy

Macroeconomic policy is concerned with the ways in which certain policy instruments such as fiscal policy, monetary policy, prices and incomes policy, and the exchange rate are used by government to achieve stated macroeconomic targets. These targets can include full employment, low inflation, balance of payments equilibrium and economic growth. In postwar Britain, fiscal and incomes policies have generally been favoured by Labour Governments, while Conservative Governments have emphasized the importance of monetary policy.

Fiscal policy deals with changes in taxation and government spending. Its aim is to manage the level of total or aggregate demand for goods and services in the economy, and thereby determine employment levels. It was John Maynard Keynes who drew attention to the association between total demand and the level of employment in the trade cycle. Stabilization of economic activity through fiscal policy is directed at stimulating aggregate demand when it is lagging behind output and inhibiting demand when it is pushing ahead of output. In using fiscal policy, government seeks to encourage firms to invest when consumer demand is low, with savings too high. Conversely, it seeks to discourage firms from investing when consumer demand is high and savings are too low. Policy is directed, therefore, towards either creating employment by ensuring that savings run behind investment or increasing unemployment by allowing savings to run ahead of investment.

Fiscal policy operates in three ways. First, the Chancellor of the Exchequer may use taxes and subsidies in the budget to influence consumption and investment expenditure by firms and households. Raising taxes or lowering subsidies, for example, tends to discourage spending and is used in times of boom. Lowering taxes or raising subsidies normally encourages spending and is used when levels of economic activity are low.[10] Secondly, during booms, government can run a budget surplus to reduce the pressure on aggregate demand, whilst in recession it can run a budget deficit by raising the public sector borrowing requirement (PSBR), thus increasing demand. Thirdly, at other times, when government wishes to reduce public spending for instance, it does so by using other devices such as cash limits. Since public spending plans are long term and are difficult to stop once started, cash limits put constraints on the amount of money that can be spent annually on any particular programme, thus making public spending controls effective.

Monetary policy is the second policy instrument used by governments to manage the economy. This may influence the general level of spending of producers and consumers through the activities of the Bank of England. It has two main aspects. One is the government's attempts to control the supply of money within the economy, although in practice there is no generally agreed definition of what money supply is. The second is interest rate policy, with hire purchase and credit controls being a third arm of monetary policy.[11] Several statistics are used to measure money supply but each is based on different definitions. Sterling M1, for example, is limited to notes and coins and the current accounts of the private sector. Sterling M3 also includes deposit accounts, whilst 'high powered money' is defined as bankers' current deposits plus the note issue. Control of the money supply is based on the fact that bank deposits are the chief element in the UK's money stock. It operates by the Bank of England exerting or releasing pressure on the liquidity of the commercial banks.

Although the techniques for controlling the money supply are complex, in outline open market operations are one possible method that the Bank of England may use in attempts to control the quantity of money in the UK. If government wishes to put pressure on bank liquidity, for example, it sells Treasury bills on the open market. These are paid for out of the credit balances of the banks at the Bank of England. With their liquidity lowered, the banks are induced to reduce their loans and advances to customers, leading to a fall in total deposits and money supply. When government is trying to increase spending, the Bank buys short term government securities, thereby increasing bank liquidity. Since bank balances at the Bank of England are not their only liquid assets, open market operations are supplemented by other monetary measures. These include special deposits and monetary targets centring around high powered money. Special deposits, for example, are called in from the banks by the Bank of England when it wishes to put pressure on bank liquidity and are released to increase it.

Whilst open market operations act directly on the quantity of money supplied by the banks, the second mechanism of monetary policy, changes in interest rates, aims to influence the demand for bank loans. The distinctive feature of interest rate policy is that it acts not on the willingness of banks to make loans but on the desire of firms and households to raise them from the banks. Borrowing money is expensive since interest has to be paid on loans and the higher the rate of interest, the more costly it is to borrow. A rise in interest rates, for example, tends to discourage borrowing, whilst a fall in them encourages it. The Bank of England as the bankers' bank acts as a lender of last resort so it may charge a rate of interest above the market rate. When it does this, these higher rates filter through the banking system into the financial markets.

A third macropolicy instrument which has been used by government is prices and incomes policy. Prices and incomes policies have a long history and can be traced back to the late 1940s when the Attlee Labour Government first pressed the trade unions for a pay freeze. The main aim of a prices and incomes policy is to reduce the rate of inflation by keeping pay and price increases in line with productivity rises in the economy as a whole. But it also aims at reducing restrictive labour practices, increasing labour productivity generally, encouraging a shift in internal and external pay relativities and improving industrial competitiveness. The essence of such a policy, says Robinson (1979), is that those responsible for pay and price decisions 'are expected to take decisions which are different from those which they would take in the same economic circumstances but without the existence of the prices and incomes policy'.[12]

The balance of payments is a record of all the payments and receipts made between UK firms and households and other countries over a year. There are a number of economic factors helping to maintain some degree of equilibrium in a country's balance of payments. One is national income changes. If the UK's exports fall, for example, the falling incomes of its exporters may lead to falling imports. Changes in relative prices also play a role in determining the volume of international trade. Thus the prices paid by UK importers are affected not only by the domestic prices of overseas exporters but also by the rate of exchange between UK and foreign currencies. In the absence of government intervention, exchange rates are determined by the interplay of demand and supply in foreign exchange markets. Exchange rates also move to compensate for changes in domestic prices. If the UK, for instance, has a persistently higher rate of inflation than do other countries, it experiences a fall in the value of its currency *vis à vis* other currencies and *vice versa*.

Countries experiencing pressure on their balance of payments, such as the UK in recent years, have a number of policy alternatives to choose from. First, governments can use their gold and foreign exchange reserves to tide them over any temporary difficulties. Secondly, they can borrow from abroad or from the International Monetary Fund (IMF). Thirdly, they may deflate the economy, so helping to reduce imports and stimulate exports. Fourthly, they can put restrictions on foreign trade and international payments through: tariffs or duties; quotas and subsidies; and exchange controls. Fifthly, governments can fix the exchange rate for their currencies and use it directly as a balance of payments policy instrument. Since 1972, however, the UK has adopted a floating exchange rate policy, with the pound rising and falling in foreign exchange markets according to changing economic circumstances.

From the preceding analysis, it is evident that government macroeconomic policy is both a complex and a controversial issue. Cuthbertson (1979) argues that there are three theoretical approaches to macroeconomic analysis. First, there are the Keynesians who provided the dominant academic and policy orthodoxy in the UK during the 1950s and 1960s and who are still particularly associated with the views of the National Institute of Economic and Social Research (NIESR). The second group are the Monetarists. They came to the fore in the early 1970s under the influence of Milton Friedman and his colleagues at the University of Chicago in the United States. They are strongly represented at the London Business School (LBS) and, since the late 1970s, at the Treasury. Thirdly, there is the New Cambridge School which came to prominence in the 1970s. Their views are associated with the work of the Cambridge Economic Policy Group (CEPG) in the Department of Applied Economics at the University of Cambridge.[13]

In outline, Keynesians argue that since employment levels are primarily determined by output, fiscal policy rather than monetary policy is the major instrument to be used in achieving particular employment targets. In accepting that price rises are caused largely by trade union bargaining power, Keynesians view fiscal policy as being ancillary to controlling inflation which, they believe, needs to be tackled 'by some kind of long-term incomes policy'.[14] Because Keynesians do not believe that the money supply has any significant impact on prices and output, they do not regard fixed targets for the rate of growth in the money supply as particularly crucial. On the other hand, they consider the exchange rate to be an important policy instrument in achieving a balance of payments target. They also believe, if a range of macropolicy targets are to be achieved, in using a variety of policy instruments to influence the economy, both in the short term and long term.

Central to Monetarists' models of the macroeconomy is their view that in the long run the level of real output in the economy is determined 'by the profit-maximizing decisions of the *suppliers of goods*'.[15] For Monetarists, the prime target of macroeconomic policy is control of inflation. In contrast to Keynesians, Monetarists see the money supply as the key policy instrument, with fiscal policy being relatively unimportant unless it leads to changes in the money supply. They also reject prices and incomes policy as a means of controlling inflation. Some Monetarists put forward an additional reason for the ineffectiveness of fiscal policy in influencing output and controlling inflation. For them, increases in government expenditure, by raising interest rates, crowd out private consumption and private investment expenditure. The Monetarist school also believes that exchange rates should be flexible and determined by demand and supply in the foreign exchange market, not by the public authorities. Finally, the rate of growth in the money supply, they argue, 'should be set according to rules based on the authorities' policy targets; they should not be changed by discretionary action based on the results of short-term forecasting exercises'.[16]

The policy conclusions of the New Cambridge School focus on the long term behaviour of the economy. Like the Keynesians, for example, they argue that inflation is largely caused by trade union bargaining power. But they also believe that it is triggered off by rises in import prices caused by increases in world commodity prices or by devaluation. For them, devaluation does not affect the balance of payments in the long run, whilst a permanent prices and incomes policy is impracticable. They argue, again like the Keynesians, that control of the money supply is relatively unimportant and that an expansionary fiscal policy is a necessary condition for raising employment and for lowering the rate of inflation, though this is bound to come up against a balance of payments constraint eventually. If the public authorities wish to achieve full employment, low inflation and balance of payments

Table 25
Key UK economic statistics, 1982–90

Year average	1982–86 average	1987 out-turn	1988 out-turn	1989 forecast	1990 forecast
% Change over previous year:					
GDP (output measure)	2.9	4.8	4.5	2.5	2.5
Consumers' expenditure	3.3	5.3	6.4	2.7	1.1
Government consumption	1.1	1.1	0.5	0.5	1.1
Fixed investment	4.9	8.0	12.2	7.1	3.9
Export volumes (goods and services)	3.9	5.4	−1.1	5.8	6.3
Import volumes (goods and services)	6.0	7.4	12.0	6.7	2.2
Average earnings	8.1	7.8	8.8	9.3	8.3
Real personal disposable income	2.0	3.4	4.7	4.0	3.0
Retail prices	5.5	4.1	4.9	7.7	5.5
Levels:					
Unemployment (million adults)	2.88	2.82	2.29	1.80	1.85
Current account (£billion)	2.7	−2.9	−14.9	−16.3	−11.7
Sterling exchange rate index (1985=100)	102.2	90.1	95.5	94.0	94.0
Dollar/sterling	1.47	1.64	1.78	1.67	1.75
Deutschmark/sterling	3.77	2.94	3.12	3.14	3.10
PSBR (£billion)	7.6	−3.5	−14.4	−16.0	−13.0
Interest rates (%)	11.1	9.7	10.3	14.0	N/A

Source: Barclays Bank, *Economic review*, August 1989.

equilibrium at the same time, the CEPG claim, it is 'necessary to introduce long-term import controls on manufactured goods'.[17] They also support stable tax rates which should only be altered when government's long term policy targets are changed.

Turning to Table 25 and key UK economic indicators for the period 1982–90, we observe that the growth rate in the early 1980s and mid 1980s increased by just under three per cent per year, rising to almost five per cent per year in 1987 and 1988 but falling back to 2.5 per cent for the years 1989 and 1990. Fixed investment averaged an increase of some five per cent per year in the period 1982–86, rising steadily to an increase of over 12 per cent for 1988. By 1990, however, the annual rate of change in investment spending was projected to fall to under four per cent. To put the early 1980s into context, it needs to be recalled that there was a fall in manufacturing output of 17 per cent between 1979 and 1981, whilst gross domestic product fell by 4.5 per cent over the same period.[18]

The annual rate of change in consumption spending rose steadily throughout the 1980s, only to fall away dramatically in 1989 and 1990, after peak years in 1987 and 1988. This steady rise in the annual rate of consumption spending for most of the 1980s is reflected in annual rates of change in average earnings and in real disposable incomes. The annual rate of change in average earnings was about eight per cent for most of those years, rising to about nine per cent in 1988–89. The annual rate of change in real disposable income was about two per cent in the early 1980s and then rose to some four per cent in the last years of the decade. Recorded unemployment, in contrast, did not fall below the two million mark till 1989, with a forecasted increase for 1990.

The annual rate of change in government spending remained fairly constant throughout the period, varying between the limits of a half to one per cent per year. The PSBR, in contrast, averaged some £7.6 billion in the years 1982–86 but was being repaid at a rate of some £14 billion per year in the late 1980s. The annual rate of change in imports rose from an average of six per cent in the period 1982–86 but had doubled to a 12 per cent annual increase in 1988, with a projected fall to a two per cent change for 1990. The annual rate of change in export sales over the decade was less dramatic at about five per cent per year, except in 1988 when exports and services fell by some one per cent over the previous year. These developments were reflected in the steadily deteriorating balance of payments on current account from a positive annual balance averaging about £3 billion in the early 1980s to a £16 billion deficit in 1989. At the same time, the sterling exchange rate index which stood at 100 in 1985 had fallen to 94 by 1989–90.

Finally, the annual rate of increase in retail prices between 1982–86 averaged 5.5 per cent, was 4.9 per cent in 1987 and was projected to rise to 7.7 per cent in 1989 and 5.5 per cent in 1990. Throughout the 1980s, UK interest rates were on average continuously in double digits, except in 1987 when they averaged 9.7 per cent. In 1988 they rose again, reaching a peak of 15 per cent in 1989–90.

Employment trends and the labour market

Employment levels within the economy are ultimately dependent on labour demand by employers. In outline, labour demand and employment levels increased in the UK between 1960 and 1966, fell between 1966 and 1971 and rose steadily, but with fluctuations, from 1971 until 1979. Three main labour market changes took

Table 26
Employment and unemployment in the UK 1979–89

Year	Working population 000's	Labour force 000's	Employees in employment 000's	Unemployed 000's
1979	26,433	25,089	22,919	1,344
1980	26,347	24,687	22,508	1,660
1981	26,063	23,382	21,192	2,680
1982	25,761	22,700	20,520	2,878
1983	26,986	23,906	21,222	3,079
1984	27,519	24,300	21,423	3,219
1985	27,851	24,578	21,590	3,273
1989	28,183	26,487	22,562	1,696

Source: Central Statistical Office, *Economic trends: annual supplement 1983 edition,* HMSO 1982 and *Employment Gazette,* various

place between 1979 and 1989 (Table 26): first, the size of the working population rose from 26.4 million to 28.1 million; secondly, the labour force increased from 25 million to 26.4 million; and thirdly, employees in employment stabilized around the 22 million level.

An analysis of categories of employment in the UK between 1981 and 1989 is provided in Table 27. This shows that the total of those in civil employment, self employment and the armed services, including part timers, rose from around 24 million to 26 million, with the self employed increasing. In 1989 out of 25.8 million, an estimated 20 million or three quarters of the total were employed in the private sector, including over three million self employed persons, with the remaining six million in the public sector. The public sector consisted of 844,000 or two per cent in the public corporations, two million or eight per cent in central government and just under three million or 12 per cent in the local authorities. Within the public services, education and the National

Personnel in Context

Table 27
Employment categories in the UK 1981–89

Employment category	1981	1984	1986	1987	1989
	000's	000's	000's	000's	000's
Civil employment					
Agriculture	635	615	603	590	567
Energy, water	710	617	546	509	469
Manufacturing	6,370	5,592	5,438	5,400	5,467
Construction	1,534	1,509	1,484	1,559	1,687
Transport	1,522	1,460	1,411	1,442	1,493
Other services	13,219	13,940	14,534	14,944	15,874
(Self employed)	(2,118)	(2,496)	(2,627)	(2,860)	(3,110)
HM services	334	326	322	319	308
Total labour force	24,324	24,059	24,338	24,763	25,865

Source: Central Statistical Office, *Economic trends*, March 1985 and December 1989

Health Service were the largest employers, accounting for some 50 per cent of their five million employees.[19]

A further breakdown of the UK labour force by employees in both sectors for the years 1976–89 is shown in Table 28. This indicates that the area of increased labour demand and rising employment during the years 1983–89 was the private sector. Apart from the local authorities, all other parts of the public sector showed decreases in the numbers of employed. Evidence of the widespread shedding of labour by employers between 1979 and the late 1980s, reflecting the general decline in labour demand, is provided from a number of sources. First, job losses were particularly severe in manufacturing, such as steel making, engineering and textiles, though the downward trend in manufacturing employment had begun as early as in the mid 1960s. In the period 1979–81, the share of manufacturing employment in the economy 'had dropped to 28 per cent compared with nearly 40 per cent in 1960'.[20] Also whilst one of the most striking features of the 1960s and 1970s had been the rapid growth in service sector employment, this trend was reversed after 1979 as shown in Table 29. Taking manufacturing and production industries together, the fall in total employment in the UK for the 10 years 1979–89 was greater than any other contraction in the previous 20 years. During these 10 years, the

Table 28
UK employees by sector 1976–89

Sectors	Changes in numbers employed				Numbers employed mid 1989 000's
	1976–81		1983–89		
	000's	per cent change	000's	per cent change	
Private sector	−508	−2.9	+3,111	+18.7	19,769
Public sector	−118	−1.6	−871	−12.5	6,081
Public corporations	−113	−5.7	−818	−49.2	844
Central government	+45	+1.9	−81	−3.4	2,303
HM Services	−2	−0.6	−411	−4.3	308
NHS	+118	+10.3	−6	−0.5	1,221
Others	−71	−8.5	−61	−7.3	774
Local authorities	−50	−1.7	−28	−1.0	2,934
Education	−63	−4.0	+6	+0.4	1,440
Social services	+31	−9.7	+51	+14.2	411
Police	+13	+7.0	+9	+4.8	196
Others	−31	−3.3	−38	−4.1	887
Total employees	−626	−2.5	−871	−12.5	25,626

Source: as in Table 27

Table 29
Changes in British employment by production and service industries 1979–89

	1979 000's	1983 000's	1989 000's	Per cent change 1979–89
Manufacturing industries	7,395	5,677	5,467	−26
Service industries	14,706	14,880	17,362	+18
Others	2,978	2,732	2,734	−8
All industries	25,079	23,289	25,563	+2
Males	15,037	13,645	14,303	−5
Females	10,042	9,644	11,260	+12

Source: Manpower Services Commission, *Annual report 1985*, HMSO 1985 and Department of Employment, various

number of employees in UK manufacturing fell by 26 per cent or some two million people. The service sector rose by about 18 per cent or 2.7 million people.[21]

A second indicator of the decline in labour demand after 1979 is the number of redundancies notified to the authorities. The former Manpower Services Commission (MSC 1982), for example, claims that the number of reported redundancies reached a peak of 50,000 per month in the first halves of 1980 and 1981, with some slackening in the last six months of 1982. The stock of job vacancies at employment offices and jobcentres also declined from over 250,000 in 1979 to about 100,000 in mid 1981. Also during 1980, the rate at which new vacancies were notified to the Department of Employment was consistently some 10–15,000 per month lower than the rate at which vacancies were filled. Only after August 1981 did the inflow of new job vacancies exceed the outflow for the first time since mid 1979.[22]

Further evidence of the decline in labour demand during the 1980s is shown by the massive increase in short time working and the large fall in overtime working during that period. Whilst hours of work fluctuate a good deal from year to year, the length of the working week generally falls in recessions and rises in periods of economic expansion. In 1979 average hours worked by male manual workers were 46.2 per week, falling to 44.2 per week in 1984. According to Metcalf and Richardson (1982), 'over the same period, the percentage of operatives in manufacturing industries who worked any overtime fell from 34.2 per cent to 26.7 per cent, a postwar record low'.[23]

Turning to labour supply, we define the working population as those persons available for work within the economy. It consists of all those males and females in employment plus the registered unemployed.[24] The male working population fell by a million between the mid 1960s and the mid 1980s to just over 15.5 million. By contrast, the female working population rose steadily from about eight million in 1961 to just over 10 million in 1979, rising again in the 1980s. These trends occurred despite the growing number of people of working age in the adult population after the late 1970s. Department of Employment labour force forecasts claimed that there would be a slight fall in labour force activity rates at that time which would just offset a small growth in the population of working age. Because of this, it was assumed that the size of the labour force would remain roughly constant until the early 1980s, falling again during the early 1990s.

In the case of males, the two effects were in balance till 1980. After then, the male working population fell slightly quicker than expected. For females the pattern was even more pronounced, with the female working population falling by nearly 250,000 in the first half of 1981. One reason why female activity rates fell more than expected was that more women possibly ceased to look for work because jobs were scarcer. Another reason was that larger numbers of unemployed women may have decided not to register as unemployed, even though they were still genuinely seeking work. In general, the tendency is for the female labour force to expand when the economy is growing and to contract when the economy moves into recession. After 1979, with the economy in recession, female activity rates fell initially but recovered substantially after 1985 when the economy expanded.

A major determinant of an individual's employment prospects is that person's skills and abilities available to employers. Research by the MSC (1982) shows the particular vulnerability of unskilled male manual workers in the labour market. First, they are more likely to become unemployed than are skilled workers. In the 1980s, for example, about 50 per cent of male manual workers who were unemployed were classified as general labourers. Secondly, once unemployed, unskilled males are much less likely to find other jobs compared with skilled workers. Unskilled men, therefore, tend to be disproportionately represented among the stock of the unemployed.[25]

Unemployment

A summary of the changes in unemployment in the UK since 1964 is provided in Table 30. The steep rise in unemployment in the early 1980s can be seen as an acceleration of the upward trend of the previous 20 years, with successively higher peaks in the early 1960s, early 1970s and late 1970s. The rate of increase in the 1980s was much higher than in previous economic downturns, reaching 100,000 per month during the last quarter of 1980 but regressing to about 40,000 per month during the second half of 1981. In 1981, the number of people who were unemployed in the UK averaged

Table 30
The UK labour force and unemployment rates 1964–89

Year	Labour force	Unemployed excluding school leavers	Unemployed as propor- tion of working population
	000's	000's	per cent
1964	25,125	354	1.4
1966	25,116	444	1.8
1968	24,858	568	2.2
1970	24,678	618	2.4
1972	24,658	789	3.1
1974	25,104	655	2.5
1976	24,805	1,307	5.0
1978	25,065	1,334	5.0
1980	24,808	2,015	7.4
1982	23,794	3,097	11.5
1984	24,035	3,030	11.2
1986	28,289	3,229	11.4
1988	28,279	2,257	8.0
1989	28,183	1,696	6.0

Source: Central Statistical Office, *Economic trends: annual supplement 1985 edition*, HMSO 1985 and *Employment gazette*, various

2.7 million, a proportion equivalent to over 11 per cent of the labour force. By the first quarter of 1986, the total number of registered unemployed in the UK was over three million, an unemployment rate of 13 per cent, having more than doubled since 1980. It was only post 1986 that unemployment levels began to fall.

The impact of rising unemployment was particularly marked for certain groups. Males, for example, accounted for some 70 per cent of the total in 1985. But there are also differences by age, ethnic or minority group and region. The young and old, for instance, have a particularly high risk of unemployment. During April 1985, about 25 per cent of males and females under 25 years of age were unemployed. Generally we note the highest rates of unemployment are among the under 20s, whilst in the summer months the unemployment rate for those under 18 reaches some 30 per cent. The unemployment rate is also high among males aged 50 and over. In April 1985, it was 20 per cent of male unemployment, compared with 13 per cent for females.[26]

Members of ethnic minority groups also suffer disproportionately during periods of high unemployment. For example in the recession, between mid 1979 and mid 1981, it is estimated that unemployment among the ethnic minorities rose from some 55,000 to about 120,000, reaching over four per cent of the unemployed population which was the highest proportion ever recorded for this group. This disguised wide regional variations since ethnic minorities are concentrated in London and the South East, the East and West Midlands, Yorkshire and Humberside and the North West. In the West Midlands in the early 1980s, for example, nine per cent of the unemployed were from the ethnic minority groups. Disabled people also face problems in the labour market when unemployment is rising, over and above the usual disadvantages they suffer just because they are disabled. The MSC estimates, for example, that the number of disabled people placed by its employment service halved between 1979 and the early 1980s.

Turning to regional unemployment, we observe that the regional structure of unemployment was much more unequal between 1930 and 1970 than it is now. During much of the postwar period, for example, Wales, Scotland and Northern Ireland had unemployment rates some three times higher than those of the East and West Midlands and the South East. But in the 1970s, regional differences in unemployment tended to become less severe, though unemployment continued to be more marked in some regions than in others. In the 1980s, however, the gap between the highest and lowest regional unemployment rates widened significantly. This was because regions with relatively low rates of unemployment had generally smaller increases in unemployment than those with higher levels of unemployment. The largest increases were in the Midlands and the North where large job losses in manufacturing occurred. Unemployment there continued to rise faster than in other regions. But there was also a relatively larger increase in unemployment in the South East, especially in Greater London, where unemployment had generally been low in the postwar years. Metcalf and Richardson conclude that 'unemployment in the central areas of our great conurbations is now seen to be the major spatial labour-market problem'.[27]

Although the number of people out of work has increased steadily in recent years, the unemployed are not a static group. What determines whether the stock of unemployed people rises or falls is the average duration of unemployment and whether unemployment inflows exceed or are less than their outflows. The steep rise in unemployment in the early 1980s, for example, was mainly a result of an increased inflow into the unemployment register. With little change in the rate of outflow, but with a stock of unemployed persons more than twice the mid 1979 figures, an individual's chance of leaving the unemployment register was severely diminished. As Metcalf and Richardson indicate: 'since 1966 flows into unemployment have been remarkably stable at around 4m per year, so the higher unemployment rates primarily reflect longer-spell durations'.[28]

According to the MSC, long term unemployment started to rise in the second quarter of 1980, nine months after total unemployment had increased. Two factors affect the number of long term unemployed persons: first, the level of total unemployment and, secondly, the chances of leaving the unemployment register in a given period. Employment prospects vary according to age and sex, with younger people normally having a better chance of obtaining jobs than older ones and females having a slight advantage over males. By the early 1980s, over 25 per cent of the unemployed had been on the unemployed register for more than a year. Clearly, the incidence of unemployment among people is very unequal, with a proportion of the labour force constantly at risk of long term unemployment or of recurrent spells of being out of work.

Unemployed claimants are those individuals entitled to unemployment benefit. In the early 1980s, the number claiming benefit rose sharply, with recorded unemployment around, or in excess of, three million for most of the period. It was not until May 1987 that the number of claimants fell below the three million mark, the lowest it had been for four years. Table 31 shows the fall in unemployed claimants since 1984. The figures must be treated with some caution, since the government changed the method of calculating unemployment 24 times between 1979–89.

As we have seen, unemployment rates for both males and females rose very sharply in 1981 and 1989. The upward trend continued subsequently, though the rate of increase slowed down in the period up till 1986. After then there was a steady fall, although the male rate was consistently higher than the female rate. By 1983, it had risen to almost 13 per cent but fell slowly to

Table 31
Unemployed claimants in the UK: annual averages 1984, 1986 and 1988

Type of claimant	1984 (000's)	1986 (000's)	1988 (000's)
Males			
Under 25	753	727	558
25 and over	1,445	1,539	1,335
Females			
Under 25	479	461	340
25 and over	481	585	497
All claimants	3,158	3,312	2,730

Source: Central Statistical Office, *Social Trends 19,* HMSO, 1988

around eight per cent by 1988. Since 1986, there has been a proportionally larger fall in unemployed claimants for both sexes in the under 25 age groups, partly due to the introduction of youth training programmes to deal with the long-term unemployed.

After 1979, the long term unemployed – claimants unemployed for over a year – accounted for an increasing proportion of all claimants. In July 1979, for example, they accounted for some 25 per cent of the total, whilst by July 1988 they comprised nearly 41 per cent. The growth in the long term unemployed has been concentrated in the longest duration groups. The proportion of all claimants unemployed for more than five years increased from two per cent in July 1983 to 11 per cent in July 1988. The proportion of claimants who are long term unemployed increases with age. In July 1988, two thirds of unemployed males over 50 had been unemployed for over a year, whilst for males aged 16–19 the corresponding figure was 17 per cent. The durations of unemployment for females also show relatively high proportions of older women who are long term unemployed.

Two explanations have been advanced to account for the relatively higher levels of unemployment in recent years. One is that the 'full employment' or equilibrium rate of unemployment has risen. The other is that the wish to contain inflation, and to protect the balance of payments, has inhibited successive governments from using fiscal and monetary policies to reduce the unemployment resulting from lack of demand in the economy. For Beveridge (1944), full employment meant:

that unemployment is reduced to short intervals of standing by, with the certainty that very soon one will be wanted in one's old job again or will be wanted in a new job that will be within one's powers.

He estimated that the average unemployment rate under conditions of full employment would be, at a conservative estimate, around three per cent.[29]

Nickell (1982) calculates that by the late 1970s the full employment rate of male unemployment had risen to six per cent.[30] Since this was less than half the 1982 level of unemployment, Metcalf and Richardson argue that 'cyclical-deficient demand-factors are the dominant cause of current unemployment'.[31] They go on to say that there is strong empirical evidence showing that unemployment can be reduced by expansionary fiscal and monetary policy. Successive governments in the 1980s have been unwilling, however, to eliminate demand deficient unemployment by such means. The reasons for this, they claim, are first that government revenue tends to fall short of public spending thus necessitating an increase in the PSBR. Secondly, expansionary fiscal and monetary policy results in higher pay settlements so inducing inflationary pressures within the economy. Thirdly, the balance of payments deteriorates in an open economy like that of Britain, when macroeconomic policy is expansionary. Metcalf and Richardson conclude therefore that 'the main cause of [1980s] high levels of unemployment [was] deficient demand'.[32]

The implications for personnel management

The British open mixed market economy is a complex system of production, distribution and exchange. It is characterized by a high degree of import penetration, intense competition in international markets, relatively high public expenditure, steadily rising prices and government economic policy conflicts. Compared with other western economies in recent years, the UK economy has experienced fluctuating but generally lower rates of economic growth coupled with higher rates of price increase and unemployment. Furthermore, the dominant policy framework within which successive governments have attempted to manage the macroeconomy since the late 1970s has been predominantly monetarist, rather than Keynesian. Although the rate of price increases noticeably slowed down as a result of monetarist economic orthodoxy and economic recession in the early and mid 1980s, both the absolute and relative levels of unemployment in the UK dramatically increased, with no corresponding acceleration in growth rates or substantial increases in real national income till the late 1980s.

The major impact on personnel management practices of supply side economic policy between 1979–86 was managing manpower contraction within enterprises rather than, as in the expansionist days of Keynesian demand management policies, a growth in manpower demand. In consequence, the emphasis within personnel management at that time was an essentially negative and restrictive one. Recruitment and selection activities, for example, generally tended to slow down and training and development decreased. There were few innovations in health safety and welfare, or organization design and development. Also, there was little evidence of fresh initiatives being taken in personnel policy or personnel planning and research, other than those resulting from a recessionary economic climate. Only after 1986 were there innovatory approaches to personnel management practices as the economy moved into expansion.

Even in industrial relations, where the balance of bargaining power had shifted significantly towards employers and management in the early 1980s, there were few signs of determined trade union resistance to growing managerial confidence and authority at the bargaining table. As one production director put it in late 1983:

> The union came to us recently with a claim we costed at 29 per cent. Five years ago we would have been defensive, set up a management team and wasted weeks preparing a reply and giving it. This time we told them to take it away and not come back unless it's with something realistic and responsible.[33]

Also, between 1979 and the mid 1980s, the number of manufacturing plants with strong, autonomous and assertive shop steward committees declined sharply. At the same time, the shift from manufacturing to service employment quickened, continuing to weaken the base of traditional trade union bargaining power. As one national full time trade union officer commented: 'against the background of continuing high unemployment, these changes threaten the basis of union power'.[34]

During the early and mid 1980s, it appears, the locus of personnel management activities within organizations was control of manpower numbers and the rationalization of labour costs. Throughout private industry and, to a lesser extent, public industry, jobs of various kinds, levels and degrees of skill were lost by a variety of procedural means. These included: redundancy; redeployment; natural wastage; early retirement; non-replacement of posts and so on. The impact was especially severe on manufacturing employment which lost over one million jobs alone in the period from 1979 to the mid 1980s.[35] Added to this, although the evidence is inconclusive, there were the possible negative effects of the new microelectronic technologies on certain types of employment and occupational skill during the same period. Those involved in personnel work have had to manage these changes too.

The economic context of personnel management between 1979–86, in short, was dominated by change, recession, and monetarism. In the process, personnel management policies and practices tended generally to be inward looking rather than outward looking, regressive rather than progressive and safe rather than innovatory. Opposition from a variety of sources to monetarist economic policies grew more vociferous and coordinated after 1986. More importantly, research by Hendry and Ericsson (1983) severely challenged one of the major academic studies upon which the reputation of Milton Friedman and the Monetarist school rests.[36] Their conclusion was that the empirical evidence failed to support the claims made by Friedman about monetary trends in the UK. With an expanding economy in the late 1980s, we observe renewed optimism in the personnel function and more proactive personnel policies. One manifestation of this was the emergence of a 'human resource management' emphasis in some organizations, with the personnel function more closely integrated with corporate management and corporate policy making.[37]

References and footnotes

1 Land incorporates all of society's natural resources, capital is its man made aids to production and labour is its stock of human resources and skills.

2 Wealth is the stock of economic commodities and assets in society that are capable of satisfying wants at a given time. Such assets can be owned by individuals (personal wealth), by companies and firms (corporate wealth) and by municipal or state authorities (public wealth).

3 GROSSMAN G. *Economic Systems*. (NJ, Prentice-Hall, 1967). p14.

4 The UK came nearest to the 'command' economy during the second world war when production, distribution, consumption and labour mobility were firmly directed and controlled by the wartime government and its various ministries.

5 The phrase is first attributed to some French merchants in the eighteenth century who, when asked what government help they might need, are said to have replied: *'nous laissez faire'*.

6 See chapter 2 above.

7 HARBURY C. *Descriptive Economics*. 6th ed. (London, Pitman, 1981). p204.

8 SURREY M J C. 'The domestic economy' in MORRIS D (ed). *The Economic System in the UK*. 2nd ed. (Oxford, OUP, 1979). p83.

9 They should be identical. In practice, however, total expenditure and total income do not come to the same total. In this case, national expenditure is assumed to be correct and a 'residual error' is added to or subtracted from the national income figures.

10 The government can also use the 'regulator' which enables it to vary tax rates on customs and excise duties by up to 10 per cent, in either direction, without the prior approval of Parliament.

11 In practice, of course, changes in money supply affect changes in interest rates.

12 ROBINSON D. 'Government pay policy' in MORRIS. *opcit*. p297. This provides a useful description and evaluation of prices and incomes policies in the UK up till 1977.

13 CUTHBERTSON K. *Macroeconomic Policy*. (London, Macmillan, 1979). pp1–15. Each group presents its own current review of the economy. Their respective publications are: the *National Institute Economic Review; Economic Outlook;* and the *Cambridge Economic Policy Review*.

14 *ibid*. p5.

15 *ibid*. p8. For this reason, monetarism is sometimes described as 'supply side' economics.

16 *ibid*.

17 *ibid*. p14.

18 MACINNES J. *Thatcherism at Work*. (Milton Keynes, Open University Press, 1987). p65.

19 See also MORRISON M. 'Employment in the public and private

sectors 1976 to 1982' in CENTRAL STATISTICAL OFFICE. *Economic Trends*. No. 352, February 1983. p82ff.

20 MANPOWER SERVICES COMMISSION, *Manpower Review 1982*. (London, HMSO, 1982). p4.

21 See also *ibid*. p3.

22 *ibid*. p4f. Notified vacancies, in fact, only represent about 25–30 per cent of total vacancies at any one time.

23 METCALF D *and* RICHARDSON R. 'Labour' in PREST A R and COPPOCK D J (eds). 9th ed. *The UK Economy*. (London, Weidenfeld and Nicolson, 1982). p255.

24 Those seeking work also include persons not registered as unemployed at employment offices. In 1980, there were about 300,000 'unregistered' unemployed who were mainly women, many of them married and not normally eligible for unemployment benefit.

25 See MANPOWER SERVICES COMMISSION. *Cohort Study of the Unemployed*. (London, MSC, 1981a).

26 CENTRAL STATISTICAL OFFICE. *Social Trends*. No. 16, 1986. (London, HMSO). p73.

27 METCALF *and* RICHARDSON. *opcit*. p261.

28 *ibid*. p259.

29 BEVERIDGE W H. *Full Employment in a Free Society*. (London, Allen and Unwin, 1944). pp18 and 128.

30 NICKELL S J. 'The determinants of equilibrium unemployment in Britain'. *The Economic Journal*. Vol. 92, No. 3, September 1982.

31 METCALF *and* RICHARDSON. *opcit*. p264.

32 *ibid*. p269.

33 Quoted by FAZEY I H. 'A growing confidence'. *Financial Times*. 4 January 1984. p7.

34 EDMONDS J. 'Time to rethink': a role (for unions) for the 1980s'. *Financial Times*. 21 December 1983. p13.

35 See Chapter 1 pp11ff above.

36 See HENDRY D *and* ERICSSON N. Quoted in note of a meeting of the Bank's panel of academic consultants. *Bank of England Quarterly Bulletin*. Vol. 23, No. 4, December 1983.

37 For the development of those ideas, see Chapter 12.

9

The social context

The individuals making up the total population of Britain constitute a variety of overlapping and complementary social groups. Some of these are based on the family, others on class and status, others on sex or ethnic origin and so on. Groups also arise out of common educational experiences, occupational self interest and party politics. Many of the individuals making up these social groupings are employees and they bring their social allegiances, and the attitudes and values associated with them, into their places of work. It is these powerful social forces, external to organizations and beyond the control of those who manage them, which provide the social context of personnel management.

Population and demographic trends

Any analysis of the social context of work must start by considering demographic trends. Table 32 (p. 214) shows that the enumerated population of Britain on census day, 5 April 1981, was just under 54.3 million. It comprised 26.3 million males and almost 28 million females. This represented an overall increase since the 1971 census of around 0.6 per cent, which is the smallest change ever recorded between censuses. It compares with an increase of just over five per cent between 1961 and 1971. Within these overall population changes since 1971, Wales showed the largest proportionate increase of just over two per cent. By 1988, the population of Britain had risen to 55.5 million and was projected to rise to some 56.8 million by 1996.[1]

Table 33 shows recent changes in the population of Britain's constituent countries since 1961. England is by far the most densely populated country, with Greater London the most densely populated metropolitan area. Apart from the South East region,

Table 32

Population present on census night: change in Britain 1961–81

Area	1961 000's	1971 000's	1981 males 000's	1981 females 000's	1981 total 000's	1961–71 rise/fall per cent	1971–81 rise/fall per cent
England	43,460	46,018	22,521	23,824	46,363	5.89	0.75
Wales	2,644	2,731	1,353	1,439	2,742	3.30	2.22
Scotland	5,179	5,229	2,466	2,664	5,130	0.96	−1.88
Total	51,283	53,978	26,340	27,927	54,235	5.25	0.57

Source: Office of Population Censuses and Surveys, *Census 1981. National report. Great Britain Part 1*, HMSO 1983

Table 33

Population and population density in Britain: countries, regions and metropolitan counties 1961–88

	Year 1961	Year 1971	Year 1983	Year 1988	Population density Numbers per square km
England	43.6	46.2	46.8	47.5	359
North	3.1	3.1	3.1	3.1	200
Yorkshire and Humberside	4.7	4.9	4.9	4.9	317
South Yorkshire MC	1.3	1.3	1.3	1.3	835
West Yorkshire MC	2.0	2.1	2.1	2.1	1,014
East Midlands	3.3	3.6	3.9	4.0	242
East Anglia	1.5	1.7	1.9	2.0	150
South East	16.1	17.0	17.0	17.3	621
Greater London	8.0	7.4	6.9	6.7	4,338
Outer London	4.4	5.2	5.4 } 10.6		593
Outer South East	3.7	4.2	4.7 }		289
South West	3.7	4.1	5.2	4.6	182
West Midlands	4.8	5.1	5.2	5.2	396
West Midlands MC	2.7	2.8	2.7	2.6	2,989
North West	6.4	6.6	6.4	6.7	880
Greater Manchester MC	2.7	2.7	2.6	2.6	2,048
Merseyside MC	1.7	1.7	1.5	1.5	2,329
Wales	2.6	2.7	2.8	2.9	134
Scotland	5.2	5.2	5.2	5.1	66
Clydeside	1.8	1.7	1.7	1.6	997

Source: Central Statistical Office, *Social Trends*, HMSO 1983 and 1985 and OPCS, *Population Trends 58*, HMSO 1989

where the population is increasing, the current annual change for each region is much the same as the average change since 1971. The general pattern to emerge during the 1980s is that of a continual decline in the population of the big cities. For example, the 1981 census was the first to record a population of under seven million for Greater London. Since 1971, the population of Greater London has fallen by around 10 per cent and that of Inner London by nearly 18 per cent. For other metropolitan counties the overall decrease since 1971 has been around 4.5 per cent. By contrast, the South West and East Anglia, which are the least densely populated areas of England, are its fastest growing regions.

Another trend is that of an ageing population. Since 1971, for example, the number of children under the age of 16 has fallen by around 12 per cent. There has also been an increase of 10 per cent in the population aged 75 and over, during the same period. Indeed, the number of people of pensionable age has risen by over 40 per cent since 1951, from 5.5 million to around 9 million in the late 1980s, or from just under 14 per cent to almost 18 per cent of the population. The increase is even more marked for those aged 85 and over. This group has risen by over 150 per cent from 0.2 million in 1951 to nearly 0.8 million in the late 1980s. During the same period, the number aged 75 to 84 also rose from 1.6 to 2.6 million, an increase of over 60 per cent. On current projections, as shown in Table 34 on page 216, it is estimated that there will be some 10 million persons of retirement age in the UK by 1991, with a substantial increase in those aged 75 and over.

Population changes and their components in England and Wales for the period 1971–88 are shown in Table 35. The number of live births declined in 1981, after increasing in the preceding three years. Live births have fallen fairly steadily from a peak of 876,000 in 1964 to 568,000 in 1977, rising to 647,000 in 1980. The number of legitimate live births in 1981 was 553,000, some four per cent lower than in the previous year. There were 81,000 illegitimate live births in 1981 which was some five per cent higher than in 1980. According to the Office of Population Censuses and Surveys (1982), the illegitimacy ratio in 1981 was about half as much again as that in 1971 and double that in 1961. 'The increasing incidence of marital breakdown during the 1970s has been reflected in a rise in the proportion of mothers who were either divorced or separated and gave birth to an illegitimate child.' By 1988, over '25 per cent

Table 34
Sex and age structure of the UK population 1951–91

	0–4	5–15	16–29	30–44	45–59	60–64	65–74	75–84	85+	All ages
				Millions						
Males										
1951	2.2	3.9	4.9	5.5	4.5	1.1	1.6		0.7	24.4
1971	2.3	5.0	5.6	4.9	5.0	1.5	2.0	0.7	0.1	27.1
1981	1.8	4.7	6.0	5.5	4.8	1.4	2.3	0.9	0.1	27.4
1983	1.8	3.9	6.7	5.6	4.6	1.5	2.2	1.0	0.1	27.4
1991[1]	2.3	4.1	6.2	6.0	4.6	1.3	2.2	1.0	0.2	28.0
Females										
1951	2.1	3.8	4.9	5.7	5.1	1.4	2.1		1.1	26.1
1971	2.2	4.7	5.4	4.8	5.2	1.7	2.7	1.4	0.4	28.6
1981	1.7	4.4	5.8	5.4	4.9	1.6	2.9	1.7	0.5	28.9
1983	1.7	3.7	6.5	5.5	4.7	1.7	2.8	1.8	0.5	28.9
1991[1]	2.2	3.9	5.9	5.9	4.7	1.5	2.7	1.8	0.6	29.2

[1] Projected
Source: Central Statistical Office, *Social trends*, HMSO 1983 and 1985

Table 35
Population change and its components for England and Wales
1971–88

	Population 000's	Births 000's	Deaths 000's	Natural increase 000's	Net migration 000's	Total change 000's
1971–72	48,854	749	580	+169	−5	+172
1974–75	49,159	625	589	+36	−44	−2
1979–80	49,171	647	577	+70	+2	+73
1981–82	49,634	628	587	+41	−74	−33
1982–83	49,601	629	580	+49	+3	+52
1983–84	49,654	627	574	+53	+57	+110
1984–85	49,764	651	581	+70	+90	+160
1985–86	49,924	660	589	+71	+81	+152
1986–87	50,075	670	558	+112	+56	+168
1987–88	50,243	693	573	+120	+31	+150

Source: Office of Population Censuses and Surveys, *Population trends 30*, HMSO 1982 and *Population Trends 58*, HMSO 1989

of all births in England and Wales . . . occurred outside marriage.'[2]

When the current pattern of childbearing in England and Wales is compared with that of a generation ago, the age specific rates for women over 30 are much lower than they were 40 years ago. The decline at these ages since the prewar period reflects three factors: the decrease in births of higher orders; the general tendency towards an earlier age at childbirth; and a shortening period during which women are actually involved in child care.

Table 36
Generation fertility in England and Wales 1935–60

Women's year of birth	Mean number of children per woman by age					
	20	25	30	35	40	45
1935	0.11	0.87	1.78	2.24	2.39	2.42
1940	0.16	1.05	1.90	2.25	2.35	
1945	0.22	1.06	1.78	2.08		
1950	0.23	0.92	1.54			
1955	0.22	0.78				
1960	0.16					

Source: Office of Population Censuses and Surveys, *Population trends 30*, HMSO 1982

Table 36 provides an analysis of generation fertility in England and Wales between 1935 and 1960. It shows the mean number of children that women born in a specific year had achieved at a given age. Its main implication is that mean completed family size is falling. It reached a peak of 2.42 children per woman achieved by women born around 1935, with childbearing now occurring at a relatively slower pace than 50 years ago.

In the 1980s, decline in all indices of infant mortality in England and Wales continued, falling to just over 11 per 1,000 births. This represents a decline of nearly 50 per cent since 1961 and of nearly 25 per cent since 1976. The rate has now fallen uninterruptedly every year since 1970, though it is still higher in Britain than in a number of other European countries. Differences between the infant mortality rates recorded for different socioeconomic groups, however, continue to persist. The mortality rate of babies born to mothers in semiskilled manual households, for example, continues to exceed that of babies born to mothers in professional households.

In the 1980s, the crude death rate in England and Wales continued to decline. The most striking feature is the virtual disappearance of deaths due to infectious diseases, notably the elimination of tuberculosis. Relatively very few young people die, particularly those aged between five and 35. But a high proportion of deaths occurring in this age group is caused by accidents and violence rather than by disease. One of the most common causes

of death is respiratory disease, with mild pneumonia, influenza
and bronchitis being the main specific causes within this group.
With rising life expectancy, deaths from pneumonia increasingly
affect the elderly. Influenza, since it is an epidemic condition,
causes appreciable swings in mortality from year to year, while
the death rate from bronchitis is appreciably higher in males at
any given age than in females. By contrast, the percentage of
deaths due to circulatory diseases and to cancer, especially among
women, is tending to increase in recent years.

In 1984–88, immigration from countries outside the UK
increased and emigration decreased. However in 1988 more people
left the UK than entered. The number of immigrants from the
European Community has more than doubled between 1974–78
and 1984–88. When analysed by citizenship there was a net outflow
of British citizens and a net inflow of non-British citizens. In 1984–
1988 46 per cent of all migrants into the UK were British citizens,
compared with 43 per cent in both 1974–78 and 1979–83. The
inflow of British citizens to the UK in 1988 was 89,000. 'Most of
these were from non-Commonwealth countries and 29 per cent
were from the European Community.'[3]

To sum up, the general demographic situation in Britain is one
in which the population has remained relatively static over the last
10 years, but is ageing. From the statistics available, fertility among
recent generations is declining and may well prove to be below
that necessary for replacement. Marriage rates at younger ages
continue to fall, with births outside marriage becoming proportion-
ately more important. Infant mortality continues to decline, though
Britain's record remains inferior to that of some other European
countries. Lastly, the number of those emigrating now tends to be
less than those immigrating.

Class, status and power

All societies are socially stratified. This means that there are
significant inequalities in the distribution of resources, of property
rights and of power within them. Such economic and social features
of human behaviour are attributes of people's positions in society
rather than of their personal qualities as such. Whilst individuals
are unequally endowed regarding health, strength, intelligence

and so on, such differences do not provide the basis from which studies in social stratification start. As Littlejohn (1972) points out, when a society is socially stratified it shows 'significant breaks or discontinuities in the distribution of one or several of the attributes mentioned above, as a result of which are formed collectivities or groups which we call strata'. In our own society, for example, 'we sometimes say that it has an upper class, a middle class and a working class'.[4]

Sociologists distinguish between two main types of social stratification. The first can be based on differences between one stratum and another which are 'expressed in terms of legal rights or of established customs which have the essential binding character of law'.[5] These include systems of 'estates' and of 'castes' which are relatively closed or immobile societies. Estates are strata distinguished from each other through differential immunities defined by law, as in feudal societies. Caste denotes the stratification most conspicuously associated with Hinduism, where differences between strata are defined largely in religious terms by degrees of 'purity' and 'impurity' between social groups.

The second type is found largely in industrial societies where strata 'emerge from the interplay of a variety of factors related to the institutions of property and education and the structure of the national economy'.[6] Since the study of stratification focuses on the distributive process within societies, the question of who gets what and why is a controversial one. Compared with estate or caste societies, however, industrial societies are relatively more open and more socially mobile. Within them, there is considerable mobility for a minority both upwards and downwards in the social hierarchy. Nevertheless, their main feature remains the continuity of family position between generations.

Within industrial capitalist society, the structure of social inequality derives from the different distribution of power and advantage between individuals and groups. According to Halsey (1986), power is the resources which individuals or groups command to achieve their economic and social objectives. Advantage is their control over those things which are valued and scarce in society, such as property, human skills, education and so on. 'Power and advantage are controvertible. Together they define the character of strata and the relations between them in a stratification system'.[7] Social stratification of this sort has three main dimensions: class, status and power. Class arises out of the social division of labour and comprises those occupational groups and families which share like work and similar market positions within society. Status is formed out of the human tendency to attach positive and negative values to certain human attributes such as personal worth and social position. Power is concerned with the organized pursuit of economic and social goals through political means. To quote Halsey again: 'classes belong to the economic, status groups to the social, and parties to the political structure of [modern] society'.[8]

Though social class is an imprecise concept which means different things to different people, the anatomy of class in industrial capitalism is displayed essentially in the occupational structure. Its foundation lies in the market, not in the law. Since occupation is its key indicator, one of the two principal classifications currently in use in Britain is the Registrar General's classification based on socio-economic groups. The other is his definition of social class. Both are used as statistical concepts for classifying data, rather than as means for explaining why or how social differences exist.

The social class definition first appeared in the Registrar General's annual report of 1911. There, a number of occupational groups were formed to show variations in infant mortality. The principle of linking social to occupational groupings was continued in the 1921 Census and, with a few modifications, the five-fold social class classification has retained its basic structure ever since. The Registrar General's current classification of social class is as follows:

I Professional, etc., occupations (including doctors, lawyers, chemists and clergymen)

II Intermediate occupations (including most managerial and senior administrative occupations, eg sales managers, authors, MPs, colliery managers, personnel managers, senior government officials, school teachers, farmers, physiotherapists, and nurses)

III Skilled occupations
  (N) Non-manual (including typists, clerical workers, sales representatives, and shop assistants)
  (M) Manual (including cooks, foreman packers, and foremen in the engineering and allied trades)

IV Partly-skilled occupations (including barmen, bus conductors, canteen assistants, and telephone operators but not supervisors, who are IIIN)

V Unskilled occupations (including office cleaners and stevedores (but not foremen, who are IIIM), lorry drivers' mates, and labourers).[9]

It is a very broad classification which does not take income into account. Its notable feature is the preeminence given to the professions. Overall, however, the classification has the merits of simplicity and a degree of historical continuity.

The Registrar General's socioeconomic groups (SEGs) classification was introduced in 1951. Whereas the social class classification attempts to rank occupations by skill and standing in the community, SEGs comprise groups of unranked occupations. The intention is that each SEG should contain people whose social, cultural and recreational standards are similar. The SEG classification is built up from both non-manual and manual occupational groups, distinguishing workers in agriculture and the armed services as separate categories, using employment status as a further differentiating factor. The groupings for 1981, based upon a 10 per cent employment sample, are shown in Table 37 on page 222. Its main feature is that the occupational structure is now diamond shaped, or narrow at the top and bottom and broad in the middle. In the early twentieth century, it was more like a pyramid – narrow at the top and broad based at the bottom.

An analysis of the contemporary class structure in Britain by Dahrendorf (1982) views it as 'a layer cake in which clear distinctions can be drawn between the bottom of the cake, the jam in the middle, and the chocolate on the top (if such a concoction holds together)'.[10] He divides Britain into a very old, an old, and a more recent upper class; an upper middle, middle middle and a lower middle class; and a skilled, semiskilled and unskilled working class. He goes on to argue that the relative distribution among these classes has changed over time, especially since the 1960s. 'The working class has shrunk, and the upper class has diminished in importance. By sheer weight of numbers, the middle class has gained ground'.[11] It is not a homogeneous middle class, however, it is fundamentally divided, he argues, between what may be described as the radical egalitarians on the political left, and the radical market liberals on the right. In his view, if there are any signs of anything approaching class conflict in contemporary Britain, its origins lie in the new middle classes, left and right, and not in the working class.[12]

Historically, according to Halsey, certainly up till the first world war, an integrated inequality was a central principle of British social life. Britain's class system, rooted at that time firmly in the market place, he argues, was fully congruent with the status system which supported it. Slowly and imperceptibly during the twentieth century, however, a new form of status has emerged. This has been achieved by the redistribution of goods and services through the agency of the state, based on the criterion of need rather than on purchasing power. Whilst a class society uses the market place

Table 37

Socioeconomic groups by occupational category in Britain 1981:
10 per cent employment sample

Socioeconomic group	Total	per cent
1 Employers and managers (large establishments)	103,344	4.5
2 Employers and managers (small establishments)	170,083	7.4
3 Professional workers (self employed)	15,536	0.7
4 Professional workers (employees)	76,547	3.4
5.1 Ancillary workers and artists	224,234	9.8
5.2 Foremen and supervisors (non-manual)	23,349	1.0
6 Junior non-manual workers	492,621	21.5
7 Personal service workers	130,069	5.7
8 Foremen and supervisors (manual)	58,798	2.6
9 Skilled manual workers	399,887	17.4
10 Semiskilled manual workers	277,990	12.1
11 Unskilled manual workers	133,129	5.8
12 Own account workers (other than professional)	93,629	4.1
13 Farmers – employers and managers	11,568	0.5
14 Farmers – own account	11,523	0.5
15 Agricultural workers	22,684	1.0
16 Armed Forces	24,870	1.1
17 Others	20,518	0.9
Total	2,290,379	100.0

Source: Office of Population Censuses and Surveys, *Census 1981. National report. Great Britain part 2*, HMSO 1983

as a distributive mechanism, citizenship according to Halsey 'is a special form of status which looks to the state and seeks a different type of distribution which . . . is intrinsically levelling'.[13] Hence just as the old bonds of social class in Britain are weakening, so new social groups are coming to the fore and the old status structure is weakening too. This has resulted in the creation of, not only new vested interests in society, but also critical attitudes towards the existing social structure. Yet as Dahrendorf points out, 'the question remains whether it must also mean that the sense of solidarity and cohesion which went with the old structure is breaking up [too]'.[14]

Women and employment

Every society allocates social and economic roles to men and women and designates activities and tasks to one sex or the other. This sexual division of labour is found in the family, at work and in the wider functions of society. Yet as a Department of Employment (1975) research paper points out: 'in the home most of the responsibility of caring for children and elderly relatives and for the general household duties is traditionally regarded as women's province'. Further 'girls may enter employment below their potential without regard to the work they will do later in life'.[15]

Despite these forces of tradition, significant changes have taken place in the pattern of women's lives as wives, mothers and workers over the past few decades. More women are now married than was the case earlier this century, and they live longer. Childbearing is normally compressed into a short period relatively early in life. In 1901 women comprised about 29 per cent of Britain's labour force, by 1989 this had risen to over 40 per cent. In short, the pressure for women's rights whether in the home, at work or in society has been both inexorable and inevitable in recent years. Although full equality of opportunity between the sexes is not yet a social and economic reality, progress towards greater sexual equality in Britain is slowly taking place. It is being incrementally facilitated not only through more liberal social attitudes to women's rights in society generally, but also by institutional pressures. These include the Equal Pay Act 1970 (EPA 1970), as amended by the Equal Pay (Amendment) Regulations 1983, the Sex Discrimination Act 1975 (SDA 1975), and the influence of the Equal Opportunities Commission (EOC).

The EPA 1970, for example, provided for individuals of one sex to be treated not less favourably than persons of the opposite sex in the same employment, regarding their pay and conditions, where they were employed either on like work or on work which had been given an equal value under a job evaluation scheme.[16] The Equal Pay (Amendment) Regulations, which came into effect on 1 January 1984, now enable women workers to claim the same pay and conditions as male workers doing totally different work, provided that the two jobs are of equal value in terms of their skill, training, physical or mental effort, and decision making (ie job content). The SDA 1975 covers a wide range of benefits, in addition to covering practices and procedures relating to recruitment, training, promotion and dismissal at work. The provisions of the SDA 1975 apply to both women and men and it is unlawful to discriminate, directly or indirectly, against a person on the grounds of sex or marriage, unless the situation is covered by one of the exemptions within the Regulations. It is also unlawful to instruct or bring pressure to bear on others to discriminate sexually or maritally.

The main tasks of the EOC are to work towards the elimination of discrimination between the sexes and to promote equality of opportunity between men and women, including employment opportunities. It also keeps the legislation under review and makes proposals for changes in the law.

In 1988 women made up about 43 per cent of those in employment. This comprised almost 12 million female workers, compared with 15 million men. Of these female employees five million were full time workers and 4.2 million part timers, with 90,000 in the primary sector, 1.8 million in manufacturing and seven million in service industries. The corresponding figures for men were 270,000, 5.3 million and six million respectively. The economic activity rates of British women aged 16–59 by marital status for 1987 are shown in Table 38. They indicate wide variations in labour force participation among women of different marital status.[17]

Despite the EPA 1970 and the SDA 1975, there are a number of areas where women continue to be occupationally disadvantaged and unequally treated compared with men. The main areas are: earnings; job segregation, recruitment, promotion and transfer; and redundancy. Women's earnings, for example, remain significantly below those of men. According to a study by the Low Pay Unit (LPU 1980), the period from 1970 to 1976 produced a substantial improvement in women's relative pay which, as illustrated in Table 39, seems subsequently to have regressed. Indeed, between 1977 and 1979, there was a slight decline in women's

Table 38
Economic activity rates for women aged 10–59 by marital status in Britain 1987

Marital status	Full time employees 000's	Part time employees 000's	Self employed	Economically active per cent
Non-married	2,266	744	145	44.3
Married	2,874	3,469	615	54.3
All women	5,140	4,213	760	50.5

Source: Department of Employment, *Labour force survey*, HMSO 1987

Table 39
Gross median weekly earnings: males and females 1971–88

Year	Gross median weekly earnings Males	Gross median weekly earnings Females	Females' earnings as % of males'
1971	£29.4	£16.7	56.8
1981	£124.6	£82.8	66.5
1986	£185.1	£123.4	66.6
1987	£198.4	£132.9	66.9
1988	£215.5	£145.3	67.4

Source: Central Statistical Office, *Social trends 20*, HMSO 1990

earnings relative to those of men, with adult women having weekly earnings less than two thirds of those of their male counterparts. Further, women form the largest proportion of the low paid. The LPU accounts for this by differences in patterns of overtime and shiftwork between the sexes; by differences in skill and training; and by a higher incidence of low paid part time work among women.[18] By 1988 women's gross weekly earnings were 67 per cent of those of men's, with median female earnings £145.3 per week and males' £215.5.

The EOC (1982) shows that the segregation of work into jobs performed traditionally by women and men continues to be widespread. According to the EOC, the effect of this on equal opportunities in employment between the sexes is far reaching. It prevents women not only from claiming equal pay for lack of the necessary male comparison, but also from applying for jobs in traditionally male areas of work because they lack the necessary experience and qualifications. Cases have even been referred to the EOC where men have threatened to go on strike if women were recruited into so called male jobs. The EOC considers the dismantling of job segregation to be one of its main priorities.[19]

Discriminatory recruitment practices perpetuate job segregation, though it is difficult for those affected by them to prove their case. The House of Lords decision in *Norse v SRC* (1979) sets out useful guidelines on the discovery of documents but it remains difficult for unassisted applicants to prove discrimination. While some men allege sexual discrimination when applying for certain jobs, women have the additional burden of being discriminated against, even in traditionally female jobs, if they are married, have children or appear to the employer likely to have children. Sometimes one sex is not recruited because employers either want to maintain a single sex environment or believe that the existing workforce will not work with the opposite sex. When dealing with promotions and transfers, as shown in an earlier EOC (1978) study, many firms apparently see women's lack of promotion caused 'not only by unhelpful attitudes on the part of men but also of women themselves'. In other words, 'many women were seen as limiting their own progress and choice of careers, despite efforts to motivate them'.[20]

Discrimination against women continues to occur in redundancy situations. Some women, for example, have difficulty in gaining union support when threatened with redundancy. Discrimination can also result when redundancies are linked to age and pension benefits, since many women do not qualify for full pensions. Women are also particularly vulnerable when it comes to selection for redundancy. They continue to be selected for redundancy in preference to men, for example, where the remaining jobs are heavy or dirty. Further, redundancy procedures sometimes provide for part time workers, the majority of whom are women, to be made automatically redundant before other workers. In one case supported by the EOC, a woman complained that women on the day shift were to be made redundant before men with shorter service. They were told that the firm was doing this because it was changing its production to a shift system, where women could not work because the employer had not applied for the necessary exemption order from the Health and Safety Executive.[21]

Race relations

In 1987, as shown in Table 40, over 2.5 million people living in Britain were from ethnic minority groups, forming about 4.5 per

Table 40
Population: by ethnic origin 1983 and 1987

Ethnic origin	1983 000's	1987 000's
White	50,798	51,573
West Indian	503	489
Indian	791	761
Pakistan, Bangladesh	436	508
Chinese	106	126
African	91	116
Arab	69	79
Others, not stated	1,184	871
All origins	53,978	54,523

Source: Central Statistical Office, *Social trends No 16*, HMSO 1986 and *Labour force surveys*, HMSO, various

cent of the total population. Some 26 per cent of these (761,000) were Indian; 17 per cent (489,000) were West Indian; 17 per cent (404,000) were Pakistani; four per cent (120,000) were Bangladeshi, and five per cent were Chinese. Almost half of these groups were born in the new Commonwealth countries and Pakistan and a slightly low proportion – 45 per cent – in the UK, with the remaining eight per cent born in other countries.[22]

Smith (1976), in a report based on a national survey of a representative sample of 3,300 adults of West Indian, Pakistan and African origin highlights the facts of racial disadvantage in England and Wales. The report points out, for example, that the ethnic minorities consist of diverse groups, speaking different languages, belonging to different religions, are concentrated in certain areas, and generally have little in common with one another. They have mostly arrived in Britain over the past 25 years and tend to go through their worst experiences immediately after arriving here. The survey reports that there is little evidence of active discontent among the minority population as a whole. This is largely because most of them tend to evaluate their present position with that in the countries from which they have come.[23]

Inner city riots in the 1980s, however, raise doubts whether the present generation of young people from the ethnic minorities are as prepared to put up with racial discrimination in housing, environment and jobs as their parents have done during the past 20 years.

Smith also shows that the job levels of ethnic minority men are substantially lower than those of white men. In his sample, only eight per cent of West Indian and Pakistan men were doing non-manual jobs, compared with 40 per cent of white men. There are also differences in levels of academic and job qualifications between the two. Qualifications tend to be higher, for example, among the whites. This does not explain the disparity in job levels, however, since men from the ethnic minorities tend to have more inferior jobs than do white men with equivalent qualifications. The earnings of the ethnic minorities are also significantly lower than those of whites, including the earnings of black men doing the same jobs as white men. At the time of Smith's survey, for example, median gross weekly earnings for skilled manual workers aged 25–34 were £39.30 for white men, but only £33.60 for men in the ethnic minorities.[24]

According to the Commission for Racial Equality (CRE, 1983a), racial discrimination in Britain is widespread. In 1982, for example, the Commission carried out spot checks on 300 firms in London which were recruiting employees. It discovered that 50 per cent of them discriminated against black applicants at the point of recruitment. It also found evidence of discrimination in promotion and redundancies and widespread misunderstanding and intolerance of the cultural and religious needs of ethnic minority employees. Industrial tribunal decisions show that discrimination in employment is extensive and involves some very well known employers. The CRE concludes that there is a 'need for all employers to take the initiative and look closely at what is happening in their own organisations [as] underlined by these cases'. It adds that 'in 1982 the pace of improvement has been painfully slow and the pattern of racial disadvantage and discrimination has therefore remained largely unaffected'.[25]

It is the task of the CRE to work towards the elimination of racial discrimination and to promote equality of opportunity and good relations between different racial groups. It does this, first, by helping individuals who believe that they have been discriminated against and who want to take a case to court or a tribunal. Secondly, the CRE is a law enforcement agency, with powers to carry out investigations and issue 'non-discrimination' notices requiring firms to stop discriminating. Thirdly, the CRE helps employers, local government officials, educationalists and others to establish and implement equal opportunity policies. Fourthly, the CRE provides money to organizations who give advice and counselling to ethnic minorities.

The Race Relations Act 1976 (RRA 1976) strengthens the law against racial discrimination which was first enacted in 1968. Other than where exceptions apply, the Act protects individuals against racial discrimination in the following instances: as a job applicant; as an employee; as a house purchaser; as a tenant; as a customer; as a pupil or student; and as a member or prospective member of a club. Individuals who think that they have been discriminated against may take legal action to seek redress of their grievance. The Act covers discrimination on the grounds of a person's colour, race, nationality or ethnic or national origins. Direct discrimination is where a person is treated less favourably on racial grounds than others in the same circumstances. Indirect discrimination takes place when a requirement or condition is applied adversely affecting one racial group considerably more than another.

Equal treatment for different racial groups in employment requires employers not to discriminate in the arrangements they make for selecting employees, in the terms offered to them, or in refusing to offer them employment. Further, employers must not discriminate in allowing their employees access to opportunities for training, promotion, or transfer to other jobs or in their terms and conditions of employment. Similarly, trade unions must not discriminate in granting membership, in the terms of membership or in providing services to their members. Racial discrimination in employment is only lawful where: first, membership of a particular racial group is a genuine occupational qualification for a job; secondly, the employment is for the purposes of training an overseas resident in skills to be used overseas; and thirdly, where the employment is in a private household.

Education and training

Unlike certain other west European countries, such as the Federal
Republic of West Germany and Sweden, there has been historically
both an institutional and a cultural separation of the educational
and training processes in Britain. Education, for example, is still
viewed by many educationalists as being essentially knowledge
aimed at developing rounded individuals as a preparation for a
leisured life style, rather than for active work. Yet somewhat
paradoxically, education is also identified for many people with
an academic tradition, emphasizing success in written examinations
in specialist subjects which are then used as screening devices by
employers when assessing individuals for entry and preferment in
the labour market. Also, despite a small but influential number of
independent schools, the supply of education and control of its
resources, from preschool to postschool levels, are now firmly
entrenched in public sector institutions, largely financed by taxation.

Training, by contrast, has tended to have a different emphasis
and a lower status than education. Training is generally regarded
as being essentially skills centred and as preparing individuals for
jobs, work roles or the professions. It is based on the learning and
application of practical knowledge in real life situations, where
learning by experience and example is as important as understanding theoretical principles and basic concepts. Although there has
been a strong vocational element in technical education, such
as in the polytechnics and colleges, the training function has
traditionally been the responsibility of private and voluntary
sectors. In other words, it has been left largely to employers,
professional bodies and the craft institutes to undertake their own
training for future professionals, technicians, craft personnel and
others. Clearly there are examples, especially amongst higher
occupational groups such as medicine and the law, where the
separation of education and training has been less apparent. But
it is only recently that serious attempts to synthesize and integrate
the two functions in Britain have been made.[26]

The structure of the UK educational system is summarized in
Figure 22. In 1988, there were 100,000 children in maintained
nursery schools in the United Kingdom, 4.7 million in primary
schools and 3.7 million in secondary schools. In the postschool

sector there were 270,000 university students, 290,000 students studying for degrees or their equivalent in the polytechnics and colleges of higher education, with another 1.8 million part time students taking a variety of courses below degree level in the colleges of further education. The independent or so called 'public schools' in the United Kingdom had 635,000 pupils in 1988, comprising seven per cent of the total school population at that time.[27]

Recent criticisms against state schools include a claimed fall in their academic attainments and educational standards. Table 41 (p. 232) hardly supports such conclusions. Between 1970–71 and 1987–88, for example, the percentage of boy pupils with five or more ordinary level, or their equivalent, passes in the General Certificate of Education or General Certificate in Secondary Education examinations in the UK increased from seven to 10 per cent, and for girls, from nine to 14 per cent. At the advanced level, there were 16 per cent of boy pupils with two or more passes in 1987–88, compared with 15 per cent in 1970–71. For girls the figures were 13 and 16 per cent respectively. Between 1965–66 and 1983–84, the number of boys leaving school with five or more ordinary levels increased by almost two thirds, while the number of girls leaving with two or more advanced levels increased by almost 100 per cent. A consistently higher proportion of boys than girls left school with two or more advanced levels but a higher proportion of girls left with one advanced level.[28]

Other indicators of the rising level of formal educational standards in the UK are provided by the numbers of students entering and graduating in higher education during the 1970s. In the period 1971–88, for example, the numbers of full time students entering higher education increased from 254,000 to 260,000 (see Table 42 on page 234). Further, as shown in Tables 43 and 44 on page 235, the number obtaining degrees of the Council for National Academic Awards increased from 7,340 to 43,900 and of those with university degrees from 54,812 to 69,900 between 1974 and 1986.

In occupational and industrial training, important recent initiatives were taken up by the former MSC. The MSC was set up on 1 January 1974 under the Employment and Training Act 1973. Its task was to run the public employment and training services. It was accountable to the Secretary of State for Employ-

Table 41

Highest qualification of school leavers by sex: UK 1970–88

	Boys					Girls				
	1970–71	75–76	80–81	85–86	87–88	1970–71	75–76	80–81	85–86	87–88
Per cent with:										
2 or more A levels	15	14	15	15	16	13	12	13	14	16
5 or more GCSE/O levels	7	7	8	10	10	9	9	10	12	14
1–4 GCSE/O levels	17	24	25	24	24	18	27	28	29	28
Total number of leavers (000's)	368	423	442	444	409	349	400	423	427	388

Source: Central Statistical Office, *Social trends 20*, HMSO 1990

Figure 22
The UK educational system

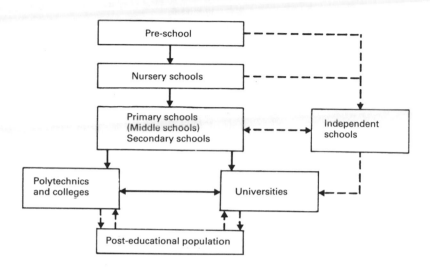

ment and, in its operations in Wales and Scotland, to the relevant Secretaries of State. The Commission had 10 members appointed for a three year period, with Committees for Wales and Scotland to advise it on manpower and training matters and the implementation of its plans in these countries. It had three operating divisions, training, employment and the Skillcentre Training Agency. Its original aims were:

(i) to contribute to efforts to raise employment and reduce unemployment;

(ii) to help assist manpower resources to be developed, and contribute fully to economic well being;

(iii) to help secure for each worker the opportunities and services he or she needs in order to lead a more satisfying working life;

(iv) to improve the quality of decisions affecting manpower;

(v) to improve the efficiency and effectiveness of the Commission.[29]

In the MSC's corporate plan for 1983–87 (MSC 1983b), the Commission stated that one of its main objectives was to develop a New Training Initiative (NTI). The NTI aims were to provide a

Table 42

Full time UK students in higher education 1970–88 (000's)

	Males					Females				
	70–71	75–76	80–81	85–86	87–88	70–71	75–76	80–81	85–86	87–88
Universities										
postgraduate	23.9	23.2	20.7	21.0	20.6	8.0	10.2	11.3	12.6	13.3
undergraduate	128.3	130.1	145.1	135.8	136.5	57.0	73.6	96.2	101.1	104.7
Polytechnics	102.0	109.3	111.9	143.5	147.3	113.1	120.1	96.4	132.2	142.8
Total	254.2	262.6	277.7	300.3	304.4	178.1	203.8	203.9	245.9	260.8

Source: Central Statistical Office, *Social trends 20*, HMSO 1990

Table 43

CNAA first degrees in the UK 1974–88

Classes	1974	1976	1977	1978	1979	1980	1983	1986
Firsts	251	700	760	809	937	864	916	N/A
Seconds	3,687	7,524	9,883	11,153	13,475	13,030	15,664	N/A
Thirds/ordinary	3,432	4,701	6,533	8,407	8,989	8,857	8,986	N/A
Total	7,340	12,925	17,176	20,369	23,401	22,751	25,566	43,900

Sources: *DES Statistics of education 1979. Vol. 3. Further education,* HMSO 1982 and *Education Statistics,* HMSO 1985 and 1988

Table 44

University first degrees in the UK 1974–88

Classes	1974	1976	1977	1978	1979	1983	1986
Honours	43,789	46,292	48,880	52,099	54,278	62,739	N/A
Pass/ordinary	11,023	10,757	11,504	11,558	11,704	12,179	N/A
Total	54,812	57,049	60,384	63,657	65,982	74,918	69,900

Sources: *DES Statistics of education 1979. Vol. 6. Universities,* HMSO 1982 and *Education Statistics,* HMSO 1985 and 1988

better trained workforce by supporting and encouraging the reform of training practices and to enable individuals to make the most of their talents. Under the NTI there were, according to the MSC (1981b), three tasks to be achieved:

(i) we must develop skill training including apprenticeship in such a way as to enable young people entering at different ages and with different educational attainments to acquire agreed standards of skill appropriate to the jobs available and to provide them with a basis for progression through further learning;

(ii) we must move towards a position where all young people under the age of 18 have the opportunity either of continuing in full time education or of entering training or a period of planned work experience combining work-related training and education;

(iii) we must open up widespread opportunities for adults, whether employed, unemployed or returning to work, to acquire, increase or update their skills and knowledge during the course of their working lives.[30]

Consultations following the NTI showed overwhelming support for all three objectives. The most important theme to emerge was Britain's need for a flexible and adaptable workforce to survive uncertainty and change in a competitive world.

The MSC's main activities were preparing young people for work, reforming occupational training and providing improved opportunities for adults. In helping young people, for example, the MSC's two main programmes were the Youth Training Scheme (YTS) and the Technical and Vocational Education Initiative (TVEI). The YTS aimed to build on the experience of the former Youth Opportunities Programme and on training schemes run by employers. It sought to do this by providing 'young people with a bridge between school and work through broad based foundation training in a range of basic skills, knowledge and experience, which will enable them to adapt to changing circumstances and opportunities'.[31] The YTS covered both employed and unemployed young people and offered a two year integrated programme with a minimum duration of off the job training reinforcing and supporting a period of practical work based experience. The TVEI was a five year pilot scheme aimed at stimulating the provision of technical and vocational education for 14–18 year olds.[32]

In seeking to reform occupational training, the MSC aimed to achieve general acceptance of training based on agreed achievement standards. In discussions with interested parties, the MSC gave priority to occupations in engineering, construction, road transport, clerical and computing. Discussions focused on three particular issues: the erosion of unnecessary barriers, such as age, to skill training and employment; the development of flexible modular programmes of training; and defined and accepted training standards. Another aim was to modernize occupational training arrangements and to deal with skill imbalances in the economy.

There are five areas where the MSC sought to improve training opportunities for adults. These were: by developing its training information network; by developing its 'Open Tech' programme; by continuing its Training Opportunities Scheme; by extending small business start up courses; and by 'expanding opportunities for women to enter occupations in which they have been traditionally under-represented and providing facilities to enable women to return to work after long absences'.[33] As the MSC said in its discussion paper on adult training strategy (1983d):

> training can no longer be a luxury for the minority: it is a necessity for all. If British industry is to compete effectively in changing markets . . . a new pattern of skills is needed rapidly.[34]

The implications for personnel management

The movement of people away from the inner cities, the ageing population, more one parent families, higher divorce rates, the falling birth rate, the 'demographic time bomb' and better educated citizens, all to varying degrees impinge on the personnel management function in organizations. The location of industry, for example, is strongly influenced by potential labour supply in the local labour market, as well as by likely attitudes towards work and employment in the area concerned. Also, other things being equal, employers want to recruit and retain the best possible personnel at the appropriate market rates to staff their organizations. Changes in social attitudes often result in employees having higher expectations in their work, employment and life styles. These include demands for higher pay, better working conditions, more job autonomy and the questioning of managerial authority within enterprises. While certain employers can satisfy these employee expectations, or some of them, others are unable or unwilling to do so.

Further, despite generally rising living standards over the past generation and the expansion of the white collar middle class, considerable inequalities of income, power and status remain in British society. The negative and obstructive attitudes associated with traditional class divisions in Britain continue to exist and are often transferred to the workplace, with deleterious effects on productivity, output and labour–management relations. As Lynne Reid Banks the novelist wrote in 1976: 'Class is so deeply embedded in our national sub-conscious it is poisoning every aspect of our lives. Not just industrial relations and politics . . . It holds back progress, destroys prosperity, impedes social and working relations on every side'.[35] Yet status differences at work persist between those earning wages and salaries, those having 'perks' and fringe benefits and those having jobs and careers respectively. Harmonization of terms and conditions between production workers and staff, and cashless pay for example, are not yet universal personnel practices.

In seeking to eliminate sex and marriage discrimination and the promotion of equality of opportunity in employment, the EOC (1982a) has issued a code of practice giving advice to employers, trade unions, employment agencies and individuals. 'It recommends the establishment and use of consistent criteria for selection, training, promotion, redundancy, and dismissal procedures which are made known to all employees'.[36] The EOC also recommends that employers should have a written policy statement setting out their commitment to equal opportunity, their opposition to sex or marital discrimination and their determination to adopt appropriate procedures and practices to achieve these. It adds: 'a published Policy which is properly monitored could well assist an employer before an Industrial Tribunal'.[37]

The Commission (1983a) further recommends that personnel departments should be responsible for monitoring the effectiveness of equal opportunity policies, 'with overall responsibility for its implementation and supervision remaining with the Personnel Director'. It also suggests that all aspects of personnel policies and procedures should be kept under constant review to ensure that they do not operate against equal opportunities. Where it appears that discriminatory practices might be taking place, the circumstances should be investigated by management and individual complaints processed through the grievance procedure.[38]

The CRE (1983b) has issued a code of practice giving practical guidance to help employers, trade unions and others on how they can best implement policies to eliminate racial discrimination and to enhance equality of opportunities in employment. Like the EOC code, it does not impose any legal obligations but its provisions are admissible in any proceedings before an industrial tribunal. It states that responsibility for providing equal opportunity for job applicants and employees rests primarily with employers. It recommends that they should adopt, implement and monitor an equal opportunity policy which should be communicated to all employees through notice boards, circulars and so on.[39]

According to the CRE (1983c), an effective equal opportunity policy enables employers to do the following: to ensure that there is no unlawful discrimination in their establishments; to develop good employment practices irrespective of an employee's colour; to identify groups who are underrepresented in certain jobs and to take any necessary action to remedy this; and, where effectively monitored, to have a defence against complaints of racial discrimination by individuals. Such a policy aims at positive measures to eliminate both overt discrimination and employment practices which are discriminating in the ways they operate. 'It is a policy which also provides special training for those employees who would otherwise be unable to enjoy the full benefits of an equal opportunity policy'.[40]

In order to ensure that an equal opportunity policy aimed at eliminating racial discrimination is fully effective, the code recommends employers to take the following actions: allocate responsibility for the policy to a senior manager; agree its contents with the trade unions; ensure that the policy is known to all employees and job applicants; provide training and guidance for supervisory staff and others; review regularly existing procedures; and make an initial analysis of the workforce and regularly monitoring the policy.[41]

Education and training continue largely to be institutionally separated. On the one side, some employees are overqualified at the recruitment stage and others, such as graduates, are in jobs below their educational capabilities. On the other hand, there are certain groups, such as school leavers, who often lack practical job skills of use to potential employers. Opportunities for continuing education, linked with either day release or sabbatical leave, are provided only to a privileged minority of employees, such as managers, in order to update their knowledge and to develop their job and life skills.

The changing social context of personnel management, in summary, is placing more pressure on employers to provide better terms and employment prospects for their employees, on the one hand, and to have more regard to their 'social responsibilities' to both employees and the wider community on the other. The areas in which personnel policy makers are having to pay attention include: the ethnic minorities; female employees; the disabled; parents wanting maternity and paternity leave; the local community; environmental conservation; the quality of working life; retirement; training and retraining; the impact of technological change on employment and so on. Given the current economic context of personnel management within enterprises, however, the major problem for employers is finding the resources to pay for implementing progressive and forward looking policies of these kinds. Yet failure to meet these demands could well result in government or the European Community placing even further restrictions on those employers claiming the unilateral right to manage subordinates in unstructured and discriminatory ways in personnel matters.

References and footnotes

1   OFFICE OF POPULATION CENSUSES AND SURVEYS. *Population Trends*. Vol. 59 (Spring 1990). p35.
2   OFFICE OF POPULATION CENSUSES AND SURVEYS. *Population Trends*. Vol. 30 (Winter 1982). p3 and Vol. 57 (Autumn 1989). p20.
3   CENTRAL STATISTICAL OFFICE. *Social Trends*. (London, HMSO, 1990). p31.
4   LITTLEJOHN J. *Social Stratification*. (London, Allen and Unwin, 1972). p9.
5   MARSHALL T H. *Citizenship and Social Class*. (Cambridge, CUP, 1950). p30.

6 *ibid.* p31.
7 HALSEY A H. *Change in British Society.* (Oxford, OUP, 1986) p21.
8 *ibid.* p22.
9 CENTRAL STATISTICAL OFFICE. *Social Trends No. 6 1975.* (London, HMSO, 1975). p29.
10 DAHRENDORF R. *On Britain.* (London, BBC, 1982). p55.
11 *ibid.* p50.
12 *ibid.* p74.
13 HALSEY. *opcit.* p56.
14 DAHRENDORF. *opcit.* p78.
15 DEPARTMENT OF EMPLOYMENT. *Manpower Paper no. 11 Women and Work: a Review.* (London, HMSO, 1975). p58. For two short, interesting but contrasting views of current feminist analyses of society see: WILSON E 'The heal of capitalism on the neck of feminism'. *The Guardian.* 3 January 1984 and MIDGLEY M. 'Why the feminists cannot succeed if they try to go it alone'. *The Guardian.* 4 January 1984.
16 See EQUAL OPPORTUNITIES COMMISSION. *Job Evaluation Schemes Free of Sex Bias.* (London, EOC, 1983b).
17 See EQUAL OPPORTUNITIES COMMISSION. *The Fact about Women is . . .* (Manchester, EOC, 1986).
18 LOW PAY UNIT. *Minimum Wages for Women.* (London, EOC, 1980). p1.
19 EQUAL OPPORTUNITIES COMMISSION. *Sixth Annual Report 1981.* (Manchester, EOC, 1982b). p7.
20 EQUAL OPPORTUNITIES COMMISSION. *Equality Between the Sexes in Industry: How Far have we Come?* (Manchester, EOC, 1978). p14.
21 EOC (1982b). *opcit.* p11.
22 HASKEY J. 'The ethnic minority populations of Great Britain'. *Population Trends 54.* (Winter 1988). p29f.
23 SMITH D J. *The Facts of Racial Disadvantage.* (London, Political and Economic Planning, 1976).
24 *ibid.*
25 COMMISSION FOR RACIAL EQUALITY. *Annual Report 1982.* (London, CRE, 1983a). pp3 and 38.
26 This is particularly the case with some of the activities of the Manpower Services Commission in conjunction with the local education authorities and their teaching establishments, though with what success it is too difficult to say.
27 CENTRAL STATISTICAL OFFICE. *Social Trends No. 20 1990 edition.* (London, HMSO, 1990). pp49–60.
28 See also DEPARTMENT OF EDUCATION AND SCIENCE. *Statistics of Education 1979 Vol. 2. School Leavers CSE and GCE.* (London, HMSO, 1981b).
29 MANPOWER SERVICES COMMISSION. *Annual Report 1982/83.* (Sheffield, MSC, 1983a). p(i).

30 MANPOWER SERVICES COMMISSION. *A New Training Initiative.* (London, MSC, 1981b). p4.
31 MANPOWER SERVICES COMMISSION. *Corporate Plan 1983–1987.* (Sheffield, MSC, 1983b). p15.
32 See MANPOWER SERVICES COMMISSION. *Technical and Vocational Education Initiative.* (London, MSC, 1983c).
33 MSC (1983b). *opcit.* p20.
34 MANPOWER SERVICES COMMISSION. *Towards an Adult Training Strategy.* (Sheffield, MSC, 1983d). p5.
35 LYNNE REID BANKS quoted in MARWICK A. *British Society Since 1945.* (Penguin, Harmondsworth, 1982). p206.
36 EQUAL OPPORTUNITIES COMMISSION. *Code of Practice: Equal Opportunity Policies, Procedures and Practices in Employment.* (London, EOC, 1982a). p3.
37 *ibid.* p10.
38 EQUAL OPPORTUNITIES COMMISSION. *A Model Equal Opportunity Policy.* (London, EOC, 1983a).
39 COMMISSION FOR RACIAL EQUALITY. *Code of Practice: Race Relations.* (London, CRE, 1983b). p8.
40 COMMISSION FOR RACIAL EQUALITY. *Equal Opportunity in Employment: a Guide for Employers.* (London, CRE, 1983c). p7f.
41 *CRE (1983b). opcit.* p8f.

10

The legal context: individual aspects

Labour or employment law is concerned with the legal relations of employers and employees at work. For analytical purposes, it is useful to separate labour law into its 'individual' and 'collective' aspects. Individual labour law deals with: the employment relationship between employers and employees arising out of the contract of employment; with employment protection rights; and with the problems of job security connected with terminating the contract. Collective labour law focuses on such matters as: collective bargaining and collective agreements; the regulation of strikes, lock outs and industrial conflict; and the status and membership of trade unions. Although some legal opinion suggests that the distinction between individual and collective labour law 'is becoming unclear',[1] for the purposes of description in this text the separation is maintained as far as possible.

The nature of law

Power is the ability to direct and affect the behaviour of others, ultimately by some sort of sanction. There are various forms of power, such as political power, economic power and social power, though they tend to be interrelated. The sanctions for enforcing power may be either positive or negative. Positive sanctions, such as an employer's power to provide more favourable terms and conditions of employment for employees, reward people. Negative sanctions, such as an employer's disciplinary powers, threaten them. Power is both a resource and a relationship. As a resource it implies that some people and groups have more power than others and that power is unequally distributed. As a relationship it implies that some people and groups are in dominant or command positions, whilst others are in dependent or subordinate ones.

In any tolerant society, naked power to make policy, to determine rules and decisions and to enforce them, whether by individuals, organizations or governments, is insufficient to maintain
consensus and social stability. The power to act needs to be
accepted as legitimate by those who are directly affected by the
decisions being made, such as employees within an enterprise,
trade union members or citizens within the state. To be acceptable
in democratic societies, power has to be legitimized and converted
into authority. This is the recognition of the right to rule of those
with power, irrespective of any sanctions which they may possess,
by those in subordinate positions. Ultimate power within society,
and the sanctions to enforce it, rest with those who control the
machinery and agencies of the state. It rests, that is, in the
legislative, executive and judicial organs of government. In Britain,
the key institutions of government are the Cabinet, the House of
Commons, the civil and armed services, and the judiciary and
bodies of law enforcement.

A major function of governing is law making, law application
and law adjudication. Kahn-Freund (1977), an eminent labour
lawyer, describes the law as 'a technique for the regulation of
social power. This is true of labour law, as it is of other aspects of
any legal system'.[2] Although the law is not the principal source of
economic and social power within the state, it can either support
such power or challenge it. Further, within the liberal democratic
state, the concept of the 'rule of law' is a fundamental one. In
Britain it reflects the preference of its citizens for 'law and order'
rather than anarchy, warfare or civil strife. It implies that conflicts
and disputes within society should be settled by peaceful and
constitutional means rather than by armed force, terrorism or
physical coercion. The rule of law also holds that both the
machinery of government and officials of the state must operate
through the law and should not be above it. More recently, the
rule of law also reflects changing social attitudes.[3]

The law has two branches: criminal and civil law. Criminal law,
which is normally enforced by the state, governs offences against
the state. Those found guilty of breaking the criminal law can be
either fined or imprisoned. Civil law is concerned with the private
rights of individuals and corporate bodies and with the legal
relations between them. Its two most important actions are those
based on the laws of contract and tort. A contract is a legally

binding agreement between two parties, such as an employer and an employee or a firm and a customer, where an offer made by one party is accepted by the other, sometimes after negotiation between them. Under a contract of employment, for example, an employer agrees to pay an individual for work done and the individual agrees to work for that employer for pay. It is both a 'pay work' bargain and a legally enforceable contract. The law of tort places a duty on individuals not to behave in ways which are injurious to others. When somebody suffers harm because of the default of another, s/he may take that person who has committed the wrongful act to a civil court and sue for damages or compensation.

From the outline provided above, it is clear that the role of law in society is both a crucial policy issue and a controversial one, especially labour law with its potentially disruptive effect on the power relations between employers and employees. Indeed, unless labour law is seen to be reasonably balanced in its impact on employers and employees, or on employers and unions, it will be viewed as being partisan by those whose power it challenges. It then lacks the legitimacy and consent which it requires for its general acceptance. Kahn-Freund argues, for example, that there can be no employment relationship without a power to command juxtaposed with a duty to obey, 'that is without [an] element of subordination in which lawyers rightly see the "contract of employment"'. For him, since the individual employee normally has very little social power, one purpose of labour law is to act as 'a countervailing force to counteract the inequality of bargaining power which is inherent . . . in the employment relationship'.[4]

Kahn-Freund goes on to argue that the law aims not only to restrain the command power of management over subordinates but also, once employees are organized into trade unions, to restrain the collective power of organized labour. How far it succeeds in achieving these ends 'depends on the extent to which the workers are organized . . . [and] on the attitude of the employers'.[5] Grunfeld (1968) is more cautious. Whilst accepting that the law has a major part to play in protecting individuals in their relationships with their employers and their unions, he concludes that 'in the sphere of the power relationship between management and organized labour, its touch should be light and sensitive'.[6]

The view that labour law can redress the imbalance in power relations of employers over employees, as advanced by labour lawyers such as Kahn-Freund, is not accepted by Marxist and some left-wing critics of industrial capitalism. They argue that the most important political fact about industrial capitalist societies is the continued existence of private and concentrated economic power within them. This economic power, they contend, is reflected in the political system, its public policies on industrial relations and its labour laws. Miliband (1973) argues, for example, that power in the capitalist state is not democratically accountable. Consequently, its labour laws are partisan rather than balanced in both their intention and their operation. In his view, the capitalist state is primarily the guardian and protector of the dominant economic interests within it. Its real purpose and mission, he claims, 'is to ensure their continued predominance, not to prevent it'.[7]

Whichever view one takes of the role of labour law under industrial capitalism, both individual and collective labour law are now playing a larger part in regulating relations between employers and employees, between employers and unions, and between unions and their members, than they did previously. Lewis (1976) claims that 'the one indubitably fundamental and irreversible trend is the ever-increasing extent of the legal regulation of the British system of industrial relations.'[8]

The sources of labour law

The main source of labour law in Britain is legislation enacted by Parliament. Each piece of legislation is normally described as an 'act' or a 'statute'. Examples include the Race Relations Act 1976 (RRA 1976), the Employment Protection (Consolidation) Act 1978 (EPCA 1978) and the Employment Acts 1980, 1982 and 1988 (EA 1980, 1982 and 1988). A second source of labour law is delegated legislation. This emanates from either Parliament or the European Economic Community (EEC). Parliamentary statutes, for example, sometimes allow the Secretary of State for Employment to issue regulations called 'statutory instruments', such as the Industrial Tribunal (Rules of Procedure) Regulations, which supplement parliamentary legislation.

Delegated legislation from the Council of Ministers or the

European Commission is of two types: regulations or directives. EEC regulations are automatically binding on member states, while directives are implemented by national legislation. In 1981, for example, the Transfer of Undertakings (Protection of Employment) Regulations, issued by Parliament, put into effect the EEC's Acquired Rights Directive. This provides most employees with automatic transfer of their employment contracts when transfers or mergers between firms take place.[9]

The feature which distinguishes the English legal system from some other legal systems is its use of case law. In England, judicial decisions in the courts have been built up to form a series of binding precedents. In addition to interpreting the law judges make law. This is judicial precedent which requires lower courts to be bound by the decisions of higher courts. In English labour law this means that while the decisions of industrial tribunals (ITs) do not themselves form legal precedents, ITs are required to follow the decisions of the Employment Appeal Tribunal (EAT), the Court of Appeal and the House of Lords. Similarly, the EAT is bound by the decisions of the Court of Appeal and the House of Lords. As Lewis (1983) points out, what constitutes the binding element in a judicial decision is for a judge or tribunal in a subsequent case to determine: 'what has to be followed is the legal principle or principles which are relied on in reaching the decision of the earlier case'.[10]

Despite its general importance in the English legal system, common law normally plays a relatively minor role in formulating the rules which regulate relations between employers and employees and between employers and unions. As Kahn-Freund shows, this is partly because 'case law can only deal with pathological conditions'. Thus while the courts interpret statutes and apply the common law, the cases they determine are concerned mainly with the unforeseen and the exceptional, rather than with the normal and commonplace. A further factor is that common law generally 'ignores the realities of social constraint and of economic power'. Employers and, where they are organized, employees normally resolve their power struggles through collective bargaining, not through common law. Common law, in other words, usually operates between individuals and 'knows nothing of a balance of collective forces'.[11]

Another aspect of labour law is the codes of practice. Their main purpose is to encourage managers and employees to follow practices and procedures in the place of work which are conducive to 'good industrial relations'. The first industrial relations code of practice was issued by the Department of Employment in 1972, and parts of it still remain in force. Other codes of practice issued with the authority of Parliament come from a number of bodies. These include: the Advisory Conciliation and Arbitration Service (ACAS); the Equal Opportunities Commission (EOC); the Commission for Racial Equality (CRE); and the Health and Safety Commission. More recently, under the EA 1980, the Secretary of State for Employment has the power to issue codes of practice, providing s/he has consulted ACAS before publishing a draft. Like the Highway Code, no one can be prosecuted or sued for breaching a labour code. But in proceedings before a tribunal or court, any relevant provisions of the codes may be taken into account.

The development of labour law

In preindustrial England, it was magistrates who were largely responsible for fixing wages by law. During the early years of the industrial revolution, however, freedom of contract between 'masters' and 'servants' became the prevailing legal doctrine. It was the terms of the 'contract of service' between the parties which determined their relationship and, by the nineteenth century, the judges were insisting that master and servant were free and equal in forming the contract and in negotiating its terms. Despite this claimed legal equality, in certain cases breach of the contract of employment by servants was, under the Master and Servant Acts, a criminal offence involving imprisonment, though not for masters. The general criminal liability arising from breach of the contract of employment was not finally repealed until the Employers and Workmen Act 1875.

The dominant power position of employers implicit in the contract of employment at that time was only partly mitigated by the growth of collective bargaining and trade unionism. As late as the 1880s, less than a million employees out of a labour force of 12 million were trade unionists. Even by 1910, only about one in six employees was a union member. Nevertheless, as a result of 'a swaying struggle between reformers, workers' unions and factory inspectors . . . and unco-operative employers, many magistrates, and pressure groups in Parliament',[12] piecemeal statutory protection for particular groups of workers was gradually enacted.

The Factory Act 1833, in establishing the first factory inspectors, provided the basis for further protective legislation. According to Lewis (1976), 'typically, the protection would originate in a statute applicable to the textile industry . . . and would then be extended on a piecemeal basis to other trades and occupations'.[13] The Factory and Workshop Act 1901 consolidated earlier legislation and was the basis of the Factories Act 1937 which was itself superseded by the Factories Act 1961. Other major protective statutes included the Mines and Quarries Act 1954, the Agriculture Act 1956 and the Offices Shops and Railway Premises Act 1963. Despite these developments, it has been estimated that prior to the Health and Safety at Work etc Act 1974, some four million workers were not covered by any statutory safety protection.

One reason why statutory protection of workers was not greatly extended from the 1880s until the 1960s was that the trade unions relied on 'free collective bargaining' as the main method of regulating their members' terms and conditions of employment. Moreover, some employers were prepared to concede to the unions and their members what Parliament denied them. Consequently, through experience, the unions became firmly attached to the 'method of collective bargaining', rather than to the 'method of legal enactment', to achieve their members' aims and objectives in the workplace. By the 1940s and 1950s, claims Lewis (1976), 'the priority of collective bargaining over legal enactment was . . . finally elevated to an ideological belief common to both sides of industry'.[14]

In the 1960s, a further series of protective statutes were enacted, though they were initiated by government not by the unions. These Acts provided individual employees with more statutory rights which might be improved on by collective bargaining but could not be undercut by it. The aim of government policy was to encourage the efficient use of manpower in industry, to promote social justice for individuals and to lessen industrial conflict between employers and employees. The first piece of legislation was the Contracts of Employment Act 1963. This provided for statutory minimum periods of notice and required written particulars to be given to employees of the main terms of their employment. The Redundancy Payments Act 1965 ensured minimum compensation for employees made redundant, while the Race Relations Act 1968 was the first statute which attempted to prohibit racial discrimination in employment.

By the 1970s, the Equal Pay Act 1970 banned discrimination in pay on the grounds of sex and, for the first time, the Industrial Relations Act 1971 (IRA 1971) provided the statutory right for certain classes of employees not to be 'unfairly' dismissed. Further Acts such as the Employment Protection Act 1975 (EPA 1975), the Sex Discrimination Act 1975 (SDA 1975) and the Race Relations Act 1976 (RRA 1976) were passed by Parliament. In 1978, the EPCA 1978 codified most of these individual statutory employment rights in one Act, though not those relating to sexual and racial discrimination.

Most of the measures outlined above, apart from the collective aspects of the 1971 Act, were largely uncontroversial. It is in the area of collective labour law, especially regarding trade union organization and industrial action, that some of Britain's most bitter industrial and political conflicts have taken place. As Lewis (1976) points out, legal regulation in this field has been determined mainly 'by the interplay of judicial innovations, public policy controversy, the relative power of management and labour interests, and party politics with a view to electoral advantage'.[15]

During most of the nineteenth century, trade union organization and activities were at risk from the criminal law. Those who went on strike, for example, or threatened to do so, risked criminal prosecution for offences such as obstruction, molestation and intimidation. Until the Trade Union Act 1871, the purposes of trade unions were regarded as unlawful at common law because they were 'in restraint of trade' and those taking part in trade union activity risked prosecution for criminal conspiracy. Further protection for trade unions and their members was provided by the Conspiracy and Protection of Property Act 1875. This Act provided legal immunity from the crime of 'simple' conspiracy when the combination was 'in contemplation or furtherance of a trade dispute'. It also gave some legal protection for peaceful picketing.

Having survived the threats posed to them from the criminal law, the trade unions now found their activities increasingly at risk from the civil law. In a series of judgments in the courts between

1890 and 1906, such as the *Taff Vale Railway v Amalgamated Society of Railway Servants* in 1901, those organizing and taking part in industrial action were successfully sued in tort and damages were awarded against them. There was, it seemed, a new civil liability for conspiracy. This meant that anyone who joined with another for the purposes of striking, which the courts regarded as unlawful, could be sued for damages. It also appeared that organizers of industrial action might be liable for inducing breaches of the contracts of employment of those whom they called out on strike.

It was the Trade Disputes Act 1906, enacted by the newly elected Liberal Government, which reversed the Taff Vale judgment and established immunity from action in tort for acts done in contemplation or furtherance of a trade dispute. Provided industrial action was in contemplation or furtherance of a trade dispute, the 1906 Act afforded legal protection against liability for civil conspiracy; immunity for persons inducing others to break their contracts of employment; and immunity against a tort of interference with the business or employment of another person. It also provided that an action in tort could not be brought against a trade union for acts done by its members or officials, even if they were carried out on its behalf.

As Lewis (1976) concludes, 'the Act of 1906 remained the bedrock of trade union freedoms for over half a century, partly because the judges eventually exercised some self-constraint in limiting the scope of common law liabilities'.[16] From 1952, however, a series of cases resulted in the further development of common law liabilities which the 1906 Act had not anticipated. One was the development of the indirect tort of inducing a breach of contract. The other was the development of liability for the tort of intimidation.

In the case of *Rookes v Barnard* in 1964, the House of Lords decided that threatening a strike if a non-unionist was not removed from his employment constituted unlawful conspiracy by union officials to commit the tort of intimidation. Consequently whenever a trade union official threatened strike action, it seemed that s/he might be liable to be sued for intimidation. It was left to the newly elected Labour Government of 1964 to introduce the Trade Disputes Act 1965. This provided that an act done by an individual in contemplation or furtherance of a trade dispute should not actionable in tort only on the ground that it consisted of a threat to break a contract of employment, or that it would induce another individual to break a contract of employment to which that individual was a party.

Although the Donovan Commission wished to extend immunity for inducing a breach of contract of employment to all contracts, and the white paper *In place of strife* incorporated this proposal, the Labour Government failed to enact its policy and the Conservatives won the General Election of 1970. Soon after taking office, the Conservative Government repealed the 1906 Act and enacted the Industrial Relations Act 1971, placing a number of legal restrictions on industrial action. Bitter conflict ensued between the Government and the trade unions which was only resolved when the Conservatives lost the February and October Elections of 1974. The incoming Labour Governments in turn repealed the 1971 Act and, through TULRA 1974 and 1976, in effect returned to the system of trade union immunities which the 1971 Act had removed.

In winning the General Elections of 1979, 1983 and 1987, however, successive Conservative Governments, led by Margaret Thatcher, were committed to a radical programme of labour law reform. In 1980, 1982 and 1988, the Conservatives enacted three Employment Acts, accompanied by the Trade Union Act 1984. These statutes, whose provisions are considered in Chapter 11, have effectively narrowed the definition of a lawful trade dispute and the circumstances in which trade unions are immune from the civil consequences of their actions, when striking or engaging in other industrial action against employers.[17]

The contract of employment

Since the nineteenth century, the working relationship between employers and employees has been embodied in the contract of employment. The employee agrees to work for the employer who agrees, in return, to pay for the work done. Formation of the contract of employment is according to the general law of contract. Apart from merchant seamen and apprentices who are covered by special provisions, the contract may be oral or in writing or both. Until fairly recently it was usual to find only a few terms of the contract specified, such as rates of pay and hours of work. Today the modern employment contract contains a number of terms and conditions derived from several sources. These have developed from the law, collective bargaining and custom and practice over the years.

The main sources of the contract of employment are shown in Figure 23 (p. 254). As O'Higgins (1976) states: 'the express terms pose few problems'.[18] These are the terms of the contract which are spelled out, either in writing or verbally, and normally include the following: the date of starting work; the terms of payment; hours; holiday entitlements; holiday pay; sickness pay; grievance and disciplinary procedures; pensions and so on. Some of these terms may be expressly incorporated in the contract of employment by reference to other documents such as collective agreements or works rules. Express terms take precedence over all other sources of the contract, apart from statutorily implied terms. Under the EPCA 1978, employers are now required to provide employees with a written statement of the main terms and conditions of their contract within 13 weeks of commencing work. Although this contractual statement is not the contract of employment itself, it is normally the best evidence of the express terms in question.

The implied terms of the contract are those inferred by the courts. Both employers and employees, for example, have certain common law duties which are implied in the contract of employment. In the employer's case, there is the duty to provide agreed pay, to take reasonable care of the employee's safety, to cooperate with the employee, and not to expose the employee to grave danger of health or person. On the employee's part, s/he has a duty to give honest and faithful service to the employer, to use reasonable skill and care when working, and to obey all lawful and reasonable instructions given by the employer or its agents. The latter is sometimes known as the duty of cooperation and it provides the basis of the employer's common law powers of discipline.

A collective agreement or particular terms of it may be incorporated into the individual contract of employment, either by express words or by implication. It is quite common in the individual contract, for example, to find words stating that the employee's pay and hours of work are to be determined in accordance with the relevant collective agreement. Even where no express words

Figure 23
Main sources of the contract of employment

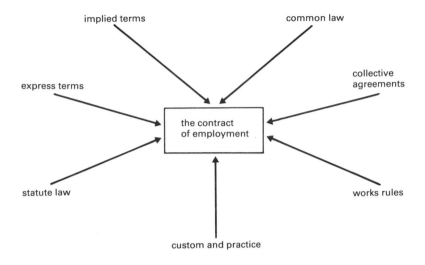

are used, and the normal practice is to pay wages and provide conditions negotiated with union representatives, there is no difficulty in implying a term that pay and conditions are to be provided in accordance with the collective agreement. Normally this applies to both union members and non-unionists working for the same employer.

Works rules also become terms of the contract of employment. Like collective agreements they may be either expressly or impliedly incorporated into the contract. Where employees sign a document saying that the works rules form a part of their contract, for example, they become express terms and the signatories are bound by them. Works rules may also become part of the contract by being prominently displayed in the workplace, or where they are proved to be the local custom in the establishment. Moreover, as Lewis (1983) points out, works rules offer an advantage to the employer: 'whereas a collective agreement can only be altered with the consent of the parties to it, management can lawfully change the content of the works rules at any time'.[19]

A custom and practice may be implied as a term of the contract if it is 'reasonable, certain and notorious'. To be reasonable it must be approved of by the judges. To be certain it must be precisely defined. To be notorious it must be well known. Not every custom and practice, therefore, can be considered as part of the contract of employment. 'Many practices are followed by employers as management policy and not because they accept that they are obliged to behave in that way'.[20]

Lastly, since the 1970s, the contract of employment is now regulated by a number of statutory requirements. The main provisions of this legislation, particularly in relation to employment protection and union membership rights, are considered in the next two sections. Generally, the enforcement of these statutory rights is kept separate from enforcing the contract. Since the mid 1970s, however, new developments have occurred. Under the provisions of the equality clauses of the amended EPA 1970, and the disclosure of information requirements of the EPA 1975, for example, those terms and conditions of employment determined by awards of the Central Arbitration Committee (CAC) operate as statutorily implied terms for the employees concerned.

Statutory employment rights

Individual employees now have a number of important statutory rights at work. Where an employee considers that any of these rights have been infringed by an employer or another party, s/he may make a claim to an industrial tribunal (IT). The Acts of Parliament conferring these rights are: the Equal Pay Act 1970 as amended by regulation in 1983; the SDA 1975; the RRA 1976; the EPCA 1978; the EA 1980; and the EA 1982. The main statutory employment rights of individuals under these Acts are summarized below.

1 The right to a written statement of the main terms of employment

Within 13 weeks of starting work, employees are entitled to a written statement from the employer setting out the main terms and conditions of their employment. The information to be given includes: identity of the parties; job titles; pay; hours of work;

holidays and holiday pay; sick pay; periods of notice; periods of continuous employment; pension scheme; details of grievance and disciplinary procedures.

2 The right to an itemized pay statement

Employees are entitled to receive an itemized pay statement at regular intervals from their employers setting out their gross pay, net pay and the amounts of and reasons for any deductions.

3 The right to a guarantee payment

After one month's service,[21] employees are entitled to receive a fixed payment, reviewed annually by the Secretary of State for Employment, for up to five days in any three month period in which they would normally work but do not do so because their employer is unable to provide work.

4 The right to payments due to medical suspension

If an employee with at least one month's service is suspended from employment on medical grounds, such as under the provisions of health and safety legislation, s/he is entitled to receive a week's pay for each week's suspension, subject to a maximum of 26 weeks.

5 The right to equal pay

When employed by the same or an associated employer, men and women have the right to equal treatment in respect of their terms and conditions of employment. Women normally earn less than men but they can claim the same pay and conditions as men in certain circumstances, even where they are doing different jobs. This is provided that the jobs the two sexes are doing are of equal value in terms of such factors as their skill, training, effort or decision making. Further, the CAC has the power to remove discrimination in employment in collective agreements, employers' pay structures and statutory wage orders where these contain any provisions applying either to men or to women alone.

6 The rights of expectant mothers

Employees who are expectant mothers have the following rights: not normally to be dismissed because of their pregnancy; to time off work for ante-natal care; to receive maternity pay; and to return to work after confinement. Any woman who has worked for an employer for two years can claim unfair dismissal if she is dismissed because of her pregnancy, or for reasons connected with it. But firms with five or fewer employees are excluded from these provisions. Pregnant women are also entitled to time off with pay for ante-natal care. Where a woman has two years' continuous service, and earns above the lower limit for national insurance purposes, she qualifies for six weeks' higher rate payment at nine-tenths of average earnings, plus 12 weeks at the lower rate for Statutory Maternity Pay. Those not qualified for the higher rate are paid the lower rate for the whole 18 week period. This is provided that they work until the eleventh week before their expected confinement. Women satisfying these conditions, and writing to their employers at least 21 days before their leave begins of their intention to return to work, can return to their jobs up to 29 weeks from the beginning of their confinement.

7 The right not to be dismissed or to have action short of dismissal taken because of trade union membership or activities

Employers may not dismiss or take any form of action short of dismissal against employees who either are members of an independent trade union or take part in its activities. Nor are employers allowed to take action against their employees to compel them to join a union whether independent or not.

8 The right not to be discriminated against on the grounds of sex, marital status or race

It is unlawful for employers, and for trade unions, vocational training organizations and other bodies, to discriminate either directly or indirectly against individuals on the grounds of their sex or marital status. It is also unlawful for these and similar organizations to discriminate against individuals on the grounds of race, colour, nationality, ethnic or national origins. Complaints under these provisions as in other instances are heard by ITs, but both the EOC and the CRE have discretion to advise and assist complainants and to arrange representation for them at IT hearings.

9 The right to minimum periods of notice

Employees with at least one month's service are entitled to at least one week's notice of the termination of their contract by the employer. This rises to two weeks' notice after two years' service and then goes up by one week for each additional completed year of service, up to a maximum of 12 weeks.

10 The right to time off without pay for public duties

Employees holding certain public offices, such as local councillors, justices of the peace and members of water authorities, are entitled to reasonable time off without pay to undertake the duties associated with these posts, irrespective of their length of service.

11 The right to a redundancy payment

Employees who have at least two years' service are entitled to a lump sum payment if their jobs disappear. The amount of payment depends on the employee's age, weekly pay and length of service with the employer.

12 The right to time off with pay to look for work in a redundancy situation or to arrange training

Employees who have worked for an employer for two years and are made redundant are entitled to reasonable time off with pay to look for work and to make arrangements for training for any future employment.

13 The right to payments in the event of employer insolvency

If an employer cannot pay certain debts to its employees because of insolvency, the employees may apply for payment, subject to certain limits, from the Redundancy Fund.

14 The right not to be unfairly dismissed

Employees who have worked for two years for an employer have the legal right not to be unfairly dismissed. But firms with up to five employees are excluded from this. Dismissal is only legally fair where the reason for it relates to: redundancy; the capability, qualifications or conduct of an employee; for some other substantial reason; or where continued employment would contravene a statutory duty. Further, if taken to an IT, the employer must demonstrate that it has acted reasonably in all the circumstances. Dismissal is always unfair if it is because the employee is a member of an independent trade union[22] or is taking part in its activities, or if s/he refuses to become a member of a non-independent union.

It can also be unfair to dismiss an employee for not belonging to a union specified in a closed shop or union membership agreement (UMA). This is providing: first, the employee genuinely objects on grounds of conscience or other deeply held personal conviction to joining a union; secondly, the employee has been employed since before the UMA took effect but was not a member of the union whilst it was in effect; and thirdly, after 1 November 1984, the UMA has not been approved in a secret ballot. The legal requirements are that a UMA is only approved where, in the previous five years, it is supported in a secret ballot either by 80 per cent or more of those affected by the agreement, or by 85 per cent or more of those voting. UMAs which came into effect after 14 April 1980 are only approved where they have been supported at least once in a secret ballot by 80 per cent or more of those affected by it.

15 The right of a written statement of the reasons for dismissal

Employees with a minimum of six months' service are entitled, on request, to receive a written statement from their employer giving the reasons for their dismissal.

Union membership rights

In addition to their statutory rights as employees, trade union members have a number of further statutory rights relating to their trade union membership. These are embodied in the EPCA 1978, the EA 1980, the EA 1982, the EA 1988 and the Trade Union Act 1984 (TUA 1984).[23] The main statutory rights of trade union members under these Acts are summarized below.

1 The right to time off with pay for trade union duties and training

Employees who are lay officials of recognized independent trade unions are entitled to reasonable time off with pay during working hours to carry out their trade union duties. They are also entitled to time off with pay for approved training in industrial relations.

2 The right to time off without pay for trade union activities

Employees who are members of recognized independent unions are entitled to reasonable time off without pay during working hours for certain trade union activities. Trade union activities are not statutorily defined but normally include taking part in union policy making bodies, such as an executive committee or annual conference, or representing the union on external bodies.

3 The right to time off with pay for safety representatives and for safety training

Safety representatives of recognized independent trade unions are entitled to time off with pay during working hours to perform their safety functions and to undergo appropriate training in health and safety matters.[24]

4 The right not to be unreasonably excluded or expelled from a trade union

Where a closed shop or UMA exists, employees have the right not to be unreasonably excluded or expelled from a trade union party to the agreement. Where these rights are infringed, and a complaint is upheld by an IT, individuals have the right to claim compensation from the union concerned.

5 The right to elect trade union officeholders by secret ballot

Trade union members have the right to elect directly, at least once every five years, all voting members of their union executives including general secretaries by individual secret ballot. Under such arrangements, individuals must be provided with a fair and convenient opportunity to vote at no cost to themselves. Any union member who considers that s/he is unfairly denied a vote can take legal action against the union, even though the inability to vote has not materially affected the outcome of the election.

6 The right to secret ballots endorsing official industrial action

Trade union members have the right to endorse, by secret ballot, officially backed industrial action. Where no such endorsement is made within at least four weeks of the industrial action taking place, the civil immunities of the trade union from legal action, provided by TULRA 1974, are removed.

7 The right to secret ballots on trade union political funds

Trade union members are entitled, every 10 years, to be balloted where trade union political funds are established under the Trade Union Act 1913. Where there is no longer support for union expenditure on political objectives, a union must take steps to end the collection of contributions for its political fund as soon as practicable.

8 The right not to be unjustifiably disciplined by a union

Trade union members have the right not to be unjustifiably disciplined by their union. The EA 1988 specifies the union actions counting as discipline and the conduct for which discipline is justifiable. Previously, union members could be disciplined for working during a strike or other industrial action. Union discipline for such conduct is now unjustifiable and individuals have the choice whether to work during a dispute or not. Protection for individuals is provided when: going to work despite a union call to take industrial action; crossing a picket line; speaking out against a strike call or other industrial action; and refusing to pay a levy to fund a strike or other industrial action.

9 The right to stop deductions of union subscriptions at source

Individuals informing their employer that they have left or are about to leave their union have the statutory right to have arrangements for deductions for union subscriptions stopped in certain circumstances. The conditions are that the employees must notify their employer, in writing, that membership of the union has ended, or will end, and that the union is aware of the fact.

Courts, tribunals and appeal bodies

The structure of the civil courts in England and Wales is shown in Figure 24 (p. 264); Scotland has a separate structure. ITs hear cases from individuals who claim that some party or person has infringed any of their statutory rights covered by employment legislation. ITs were originally established to hear appeals by employers against assessments of training levies under the Industrial Training Act 1964. Since then, their jurisdiction has widened dramatically. Their aim is to provide informal, quick and low cost access to the law for individuals whose legal rights at work are infringed. As independent judicial bodies, ITs have permanent offices in the larger centres of population in Britain and they sit in most parts of the country. Each tribunal is chaired by a barrister or solicitor of seven years' standing who is appointed by the Lord Chancellor for a five year period. Sitting with the legal chairman are two lay members drawn from panels appointed by the Secretary of State for Employment, after consultation with appropriate employer and employee organizations.

Applicants claiming their statutory rights usually complete an application form, an IT1, which may be obtained from any local employment office, jobcentre or unemployment benefit office. Originating applications are then sent to the relevant tribunal office which in turn sends a copy of the application to the respondent. The respondent, normally an employer, is then asked to complete a 'notice of appearance' stating whether it intends to contest the claim and the reasons for doing so. If the respondent does not send in a notice of appearance, it is not entitled to take part in any tribunal proceedings. Normally copies of all the relevant documents are also sent to local ACAS conciliation officers who try to assist the parties to reach a voluntary settlement. Any information given to a conciliation officer is confidential and is not admissible in evidence at an IT, unless both parties consent to this.

Some idea of ACAS's success in individual conciliation can be seen in Table 45. This shows that in 1988 ACAS successfully settled 25,654 claims out of the 44,443 it received, or some 58 per cent of the total. Indeed, only 8,297 of these claims went to ITs during that year. By far the largest proportion of cases going to ITs relate to unfair dismissal. In 1988 these accounted for 6,479 cases or 78 per cent of the total compared with 12 per cent under the EPCA 1978, and 10 per cent discrimination cases.

The procedure used at IT hearings is orderly, simple and flexible. The parties may give evidence and may question their own witnesses and those brought by the other party. Employees are usually represented by trade union officers or by lay spokesmen. Employers, on the other hand, often seek legal representation, though some of them continue to use personnel managers or employers' association officials. The order in which evidence is given varies at the discretion of the IT. Hearings are normally in public and the press may attend. An IT often announces its decision and the reasons on which it is based at the end of a hearing. In other cases they are given later.

As indicated above, by far the largest number of cases going to ITs annually concern unfair dismissal. If a tribunal upholds a

Figure 24
The civil courts in England and Wales

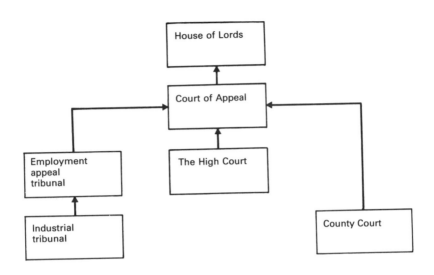

Table 45
Individual conciliation claims received and dealt with by ACAS 1988

	Unfair dismissal	Discrimination cases	EPCA 1978 and Others[1]	Totals
Claims received	36,340	2,465	5,638	44,443
Settled by ACAS	23,582	606	1,466	25,654
Withdrawn	5,160	1,777	1,283	8,220
To Tribunal	6,479	853	963	8,297
Totals	35,221	3,236	3,712	42,171

[1] Including the Transfer of Undertakings Regulations 1981
Source: ACAS, *Annual report 1988*, 1989

complaint of unfair dismissal, it may offer reinstatement, re-engagement or compensation to the applicant. But compensation may be reduced where the action of the applicant is shown to have contributed to the dismissal or where s/he fails to mitigate any loss suffered. Of the unfair dismissal cases going to ITs, only about a third find in favour of the applicant. Of these as little as one per cent result in either reinstatement or re-engagement.

The EAT was established by the EPA 1975. The EAT is a superior court of record and is the appellate body on questions of law from ITs. Prior to its establishment, appeals from ITs were dealt with by a Divisional Court of the Queen's Bench, though 'from 1972 until 1974, appellate jurisdiction from the decisions of industrial tribunals was available through the National Industrial Relations Court'.[25] A second function of the EAT is to hear appeals against the decisions of the Certification Officer on questions of law or of fact in the granting of certificates of independence to trade unions. The EAT also has appellate jurisdiction on matters of law concerning the political levy and trade union political funds under the Trade Union Act 1913 and union amalgamations under the Trade Union (Amalgamations etc) Act 1964. 'Appeals can also be made to the EAT on certain trade union ballots arising out of the Employment Act 1980'.[26]

The EAT consists of judges and lay members. In England and Wales, the judges are nominated by the Lord Chancellor and from among judges of the High Court. The panel of lay members has experience of industrial relations, as either employer or employee representatives, and is appointed on the joint recommendation of the Lord Chancellor and the Secretary of State for Employment. Appeals are heard by a judge sitting with either two or four lay members, all of whom have equal voting rights. As in ITs, the parties can choose either legal or non-legal representation. Further appeals on points of law can be made to the Court of Appeal and to the House of Lords, providing permission is granted by the body which made the decision or by the court hearing the appeal.

The implications for personnel management

The contract of employment between employer and employee is the core of the employment relationship. Although the ways in which the contract is agreed, applied and terminated have radically changed since the nineteenth century, it is still basically a power relationship implying a command position for employers and their managerial representatives and a subordinate one for employees.

Whilst ultimate power within an enterprise rests with the employer and its representatives, individual employees now have a wide range of legal rights enforceable by ITs and trade union representation, both providing valuable redress against unreasonable managerial authority. In planning and implementing its personnel policies, therefore, management now has to take into account not only trade union power but also the law regulating management's right to manage and protecting individual rights at work.

As far as individual labour law is concerned, the common law duties of employees remain. But their common law rights have effectively been superseded by a series of statutory rights covering amongst other things: minimum periods of notice and written particulars of employment; redundancy pay; unfair dismissal; equal pay; trade union membership and activities; time off work; maternity pay and leave; and protection from employer discrimination based on sex, marital status and race. All these measures necessitate more time being spent by personnel managers in servicing, detailing, recording and administering contracts of employment within their enterprises.

Of the legislative provisions aimed at promoting greater job security of individuals, the one which has had the most impact on employers and employees is the unfair dismissal requirements. A survey conducted by Daniel and Stilgoe (1978), for example, suggests 'that unfair dismissal measures have reduced rates of dismissal in establishments where levels were relatively very high prior to the legislation'.[27] If employers are to minimize the risk of being taken to ITs for claims of unfair dismissal, it is now necessary for them to have properly designed and administered disciplinary and dismissal procedures, and to train their managers in using them. In this way, consistency and equity for employees and legal protection for employers can be achieved in the disciplinary and dismissal processes.

It is also necessary for employers to exercise greater care in recruiting and selecting new employees and in appraising the performance of existing ones than they may have done in the past. Previously, employers could take risks in recruitment and selection on the grounds that they could readily dismiss unsuitable employees. Nowadays they need to be fairly certain before engaging anyone that s/he is suitable for the job. Properly monitored induction and probationary periods are also part of this process.

One implication is that recruitment and selection now take longer and are more costly in real terms than in the past. Another implication is that greater managerial attention is being devoted to human resource management than before.

Where they bargain with trade unions, employers must also consider the legal obligations placed on them to provide time off for trade union lay officials at the workplace under the EPCA 1978. According to the code of practice on time off, employers and unions are recommended to review jointly their current arrangements for trade union representatives, 'bearing in mind the statutory requirements, [the] Code of Practice and the particular workplace circumstances'. Under the Code, management is expected to make available to officials: 'the facilities necessary for them to perform their duties effectively and to communicate effectively with members, fellow lay officials and full-time officers'. Management also needs to be familiar with the agreements and arrangements relating to time off. It should also provide adequate facilities for time off including: meeting rooms; telephone access; notice boards; and the use of office facilities.[28]

The general indication is that employment legislation has 'in many instances increased the influence of the personnel function and in some instances it [has] resulted in more resources being devoted to personnel management'.[29] Demonstrating the financial benefits to senior management of improved and more effective recruitment, selection, training, appraisal and manpower planning, not to mention a more professional personnel function, is a difficult task, even for the most skilled personnel practitioners. Nevertheless, there is some evidence to suggest that employment protection legislation is encouraging 'management to pay more attention to human resources . . . that many management critics have long thought necessary'.[30]

References and footnotes

1 LEWIS R. 'Kahn-Freund and labour law: an outline critique'. *Industrial Law Journal.* Vol. 8, 1979. p219.
2 KAHN-FREUND O. *Labour and the Law.* 2nd ed. (London, Stevens, 1977). p3.

3 The law also incorporates social values extending beyond those typically held by the legal profession. See FARNHAM D *and* McVICAR M. *Public Administration in the United Kingdom.* (London, Cassell, 1982). p23.

4 KAHN-FREUND. *opcit.* p6.

5 *ibid.* p9. For a critique of Kahn-Freund see LEWIS R (1979). *opcit.*

6 GRUNFIELD C. 'Donovan – the legal aspects.' *British Journal of Industrial Relations.* Vol. VI, No. 3, 1968. p329.

7 MILIBAND R. *The State in Capitalist Society.* (London, Quartet Books, 1973). p238. See also HYMAN R. *Industrial Relations: a Marxist Introduction.* (London, Macmillan, 1975). pp121–49.

8 LEWIS R. 'The historical development of labour law'. *British Journal of Industrial Relations.* Vol. XIV, No. 1, 1976. p15.

9 Where there is a conflict between UK and EEC laws, community laws take precedence over those enacted by Parliament.

10 LEWIS D. *Essentials of employment law.* (London, IPM, 1983). p4.

11 KAHN-FREUND. *opcit.* pp18 and 22.

12 WEDDERBURN K W. *The Worker and the Law.* 2nd ed. (Harmondsworth, Penguin, 1971). p239.

13 LEWIS R. (1976). *opcit.* p7.

14 *ibid.* p9.

15 *ibid.* p1.

16 *ibid.* p5.

17 Prior to this legislation, some observers believed that trade union immunities allowed too wide a scope for industrial action without regard for its consequences. See DEPARTMENT OF EMPLOYMENT. *Trade Union Immunities.* (London, HMSO, 1981). p25f.

18 O'HIGGINS P. *Workers' Rights.* (London, Arrow, 1976). p28.

19 LEWIS D. *opcit.* p20.

20 O'HIGGINS. *opcit.* p31.

21 All qualifying service requirements under the various Acts must be continuous and unbroken periods of employment with the employer.

22 An 'independent' trade union is one granted a certificate of independence by the Certification Office. This confirms it as being independent of employer financial control and influence.

23 The Trade Union Bill received the Royal Assent in the 1984 session of Parliament, after much debate and discussion.

24 These provisions derive from the *Safety Representatives and Safety Committee Regulations* (1978).

25 FARNHAM D *and* PIMLOTT J. *Understanding Industrial Relations.* 2nd ed. (Eastbourne, Cassell, 1983). p206.

26 *ibid.*

27 DANIEL W W *and* STILGOE E. *The Impact of Employment Protection Laws.* (London, Policy Studies Institute, 1978). p74.

28 ADVISORY CONCILIATION AND ARBITRATION SERVICE. *Code of Practice 3. Time off for Trade Union Duties and Activities.* (London, HMSO, 1978). pp3 and 6.

29 DANIEL *and* STILGOE. *opcit.* p78.

30 *ibid.* p79.

11

The legal context: collective aspects

Lewis (1976) claims that the Trade Disputes Act 1906 'was of great importance in the historical development of labour law as it entrenched a legal structure and tradition that would subsequently be described as "abstentionist"'.[1] The essence of legal abstentionism, or 'voluntarism' as it is sometimes called, is a preference for collective bargaining between employers and unions as a method of job regulation, with legal enactment 'accorded a necessary but secondary role'.[2] Two other related principles of abstentionism are, according to Flanders (1975), keeping industrial disputes out of the courts and an insistence by both employers and unions 'on their complete autonomy (the notion of "free" collective bargaining) which leads them to resent any outside interference in their affairs'.[3]

Apart from the two world wars, from 1906 until the enactment of the Industrial Relations Act 1971 (IRA 1971), abstentionist legal policy was central to the voluntarist ideology held by employers, unions and government alike. As collective organizations of employers and employees became firmly established in twentieth century Britain, the nineteenth century concept of individual *laissez faire* in industrial relations gave way to an acceptance of a new principle, collective *laissez faire*. Its heyday was during the economic expansion of the 1950s and 1960s but by the early 1970s this had changed. Hawkins (1971) argues that government and legal intervention in industrial relations, at both the individual and collective levels, was more a symptom of the steady decline of voluntarism rather than its cause. In his view, voluntarism was no longer a feasible principle on which to reconstruct the industrial relations system 'primarily because the parties themselves no longer [appeared] to be believe in it'.[4]

This chapter shows how extensively the voluntarist tradition has been challenged by collective labour law. Collective bargaining between employers and unions may still be the most characteristic method of determining terms and conditions of employment. Yet, as Lewis (1979) writes, 'its content and procedures are more and more influenced by legal norms and machinery which may sometimes operate as an alternative to collective bargaining'.[5]

Trade unions and the law

The Trade Union and Labour Relations Act 1974 (TULRA 1974) defines a trade union as any organization of workers 'whose principal purposes include the regulation of relations between workers . . . and employers or employers' associations'.[6] This legal definition incorporates individual unions, federal unions, the union side of joint negotiating committees and the Trades Union Congress (TUC). A trade union is legally capable of making contracts, suing, being sued and being prosecuted.[7] All property belonging to a trade union must be vested in trustees and any award against a union is enforceable against the property held in trust. Although trade unions are protected in law against the 'restraint of trade' doctrine, their immunity from certain torts has been modified by the Employment Acts 1980, 1982 and 1988 (EA 1980, 1982 and 1988) and the Trade Union Act 1984 (TUA 1984).[8] Trade unions are also required by law to keep accounting records, to have them audited and to make annual returns.

Lewis (1983) writes that 'the rules of a trade union constitute a contract between the union and its members and must be strictly adhered to'.[9] It is the union rule book which largely determines admission to a union, discipline within it and expulsion from it. Providing it observes its own rules, a union is free to determine who is eligible for union membership and for union benefits. However, under the Sex Discrimination Act 1975 (SDA 1975) and the Race Relations Act 1976 (RRA 1976), it is unlawful for a union to discriminate against individuals seeking union membership, or access to any of its benefits or services, on the grounds of sex, race, colour, nationality, ethnic or racial origins. It is also unlawful, under the Trade Union Act 1913, to make contributions to a trade union's political fund a condition of membership to a union. Trade union members wishing to 'contract out' of the 'political levy' must be allowed to do so. Further, the TUA 1984 enables union members to obtain democratic consent for union political funds, permitted under the 1913 Act, every 10 years.

The EA 1980 provides that where a union membership agreement (UMA) or closed shop exists, employees have a statutory right not to be unreasonably excluded from a union party to the agreement. In handling admissions to membership in closed shop situations, unions are expected to follow the guidelines laid down by the code of practice on closed shop agreements and arrangements. This stipulates that trade unions should adopt and apply clear and fair rules covering:

* who is qualified for membership;
* who has power to consider and decide upon applications;
* what reasons will justify rejecting an application;
* the appeals procedure open to a rejected applicant; [and]
* the power to admit applicants where an appeal is upheld.[10]

In determining whom they accept into union membership, unions are expected to have regard to the individual's qualifications and to the type of work being done. They are also expected to take into account whether the number of applicants is likely to be 'so great as to pose a serious threat of undermining negotiated terms and conditions of employment', and also the TUC's guiding principles and procedures governing relations between affiliated unions.[11]

Union procedures on exclusion or expulsion are expected to comply with the rules of 'natural justice'. This requires that individuals are given: fair notice of the complaint against them; a reasonable opportunity of being heard; a fair hearing; an impartial decision; and a right of appeal. TUC affiliates are also expected to inform individuals of the appeals procedure that the TUC provides for those excluded or expelled from union membership. This body is called the TUC's Independent Review Committee (IRC). Its function is to hear appeals from individuals who have been dismissed, or who are under notice of dismissal, either because they have been refused admission or because they have been expelled from an affiliated union, where union membership is a condition of employment. Although the IRC's decisions have no legal force, affiliated unions normally abide by its decisions.

Under the EA 1980, where a UMA exists and an individual considers that s/he has had an application for membership of a specified union unreasonably refused, s/he may make a claim to an industrial tribunal (IT). Conciliation officers of the Advisory Conciliation and Arbitration Service (ACAS) have the power to conciliate between the parties but if the matter is not settled or withdrawn, the IT has to determine the issue according to 'equity and the substantial merits of the case'. Where the complaint is well founded, the IT makes a declaration to that effect. After four weeks but not more than six months, the aggrieved individual can claim an award of compensation from the union. If at the time of application the applicant has been admitted or readmitted to the union, the claim goes to an IT which can award compensation. If the individual has not been admitted or readmitted to membership, the application goes to the Employment Appeal Tribunal (EAT). The EAT can award compensation on the basis of what is 'just and equitable in the circumstances'.

A trade union taking disciplinary action (including expulsion) against members must ensure that its rule book contains the necessary provisions. If the union rules specify the grounds on which disciplinary action can be taken, it is 'unlawful for the union to rely on any other grounds, and where the rules provide for a procedure to be adopted that procedure must be rigidly followed'.[12] The code of practice advises that unions should adopt and apply clear and fair rules in handling membership discipline. These are recommended to cover:

- the offences for which the union is entitled to take disciplinary action and the penalties applicable for each of these offences;
- the procedures for hearing and determining complaints in which offences against the rules are alleged;
- a right to appeal against the imposition of any penalty;
- the procedure for the hearing of appeals against any penalty by a higher authority comprised of persons other than those who imposed the penalty; [and]
- the principle that a recommendation for expulsion should not be made effective so long as a member is genuinely pursuing his appeal.[13]

Unions are also advised that their procedures on discipline and expulsion should comply with the rules of natural justice and that 'unions affiliated to the Trades Union Congress should bear in mind its guidance on these matters'.[14]

Anyone wrongfully expelled from a union may seek their

common law rights. These include a declaration that s/he is still a union member, an injunction preventing the expulsion being put into effect, and damages for breach of contract. The EA 1980 also provides that where a UMA exists, anyone unreasonably expelled from a specific union may make a claim to an IT. The procedure for enforcing these legal provisions is the same as that taken by individuals unreasonably excluded from union membership described above, though the common law remedies may be more appropriate. According to Lewis (1983), by using the common law, an individual may obtain an injunction compelling the union to treat the plaintiff as still being a member. 'Secondly, the damages cannot be reduced on the grounds of contributory fault. Thirdly, a court is unlikely to condone breaches of the union's rules and proceedings'.[15]

One of the duties of the Certification Office (CO) under the TULRA 1974 is to maintain a list of trade unions.[16] Any union may apply to be put on the list and the CO must enter its name on the list if satisfied that the union comes within the statutory definition provided by the 1974 Act. Listing entitles a union to claim tax relief for expenditure on its provident funds. It is also the first stage in applying for a certificate of independence under the Employment Protection Act 1975 (EPA 1975). Any union which is refused listing by the CO may appeal to the EAT. Similarly, the CO is required to remove a union from the list where it appears that the organization is not a trade union, or where 'it no longer exists or if the organisation requests that he should do so'. Any union which is removed from the list has a right of appeal to the EAT. At the end of 1988, the CO listed 354 trade unions of which 83 were affiliated directly or indirectly to the TUC.[17]

An independent trade union is defined in the TULRA 1974 as one which 'is not under the domination or control of an employer or a group of employers or one or more employers' associations' and is not liable to interference by such bodies 'tending towards . . . control'.[18] The procedure for determining the independence of trade unions is laid down in the EPA 1975. This requires the CO to keep a public record of all applications for certification and of all decisions reached. The CO cannot take a decision on any application until at least a month after it has been entered in the record. In making the decision, the CO must take into account any relevant information given by third parties. The CO is also required to give any reasons for refusing to provide a certificate of independence to a union. Any union refused certification has a right of appeal to the EAT. The CO may withdraw a certificate of independence, if it is considered that the trade union concerned is no longer an independent body.

The method used by the CO in determining applications for certificates of independence is to scrutinize the rules and finances of the applicant union, followed where necessary by detailed investigations. The principal criteria used to decide whether a union satisfies the statutory definition of independence include: its history; membership base; organization and structure; finance; employer provided facilities; and collective bargaining record. According to the CO, 'decisions are reached on the basis of the criteria as a whole and not on the grounds of a union's success or failure in one area alone'.[19]

Trade union rights

In addition to the time off provisions for union members outlined in the previous chapter, recognized independent trade unions have a number of statutory rights. Under the EPA 1975, a recognized union is one recognized 'by an employer, or two or more associated employers, to any extent for the purpose of collective bargaining'.[20] The Acts and Regulations conferring statutory rights on recognized independent trade unions are: the Health and Safety at Work etc Act 1974 (HASAWA 1974); the Social Security Pensions Act 1975; the EPA 1975; the Employment Protection (Consolidation) Act 1978 (EPCA 1978); the Employment Act (EA) 1980; and the Transfer of Undertakings (Protection of Employment) Regulations 1981. The main statutory rights provided for unions under these Acts are summarized below.

1 The right to appoint safety representatives and to establish safety committees

Recognized independent trade unions may appoint employee safety representatives who, as far as is reasonably practicable, should have been employed by their employer for at least two years. Alternatively, they should have at least two years' experience in similar employment. The duties of safety representatives include: investigating dangerous occurrences and potential hazards at the workplace; investigating employee complaints about health and safety matters; examining the causes of accidents at work; making representations to the employer on health and safety matters; and carrying out routine inspections at the workplace. Employers have a duty to consult employee safety representatives in developing and checking the effectiveness of measures ensuring health and safety at work. On the written request of at least two safety representatives, employers are required to establish a safety committee after three months. Employers must also give safety representatives reasonable facilities for making inspections, and time off with pay to carry out their duties and attend training courses.

2 The right to consultation on pensions

Employers wishing to contract out of the earnings related state pension scheme are required to consult recognized independent trade unions and their representatives. Unions also have the right to be consulted either where an employer introduces pension benefits without contracting out of the state scheme, or where it wishes to replace a contracted out scheme by a new one or to amend it in certain ways.

3 The right to consultation on proposed redundancies

Employers proposing to make one or more employees redundant are required to consult recognized independent trade unions about the dismissals. Where an employer is proposing that 100 or more employees are to be dismissed at one establishment within 90 days, consultations must begin at least 90 days in advance of the dismissals. Where 10–99 employees are to be dismissed at one establishment within a period of 30 days, consultations must begin at least 30 days in advance of the dismissals. The employer must give similar notice to the Secretary of State through the local office of the Department of Employment. The employer must also disclose in writing to the trade unions: the reasons for the proposed dismissals; the number and descriptions of the employees involved;

the proposed method of selecting for redundancy; and the proposed timing of the dismissals. The employer must consider any representations made by the unions in response to its proposals. If a trade union considers that the employer has failed to comply with these requirements, it may complain to an IT. The IT may require the employer to pay the employees for up to 90 or 30 days. If the employer fails to do this, they may complain to an IT which can order the employer to pay the required amounts to the individual concerned. Employers must then comply with the order.

4 The right to information and consultation in business transfers

Employers transferring businesses or parts of a business are required to provide information to recognized independent trade unions of their intention to do so. Where employers are likely to be taking such measures, they are also required to consult with the relevant trade unions. To enable consultations to take place, employers are expected to provide information relating to: the fact of the transfer; the reasons for it; when it will take place; its implications; and the measures which the employer proposes taking in relation to the employees. Where an employer fails either to inform or consult the unions, they may make a claim to an IT. The procedure is the same as that used for enforcing trade union rights when consulting on proposed redundancies.

5 The right to disclosure of information for collective bargaining purposes

Employers have a general duty to disclose, at all stages of collective bargaining, information requested by representatives of recognized independent trade unions. The information to be disclosed is 'that without which a trade union representative would be impeded to a material extent in bargaining' and that 'which it would be in accordance with good industrial relations practice to disclose'.[21] Confidential information is protected and union negotiators are expected to take into account the size of the organization, the type of negotiations, the level of bargaining and the negotiating subject matter. The sort of information normally provided includes:

pay and benefits; conditions of service; manpower statistics; productivity and efficiency data, and financial and cost data.

Where a trade union considers that an employer has failed to disclose relevant information, it may make a claim to the Central Arbitration Committee (CAC) which may ask ACAS to conciliate. If this fails, the CAC determines the complaint. If the complaint is upheld, the CAC specifies the information which should be disclosed and the period of time in which the employer ought to disclose it. Should the employer continue to refuse to disclose the information, a further complaint may be made to the CAC requesting a claim for improved terms and conditions. If the complaint is upheld, the CAC makes an award against the employer specifying the terms and conditions considered to be appropriate. These become part of the contract of employment between the employer and employees concerned. But an employer cannot be legally forced to disclose information under these provisions.

6 The right to apply for exclusion in respect of dismissal procedure agreements

Where every recognized trade union is independent, is party to a dismissal procedures agreement, and where they apply jointly with the employer to the Secretary of State for Employment for an 'exclusion provision', this may be ordered by the minister. To do so s/he must be satisfied that: the agreement provides procedures to be followed in cases of unfair dismissal; the procedures do not discriminate amongst employees; the remedies provided for unfair dismissal are at least as favourable as those provided by legislation; and the procedures include a right to arbitration by an independent body or person.

7 The right to secret ballots on employers' premises

Recognized independent trade unions have the right to request employers with more than 20 employees to allow their premises to be used for balloting purposes. The ballot must be secret and it must relate to such matters as: decisions on strikes or other industrial action; electing union representatives; amending trade union rules; or approving union amalgamations and mergers. A union can complain to an IT that an employer has unreasonably failed to comply with a request to use its premises for such purposes. If the complaint is well founded, the IT makes a declaration to that effect and can award compensation to the union.

8 The right to public funds for secret postal ballots

The CO has the power to refund certain costs incurred by independent trade unions, not necessarily recognized by an employer, when they hold secret postal ballots for specified purposes. Payments may be made towards postal costs, the stationery and printing costs of voting papers and envelopes, and literature enclosed with the voting papers. Ballots must cover one or more of the following purposes:

(a) obtaining a decision or ascertaining the view of members as to the calling or ending of a strike or other industrial action;
(b) carrying out an election –
  (i) in relation to . . . section 2 of the Trade Union Act 1984 . . . which provides that every member of a trade union's principal executive committee must be elected by secret postal ballot of the members at least once every five years; or
  (ii) provided for by the rules of a trade union for elections to the principal committee of the union exercising executive functions . . .; or
  (iii) provided for by the rules of a trade union for elections to the positions of president, chairman [sic], secretary or treasurer of the union or to any position which the person will hold as an employee of the union.
(c) amending the rules of a trade union;
(d) obtaining a decision in accordance with the Trade Union (Amalgamations etc.) Act 1964 on a resolution to approve an instrument of amalgamation or transfer;
(e) obtaining a decision for the purposes of section 3 of the Trade Union Act 1913 as amended . . .;
(f) obtaining a decision or ascertaining the views of members of a trade union as to the acceptance or rejection of a proposal made by an employer which relates in whole or in part to remuneration, hours of work, level of performance, holidays or pensions.[22]

In the first year of the scheme, 16 applications for refund were received from 14 trade unions in respect of 19 ballots. They were

all non-TUC affiliated bodies. By 1989, however, 51 unions had
made claims for refunds of ballot costs during that year, including
30 from TUC affiliates.[23]

Statutory regulation of terms and conditions

Where there is no collective bargaining, governments have used a
number of devices to influence the settlement of terms and
conditions of employment between employers and employees.
One was the Fair Wages Resolution (FWR) which was first adopted
by the House of Commons in 1891, was strengthened in 1909 and
1946, but ceased to operate after September 1983. The FWR
required governmental contractors not party to a collective agreement to observe those terms and conditions of employment
established for their trade or industry, by either collective bargaining or arbitration. Where no such terms and conditions existed,
employers were expected to observe terms and conditions 'not less
favourable' than those provided by other employers in the trade
or industry concerned. Clauses to this effect were included in all
governmental contracts. The principle was extended to contractors
to the local authorities and nationalized industries and other public
authorities. Any contractor, trade union or individual was able to
complain to the Secretary of State for Employment that the FWR
was not being observed. Where it was not, the Department of
Employment (DE) referred the matter to ACAS for conciliation.
Failing this, the DE asked the CAC to determine the matter.
Where any breach of the Resolution was confirmed by the CAC,
it was the responsibility of the contracting authority to consider
what subsequent action to take.

Wages councils are a second device used by governments to
determine terms and conditions of employment. These exist in
certain industries where there is no voluntary collective bargaining,
normally because of lack of effective trade union organization
amongst employees and where low pay prevails. They have also
been set up in industries where the FWR did not apply covering
approximately two million employees especially in the hotel and
catering, retail, and clothing industries.[24] The main purpose of
wages councils is to fix statutory minimum pay and conditions
which must be observed by employers in the industries concerned.

Legislation covering wages councils is incorporated in the Wages Councils Act 1979 as amended by the Wages Act 1986. This enables the Secretary of State for Employment to establish wages councils either on his or her own initiative or following a recommendation from ACAS. Similarly, a wages council may be abolished or varied by the Secretary of State either on his or her own initiative, or following an application by the appropriate employers' association, trade union(s) or joint body.

Wages councils consist of equal numbers of employer and worker representatives, together with a chairman and two 'independent' members. Meetings are convened when either side requests it. The role of the independent members is to enable the two sides to reach agreement. If this is not possible, they vote with one side thus providing a majority decision. This is passed on to the Secretary of State who arranges for employers covered by the council to be informed of its proposals. After considering any representations, and making any necessary amendments, the wages council issues an order giving legal effect to its proposals. These then become legally binding on all employers within the industry. Notices are circulated to all establishments and must be placed where employees can see them. Employers are required to keep records of the wages paid and the terms and conditions observed. Wages inspectors have powers to visit employers and to act on complaints that employers are not observing required terms and conditions.

Health and safety is a third area where the state intervenes in relations between employers and employees. Prior to HASAW 1974, 'there were nearly 30 Acts of Parliament dealing either specifically or partially with industrial safety; some 500 legal regulations; and seven separate inspectorates'.[25] This legislation, though complex, was not comprehensive and parliamentary concern led to the appointment of a Royal Commission to review the provisions made for the health and safety of people at work and to consider what changes were needed in the law. It also examined the nature and extent of voluntary action by management and employees in securing safe working conditions within their enterprises. Its recommendations provided the basis for the HASAWA 1974.

The 1974 Act places a general duty on all employers to ensure, as far as is reasonably practical, the health, safety and welfare of their employees at work. These duties include:

(a) the provision and maintenance of plant and systems of work that are . . . safe and without risks to health,

(b) arrangements for ensuring safety and absence of risks to health in connection with the use, handling, storage and transport of articles and substances;

(c) the provision of such information, instruction, training and supervision as is necessary to ensure . . . the health and safety at work of . . . employees;

(d) so far as is reasonably practical as regards any place of work under the employer's control, the maintenance of it in a condition that is safe and without risks to health and the provision and maintenance of means of access to and egress from it that are safe and without such risks; [and]

(e) the provision and maintenance of a working environment for . . . employees that is . . . safe, without risks to health, and adequate as regards facilities and arrangements for their welfare at work.[26]

It is also the duty of employees to take reasonable care for their own health and safety at work and for that of other persons affected by their acts. They are expected to cooperate with their employers regarding any duties placed upon them 'to enable that duty or requirement to be performed or complied with'.[27]

The 1974 Act emphasizes the need for joint involvement by employers and employees in the development of health and safety policies and in efforts to reduce risks at work. It extends the protection of the law to large numbers of employees not previously covered by health and safety legislation. The Act also provides enabling powers for regulations to be made for appointing safety representatives by the trade unions and for setting up safety committees. Other provisions of the Act include: increased powers for the enforcing authorities to deal with dangerous situations; and means for progressively replacing existing legislation by regulations, approved codes of practice and other official guidance. The Health and Safety Commission (HSC) is responsible to the Secretary of State for taking appropriate steps to secure the health, safety and welfare of people at work. It is the Health and Safety Executive's task to carry out the HSC's programme of work, to undertake research and to provide information and advisory services to those requiring them.

The closed shop

Collective agreements are defined by the TULRA 1974 as 'any agreement or arrangement made by or on behalf of one or more trade unions and one or more employers or employers' associations'.[28] They cover any of the following matters:

(a) terms and conditions of employment, or the physical conditions in which any workers are required to work;
(b) engagement or non-engagement, or termination or suspension of employment or the duties of employment, of one or more workers;
(c) allocation of work or the duties of employment as between workers or groups of workers;
(d) matters of discipline;
(e) the membership or non-membership of a trade union on the part of a worker;
(f) facilities for officials of trade unions; [and]
(g) machinery for negotiation or consultation, and other procedures, relating to the foregoing matters including [trade union] recognition. . . .[29]

Collective agreements are not normally legally enforceable, being binding in honour only between employers and unions. Indeed, under the TULRA 1974, any collective agreement negotiated before December 1971 and after July 1974 is presumed not to be legally enforceable, unless it is in writing and contains a specific provision stating 'that the parties intend that the agreement shall be a legally enforceable contract'.[30]

One type of collective agreement which became common in the 1970s was the closed shop agreement. McCarthy (1964), in his pioneering study of the closed shop, defines it 'as a situation in which employees come to realize that a particular job is only to be obtained if they become and remain members of one of the specified number of unions'.[31] He distinguishes between pre-entry and post-entry closed shops. Pre-entry closed shops exist where employees have to join the union before being engaged by the employer. The post-entry closed shop is where 'the employer is free to engage a non-unionist, so long as he agrees to join the union immediately or shortly after engagement'.[32] Research by Gennard and his colleagues (1980) indicated that closed shops were then found in a wider range of industries than was the case in the early 1960s. They estimated that by the late 1970s closed shop practices covered at least 5.2 million employees, out of about 22 million in Britain, compared with some 3.75 million when McCarthy published his findings, some 15 years earlier. Of these, about 4.3 million employees or 84 per cent of the total were covered by post-entry shops. During the 1980s, the number of closed shops in existence declined significantly.[33]

The closed shop has always been a contentious issue, with its opponents demanding that it should only be allowed where there are specific legal safeguards protecting individuals against its potential abuses. The first statutory but largely ineffective constraints on the closed shop were contained in the IRA 1971. Although pre-entry closed shops were expressly void in law by the 1971 Act, two forms of closed shop ('agency shop agreements' and 'approved closed agreements') were in fact legally recognized by it.[34] In practice, however, agency shops were not generally accepted by either management or by trade unions as a satisfactory substitute for the post-entry closed shop, largely because they provided classes of non-union employees. Similarly, the approved closed shop was only available to trade unions able to show that it was difficult to achieve a viable union organization, and effective collective bargaining, without compulsory trade unionism. These included British Actors' Equity and the National Union of Seamen. With the IRA 1971 in force, both managements and trade unions used various devices to preserve existing closed shops and to circumvent the letter of the law. According to Weekes (1976) many managements sought and obtained an understanding with the unions 'by which it was agreed that if management protected existing practice, the unions would avoid precipitous action if the Act encouraged some small degree of non-membership'.[35]

Since the repeal of the IRA 1971 by TULRA 1974, closed shops have been described in law as 'union membership agreements' or UMAs. A UMA is any agreement or arrangement that:

(a) is made by or on behalf of, or otherwise exists between, one or more independent trade unions and one or more employers or employers' associations; and

(b) relates to employees of an identifiable class; and

(c) has the effect in practice of requiring the employees for the time being of the class to which it relates (whether or not there is a condition to that effect in their contract of employment) to be or become a member of the union or one of the unions which is or are parties to the agreement or arrangement or of another specified independent trade union.[36]

The legal definition of UMAs covers both written closed shop agreements and any unwritten arrangements between employers and unions. Pre-entry closed shops are predominantly informal and 'seldom become the subject of formal, written agreements' but this is not the case with post-entry closed shops. In the past, the typical closed shop arrangement, if written down, was contained in a single sentence. As Gennard and his collaborators (1979) report however: 'a typical UMA may be three or four pages in length, with attached schedules, notes for guidance, and recorded minutes of the negotiations clarifying the "spirit" in which the agreement is to operate'.[37]

The code of practice on closed shop agreements and arrangements recommends that any closed shop agreement 'should protect basic individual rights; should enjoy the overwhelming support of those affected; and should be flexibly and tolerantly applied'.[38] When negotiating UMAs with trade unions, the code suggests, employers should pay special attention to the interests of particular groups of staff, such as professional employees and members of professional associations, who are subject to their own codes of conduct. Before seeking a closed shop, unions are normally expected to have recruited a fairly high proportion of the employees concerned. The code also recommends that unions should not start negotiating UMAs which exclude other unions with membership interests in their area, until the matter has been resolved with the unions concerned.

Where a UMA is being negotiated, the code recommends that it should be clearly drafted and should cover a number of points. First, it should indicate clearly the class of employees to be covered. Secondly, it should make clear that existing employees who are not union members when the UMA comes into effect, and those objecting to union membership on personal grounds, will not be forced to become members. Thirdly, it should specify a reasonable period within which employees can join the union. Fourthly, where an individual is excluded or expelled by a union, it should be made clear that no action will be taken against that person until any appeal or complaint has been decided. Fifthly, it should provide that an employee will not be dismissed or expelled from a union for refusing to take part in industrial action. Sixthly, it should set out how complaints or disputes arising from the UMA are to be resolved. Lastly, the UMA should provide for periodic reviews and a procedure for its termination.[39]

The EA 1982 laid down minimum levels of support for UMAs, if employers were to be protected against claims for unfair dismissal or complaints of action short of dismissal by their employees.[40] After 1 November 1984, a UMA was only considered to be 'approved' where, in the previous five years, it was supported in a secret ballot either by not less than 80 per cent of those affected by the agreement, or by 85 per cent of those eligible to vote in the ballot. Where a UMA came into effect after 14 August 1980, it was necessary to show that it was supported, at least once in a secret ballot, by not less than 80 per cent of those affected by it. In conducting such ballots, employers and unions were advised by the DE to seek agreement on a number of points. These included: working out the terms of the proposed agreement; defining the electorate to be balloted; informing the electorate of the intention to hold a ballot; keeping the ballot as clear and simple as possible; conducting the ballot in such a way that all those eligible to vote can do so; and holding the ballot in a responsible and professional manner. It also recommended that 'all closed shop agreements, whether new or existing, or whether covering a firm or industry, should be subject to periodic review'.[41]

Two final points need to be made. First, the EA 1982 rendered void in law any term or condition in a contract for the supply of goods or services requiring the work to be done only by trade union members or by non-union employees. Secondly, any term and condition in a contract for the supply of goods or services requiring an employer to recognize a trade union, or to consult with its officials, was also void in law. Employers or trade unions infringing these legal provisions could be sued in tort by an aggrieved party.

As indicated above, earlier legal regulations embodied in the EAs 1980 and 1982 promoted secret ballots for closed shops and provided specific protections for non-union members in closed shop situations. The EA 1988 extends those provisions. It makes it unlawful for unions to organize or threaten industrial action to establish or maintain any closed shop practice. Although certain employees might previously be dismissed fairly for not belonging to a union in an approved closed shop, dismissal for any employees for not belonging to a union is now legally unfair. This is irrespective of whether or not they work in an approved closed shop. The effect of these legal provisions is to remove, in effect, all statutory support for closed shops.

In a green paper published in 1989, the government proposed further legislation proscribing the closed shop. This would provide a right of complaint to an industrial tribunal for any individuals whom an employer refuses to engage on the ground of non-membership of a trade union, or of any particular trade union, or on the ground of refusal to agree that they will become union members after their employment has started.

Trade disputes and the law

Industrial action is normally associated with the use of the strike weapon against employers by trade unions and their members. Yet 'there is a wide range of industrial sanctions, which management, unions and employees can use to further their immediate industrial relations objectives'.[42] Managerial sanctions against their employees can include: close supervision; tight discipline; demotion; speeding up work processes; withdrawing overtime; lay offs; suspension; tactically precipitating strikes; locking out; closing down enterprises, and withdrawing plant and machinery at the workplace. Employee and work group sanctions against employers, including trade union action, involve: working without enthusiasm; non-cooperation with management; going slow; working to rule; banning overtime; striking; sit ins; and work ins.

Where there is a dispute between employers and employees, ACAS can provide voluntary conciliation. ACAS was set up under the EPA 1975 and one of its duties is to offer collective conciliation either at the request of one or more of the parties to a dispute or on its own initiative. In exercising this function, ACAS must 'have regard to the desirability of encouraging the parties . . . to use any appropriate procedures for negotiation or the settlement of disputes'.[43] Another function of ACAS is to provide mediation either by an independent person appointed by ACAS or by an *ad hoc* body appointed to deal with the dispute. This normally consists of a chairman, an employer representative and a union representative, whose findings can provide a basis for settlement between the parties. Mediators do not settle disputes, they provide recommendations which the parties have to determine and implement themselves.

If a dispute cannot be resolved by either conciliation or mediation, ACAS may, at the request of one or more of the parties, but with the consent of them all, refer it for settlement to voluntary arbitration. ACAS does not provide arbitration itself. It refers disputes to independent arbitrators, boards of arbitration or the CAC. Although there is no legal obligation to accept an arbitrator's award, in practice arbitrators' decisions are normally ratified. ACAS also has the power to set up inquiries into trade disputes, where an intractable dispute has failed to be resolved. Further, under the Industrial Courts Act 1919, the Secretary of State for Employment may establish a Court of Inquiry, chaired by an eminent judge and including an employer and union representative, to investigate a dispute with a view to establishing the facts and making recommendations. Now that ACAS may establish its own inquiries, the power to set up Courts of Inquiry is seldom used.

Where employees take industrial action against an employer, it almost certainly involves committing civil wrongs not only against the employer but also against its suppliers and customers. As Lewis (1983) points out, going on strike 'breaches a fundamental term of the contract [of employment]: the essence of the employment relationship is that the employee [must be] ready and willing to work in exchange for remuneration'.[44] There is no legal 'right to strike' in Britain. All the law confers is a freedom to strike, to those participating in or organizing industrial action, by providing certain legal immunities which protect employees, union officials and trade unions from being taken to court for committing civil wrongs. These immunities only apply, however, when the strike or industrial action is 'in contemplation or furtherance of a trade dispute' – the so called 'golden formula'.

Under TULRA 1974, a trade dispute was fairly widely defined. To be lawful, action 'in contemplation or furtherance of a trade dispute' merely had to be 'connected with' one or more of the following: terms and conditions of employment; physical conditions of work; engagement or non-engagement; sacking; suspension; work duties; distribution of work; discipline; union membership;

negotiating and consultative machinery; and procedural rights. The EA 1982, however, provides that a trade dispute is only lawful, and the 'golden formula' only applies, where the dispute is 'wholly or mainly' related to the matters outlined above, and where the workers involved are in dispute with their own employer. This means that certain types of trade dispute are no longer lawful or protected by legal immunities. These include: first, disputes that are simply 'connected with' pay, terms and conditions of employment and so on; secondly, disputes between 'workers and workers' where no employer is involved; thirdly, 'secondary' and 'sympathy' disputes between a trade union and an employer whose own employees are not in dispute; fourthly, political strikes; and fifthly, disputes in connection with something occurring overseas, unless the terms and conditions of those taking industrial action in Britain are likely to be affected by the outcome of the matter.[45]

Just as there is no legal right to strike in Britain, there is no legal 'right to picket'. Nevertheless, peaceful picketing has long been recognized as being lawful. The statutory protection given to peaceful picketing, 'in contemplation or furtherance of a trade dispute', is now embodied in the EA 1980. This provides the basic rules for lawful picketing. These are:

(i) it may only be undertaken in contemplation or furtherance of a trade dispute;

(ii) it may only be carried out by a person *attending at or near his own place of work*; a trade union official in addition to attending at or near his own place of work may also attend at or near the place of work of a member of his trade union whom he is accompanying on the picket line and whom he represents; [and]

(iii) its only purpose must be peacefully obtaining or communicating information or peacefully persuading a person to work or not to work.[46]

Picketing which is accompanied by violent, threatening or obstructive behaviour is always criminal and is subject to the criminal law. Additionally, pickets committing such criminal offences may forfeit their immunities under the civil law and may be sued for inducing or threatening to induce a breach of contract.

Pickets have no legal right to stop motor vehicles. The law only allows pickets to ask a driver to stop, either verbally or by signalling at their place of work. If a driver decides to drive on, pickets may not physically obstruct the vehicle. Further, no one is required to stop when asked to do so by a picket. Everyone has the legal right, if s/he wishes to do so, to cross a picket line and to go into their place of work. Individuals also have the right to deliver goods to their customers, or to collect them from their suppliers. If pickets use means other than 'peacefully persuading' others, they may be committing a criminal offence. Since a main cause of violence and disorder on picket lines is large numbers of people, the code of practice on picketing strongly recommends that pickets and their organizers should generally ensure that 'the number of pickets does not exceed six at any entrance to a workplace; frequently a smaller number will be appropriate'.[47]

Employers suffering losses because of unlawful industrial action can seek an injunction to prevent further losses being incurred against either a union or an individual. Further, under the EA 1982, trade unions are now treated in law as 'ordinary persons'. This means that anyone suffering losses because of unlawful industrial action, including secondary action, secondary picketing and action which is deemed not to be 'in contemplation or furtherance of a trade dispute', may sue that union in its own name and claim damages from its funds. Unions can only be held liable for tortious acts of their officials or members, however, where that act is authorized or endorsed by 'a responsible person'. Such 'persons' include: a union's principal executive committee; its president or general secretary; and any other person with the authority to call industrial action under union rules. Unions can avoid liability for unlawful acts where those acts are genuinely repudiated by a union's executive, president or general secretary. Any damages for which unions can be sued are on a sliding scale, according to union size. Union political and provident funds are expressly protected from civil liability.[48]

Prior to the EA 1982, it was unfair to dismiss an employee for taking part in a strike or other industrial action, if that person was unfairly selected for dismissal. Thus to dismiss all strikers was fair, to re-engage all of them posed no problems, but to select discriminately at re-engagement counted as unfair dismissal against those not re-engaged. Under the EA 1982, however, employees who are dismissed while participating in a strike or other industrial action would not normally be able to make a successful claim for unfair dismissal. This is provided: first, that the employer has dismissed all those taking part in the action at the complainant's date of dismissal; and, secondly, that it has not offered re-engagement to any of them within three months of their date of dismissal, without making a similar offer to the complainant.[49]

The implications for personnel management

Collective labour law now impinges on a number of personnel management and industrial relations policy issues in the workplace. It is more necessary than ever, for example, that employers determine effective policies on trade union recognition, collective bargaining and joint consultation. In their dealings with recognized independent trade unions, employers have to take into account their statutory obligations. This requires them, amongst other things, to consult union representatives on a variety of employment matters including: occupational pensions: business transfers; union ballots on the employer's premises; health and safety at work; redundancies; and disclosure of information for collective bargaining purposes.

In fulfilling their duty to disclose information requested by trade union representatives, employers are expected to have regard to the code of practice issued by ACAS. This states that the information provided has to be in the employer's possession and must relate to the employer's undertaking. But some limitations are placed on disclosure. An employer is not required to disclose information: given in confidence; relating to an individual; or which would cause substantial injury to the undertaking. Unions can request information to be given in writing, whilst employers can ask union representatives to make their request in writing or to confirm it in writing. Employers need to bear in mind that if they fail to disclose requested information, a union may make a claim to the CAC.[50]

The employer's responsibilities for disclosure are clearly set out in the code of practice. First, 'employers should aim to be as open as possible in meeting trade union requests for information'. Secondly, if a request for information is refused, the employer should explain the reasons for the refusal and the reasons should 'be capable of being substantiated should the matter be taken to the CAC'. Thirdly, information agreed as relevant to collective bargaining should be provided as soon as possible after the request has been made. Fourthly, 'employers should present information in a form and style which recipients can reasonably be expected to understand'. The code also recommends that employers and trade unions should decide jointly how disclosure can be implemented most effectively. They should consider what information is required and its most relevant form. 'In particular, the parties should endeavour to reach an understanding on what information could most appropriately be provided on a regular basis'.[51]

In order to carry out their industrial relations responsibilities effectively, workplace representatives of recognized independent unions require not only bargaining information and time off facilities which, as outlined in Chapter 10, they are entitled to by law. They also need adequate facilities if they are to play their full part in collective bargaining and the improvement of industrial relations. These include: lists of new entrants to employment; facilities to explain to new employees the advantages of trade union membership; facilities to collect union subscriptions or the deduction of contributions at source; a room and means of storing correspondence and papers; ready access to telephones and secretarial assistance; and the provision of notice boards and internal posting systems. Representatives also require suitable accommodation for consulting and reporting to members and for holding meetings with other union officials.

Employers are under no legal obligation to negotiate UMAs. It is generally accepted that a union has to show a very high level of membership before an employer needs to consider negotiating a closed shop. The code of practice recommends that employers' associations may be able to advise their members on the implications of closed shop agreements and suggests that 'they should be consulted by their members at an early stage'. It is also advisable for employers to know the legal provisions relating to the closed shop, especially the provisions on ballots. The code advises that where pre-entry closed shops exist 'the need for their continuation should be carefully reviewed'. Above all, employers need to consider carefully 'the effects of a closed shop on [their] future employment policy and on industrial relations'.[52]

In dealing with trade union power, employers normally prefer a strategy of avoiding and managing conflict rather than outright confrontation and all-out power struggles. Although current labour law has narrowed the range of trade union immunities, there is little evidence to demonstrate that employers generally are prepared to settle their disputes with trade unions and their members in the courts. Collective bargaining, joint consultation and employee communication are the preferred methods of conflict resolution and conflict management or, where these have broken down, third party conciliation, mediation or arbitration is used. In these areas of employee relations at least, the tradition of voluntarism remains firmly entrenched and, with few exceptions,[53] is usually accepted by employers and unions alike.

Reference and footnotes

1 LEWIS R. 'The historical development of labour law'. *British Journal of Industrial Relations*. Vol. XIV, No. 1, 1976. p4.
2 *ibid*. p8.
3 FLANDERS A. *Management and Unions*. (London, Faber, 1975). p289.
4 HAWKINS K. 'Voluntarism'. *Industrial Relations Journal*. Vol. I, No. 2, 1971. p40.
5 LEWIS R. 'Kahn-Freund and labour law: an outline critique'. *Industrial Law Journal*. Vol. 8, No. 4, 1979. p220.
6 Section 29(1) TULRA 1974.
7 Section 2(1) TULRA 1974.
8 *See* pp286–90 below.
9 LEWIS D. *Essentials of Employment Law*. (London, IPM, 1983). p202.
10 DEPARTMENT OF EMPLOYMENT. *Code of Practice. Closed Shop Agreements and Arrangements*. (London, HMSO, 1983a). p19.
11 *ibid*.
12 LEWIS D. *opcit*. p203.
13 DEPARTMENT OF EMPLOYMENT (1983a), *opcit*. p20.
14 *ibid*.
15 LEWIS D. *opcit*. p203.
16 The CO also maintains a list of employers' associations and has other duties relating to these bodies. Its main significance, however, concerns trade unions and their responsibilities under the law.
17 CERTIFICATION OFFICE FOR TRADE UNIONS AND EMPLOYERS' ASSOCIATIONS. *Annual Report of the Certification Officer 1988*. (London, HMSO, 1989). p4f.
18 Section 30(1) TULRA 1974.

19   CERTIFICATION OFFICE. *Annual Report of the Certification Officer 1985*. (London, HMSO, 1986). p5f.
20   Section 11(2) EPA 1975.
21   ADVISORY CONCILIATION AND ARBITRATION SERVICE. *Code of Practice 2. Disclosure of Information for Collective Bargaining Purposes.* (London, HMSO, 1977b). p2.
22   CERTIFICATION OFFICE. *Annual Report of the Certification Office 1989.* (London, HMSO, 1990). p21f.
23   *ibid.* p56f.
24   See FARNHAM D *and* PIMLOTT J. *Understanding Industrial Relations* 4th ed. (London, Cassell, 1990).
25   *ibid.* p305.
26   Section 2(2) HASAWA 1974.
27   Section 7 *ibid.*
28   Section 30(1) TULRA 1974.
29   Section 29(1) *ibid.*
30   Section 18(1) TULRA 1974.
31   McCARTHY W E J. *The Closed Shop in Britain.* (Oxford, Blackwell, 1964). p3.
32   *ibid.* p16.
33   GENNARD J *and others*, 'The extent of closed shop arrangements in British industry'. *Employment Gazette.* Vol. 88, No. 1, January 1980. p21. Since this research was completed, however, the number of employees covered by closed shop agreements has declined significantly. See DUNN S. *and* GENNARD J. *The Closed Shop in British Industry.* (London, Macmillan, 1984).
34   In an 'agency shop', non-union members in a bargaining unit were required to pay an appropriate contribution to the union in lieu of union membership, or an equivalent contribution to a charity, as a condition of employment. An 'approved closed shop' required workers to be members of trade unions registered under the 1971 Act as a condition of employment, where the Commission on Industrial Relations had authorized such an arrangement.
35   WEEKES B. 'Law and practice of the closed shop'. *Industrial Law Journal.* Vol. 5, No. 4, 1976. p216.
36   Quoted in DE (1980a). *opcit.* p18.
37   GENNARD J *and others,* 'The content of closed shop agreements'. *Department of Employment Gazette.* Vol. 87, No. 11, November 1979. pp1088 and 1092.
38   DE (1983a) *opcit.* p3.
39   *ibid.* p13f.
40   See also chapter 10.
41   *ibid.* pp9 and 11.
42   FARNHAM *and* PIMLOTT. *opcit.* p343.
43   Section 2(3) EPA 1975.
44   LEWIS D. *opcit.* p30.
45   Section 18 EA 1982.

46 DEPARTMENT OF EMPLOYMENT, *Code of Practice. Picketing.* (London, HMSO, 1980b). p3.
47 *ibid*. p11.
48 Section 15 EA 1982.
49 Section 9 *ibid*.
50 ACAS (1977b). *opcit.* p1f.
51 *ibid*. p5.
52 DE (1983a). *opcit.* pp11f.
53 A major exception to this general statement was the bitter conflict which took place between the National Graphical Association (NGA) and the Stockport Messenger Group towards the end of 1983. The dispute arose from the dismissal of union members by the employer and claims that the employer had reneged on a closed shop agreement. After mass picketing and violence on the picket line, the employer took the union to court. This led subsequently to contempt of court proceedings against the union and large fines being paid by the NGA.

Part IV
Conclusion

Personnel managers or human resources managers? Responses and change in the personnel function

There is considerable debate about the changing nature of British personnel management in the 1980s. In the mid 1980s, when the first edition of this book was published, concern was expressed that personnel management was undergoing a crisis – 'a crisis of confidence about its role and a crisis in terms of the impact of the recession on the employment prospects of personnel managers.'[1] Although this crisis appears to have been exaggerated, one commentator concluded that the personnel function was shifting its focus. This was away from 'finding, training and developing human beings' to the reverse – 'assessing, excluding, exiting and retiring them.'[2] More recently, the debate itself has shifted. One of the main questions now being asked is whether a new role is emerging within the occupation – the 'human resources manager' – whose frame of reference and activities differ significantly from those of traditional personnel managers. As Storey (1989) claims 'this notion of "human resource management" has become very topical.'[3] This chapter reviews some of the evidence in this debate and examines current responses and change as we move into the 1990s.

Current conceptions of the personnel function

In their study of the changing nature of British personnel management in the 1980s, Torrington and Mackay (1986) note that there is an underlying trend for the term 'personnel management' to be substituted by that of 'human resources management' (HRM) amongst personnel specialists. They see 'personnel management' as being directed mainly at the organization's employees and not being totally identified with managerial interests. Indeed, 'there is always some degree of being "in between" the management and the employees, mediating the needs of each to the other.'[4] A similar point is made by Watson (1985) who argues that personnel managers frequently have to appear to be facing two ways at the same time. To maintain credibility with employees, they have to show concern for employee welfare. 'But to justify their existence with management they must show to their managers a concern for the *efficiency* of labour utilisation,' as well as 'ensuring that staff interests are always subservient to those of organizational *effectiveness*, and for *controlling* the workforce.'[5]

HRM, by contrast, is directed mainly towards managerial needs for people resources in organizations, with greater emphasis being placed on 'planning, monitoring and control, rather than on problem solving and mediation.' Whilst traditional personnel management is underpinned by the ideas that employees need looking after, and are only effective when their needs are being met, HRM reflects a different set of beliefs. These are 'that getting the deployment of correct numbers and skills at the right price is more important than a patronizing involvement with people's personal affairs.' Although some of Torrington and Mackay's respondents were impressed by a 'human resources' emphasis in personnel, others only 'reluctantly acknowledged its increasing importance.' Its greatest benefit appears to be the wider recognition given to the specialist personnel function by senior line management where an HRM approach is adopted.[6]

Tyson (1987) identifies four personnel 'traditions' and three 'models'. Taken together, they provide a useful framework for examining the modern personnel function. According to Tyson, the 'welfare tradition' originated in the industrial betterment movement of the late nineteenth century, whilst the 'employment management' tradition emerged out of the bureaucratization of work stimulated by two world wars. The more recent 'industrial relations' and 'professional' traditions respectively arose out of the tight labour market conditions of the post-war years and the occupational association activities of the Institute of Personnel Management (IPM). The latter encourages the view that 'personnel specialists possess a separate occupational identity, and should be accorded a professional status based on a knowledge of the social sciences, of personnel techniques and of employment law.'[7]

Tyson's three models of personnel are the 'clerk of works', the 'contracts manager' and the 'architect', also referred to as the 'administrative support', 'systems reactive' and 'business manager' models.[8] Where the specialist personnel function operates on 'the clerk of works' lines, for instance, it is an administrative support activity with no business planning involvement. Personnel authority is vested in line managers as the principal activities of personnel staff are recruitment, record keeping and welfare. The 'contracts manager' approach to personnel is a 'system model' which is part of a comprehensive policy framework acting on behalf of line managers. Personnel specialists are especially valued for their capacity to make quick decisions and informal agreements with the trade unions so that organizational harmony can be maintained. The 'architect' model of personnel aims to create and build the organization as a whole. It is a creative view of personnel and aims at contributing to corporate success 'through explicit policies which seek to give effect to the corporate plan, with an integrated system of controls between personnel and line managers.' A key feature of the architect model is that 'personnel executives take the management of change, and the use of social science techniques to be the cornerstone of their approach.'[9]

For Tyson and Fell (1986), an HRM philosophy emerges wherever people are perceived, not as a cost of doing business, but as 'the only resource capable of turning inanimate factors of production into wealth. People provide the source of creative energy in any direction the organization dictates and fosters.' For them, HRM has a base in the behavioural sciences, is concerned with the induction and development of individual employees and enhances the performance and productivity of the organization. Although this approach does not differ greatly from that of the two more traditional models of the personnel function, the architect model is a redefined and expanded one. It changes personnel from the role of a 'control-oriented supplier of labour to an overall human resource planning, development and utilization agency.' It integrates and coordinates people planning with strategy formulation and takes a realistic view of human resources activities in an organizational setting. Moreover, within the architect model, HRM 'is directed at achieving the symbiosis which is seen to exist between the organization and its goals and an effective use of the human resources the organization needs to achieve those goals.'[10]

Fowler (1987) identifies two main themes in HRM thinking. Those are, first, 'that every aspect of employee management must be wholly integrated with business management', thus reinforcing corporate culture. The second is 'a dominant emphasis on the common interests of employers and employed in the success of the business.' This, it is believed, will release 'a massive potential of initiative and commitment within the workforce.' Yet Fowler is sceptical about the concept of HRM. He argues that what is new about HRM is not what it is, but who is saying it. 'In a nutshell, HRM represents the discovery of personnel management by chief executives.' He suggests that the success of some of the companies held up as models of HRM practices and corporate excellence owes as much 'to the covert skills of their corporate lawyers and international marketeers as to the undoubted high morale of their factory and office staff.'[11]

Fowler is also cautious about two other aspects of HRM. One is whether an HRM culture is appropriate for all organizations, given that different business environments have their own organizational and cultural characteristics. His second reservation is the North American-centredness of much HRM literature and practices. 'At the heart of the concept is the complete identification of employees with the aims and values of the business – employee involvement, but on the company's terms.' He questions whether it is really possible to claim mutuality at work between managers and managed, when ultimately it is the employer which can decide unilaterally whether to close the company down or sell it to outsiders. In his view, the HRM literature largely ignores power in employee relations and the role of trade unions in protecting employee interests at work. Whilst accepting the need for compatibility between personnel practices and corporate culture, for effective leadership in personnel and for reorganizing individual potential at work, Fowler believes that some HRM enthusiasts may be oversimplifying the issues. 'Are they genuinely concerned with creating a new, equal partnership between employer and employed, or are they really offering a covert form of employee manipulation, dressed up as mutuality?'[12]

Michael Armstrong (1987) argues that Fowler's reservations are only valid 'if HRM is regarded as something completely different from personnel management, which of course it is not.' He believes that they share many of the same roots. What is needed is 'a revised concept of HRM which links its worthwhile elements with the best personnel management practices.' He does not see HRM as a threat to personnel management. In tracing the behavioural roots of HRM, Armstrong posits that 'it is possible to develop an HRM concept which is not as crude as it has sometimes been portrayed.' For him, HRM is based on four fundamental principles. First, human resources are an organization's most important assets. Second, personnel policies should make a major contribution to achieving corporate goals and strategic plans. Third, corporate culture exerts a major influence on achieving 'excellence' and must therefore be managed. Fourth, whilst integration of corporate resources is an important aim of HRM, it must also be recognized *'that all organisations are pluralist societies in which people have differing interests and concerns which they may well feel need to be defended collectively.'*[13]

Ambiguities in the personnel function

One set of reasons given to explain the changing nature of the personnel function, and its alleged shift from a personnel management emphasis, is an exogenous one. This type of explanation proposes that it is largely external factors such as changes in the business environment, governmental policy, the job structure, the technological environment and so on which have impacted on the personnel function. It is these, it is suggested, which have induced shifts within personnel towards the architect mode of delivery. These may well be necessary conditions for change in personnel practices but it is doubtful whether they are sufficient in themselves. More realistically, it might well be claimed that there are a series of endogenous factors inherent within the function which, in concert with exogenous factors, have induced changes of emphasis within some personnel management activities during the 1980s and into the 1990s.

At the core of these endogenous influences is the ambiguous nature of personnel management. Some of personnel's ambiguities are epitomized in the IPM's classic definition of the function at the time of its jubilee in 1963. For the IPM, personnel 'is a responsibility of all those who manage people, as well as being a description of the work of those who are employed as specialists.

It is that part of management concerned with people at work and with their relationships within the enterprise.' The claimed aims of the personnel function are: to achieve efficiency and justice; to develop into effective organizations those individuals making up enterprises; to provide fair terms and conditions of employment; and to provide satisfying work for those employed.[14] Superficially, it is a highly prescriptive and normative definition of the function, unitary rather than pluralist in tone, with both business-centred and humanistic orientations. It also has ethical undertones, associated with the concepts of 'justice' and 'fairness', implying certain social responsibilities by employers for employees.

One specific ambiguity within the function which, as we noted in Chapter 4, Legge (1978) amongst others has observed, is that 'personnel management' refers not only to personnel activity generally but also 'to that activity's *institutionalized* or *departmental presence* within the organization, in this case the *personnel department.*' In practice, of course, much operational personnel activity is carried out by line managers who have to work through people, as 'managers of people', in order to achieve their objectives. There are also the specialist activities of the personnel department. These are associated traditionally with managing the 'people system' within modern complex organizations. As specialist managers of employment relationships, personnel staff undertake a series of functional tasks. Since in most organizations, the personnel function comprises both 'managers of people' and specialist managers of the 'people system', operationally different aspects of the function remain ambiguous. This is 'due to the interactive and overlapping nature of different activities, carried out in different parts of the organization, but all nominally under the collective title of personnel management.'[15]

A second ambiguity in the personnel function is the problem of establishing whether corporate success, or enterprise efficiency, is the direct result of effective personnel management policies and practices or of other factors. Personnel outputs are often unquantifiable and they are difficult to relate to business outputs. Indeed, there are potential problems in establishing direct links between substantive personnel activities and contributive employee behaviour. It is this difficulty of establishing direct causal relationships between personnel activities and desired outcomes which 'contributes to the ambiguity surrounding personnel management.'[16]

Whilst some managements are committed to effective personnel practices, others are ambivalent about the personnel function or, more specifically, about the personnel department. Where personnel management is organizationally effective, the personnel department might not get the credit for it; where personnel activities are perceived as inadequate, it invariably attracts criticisms. As a result, the personnel contribution to line management effectiveness can be overlooked and marginalized in policy determination.

A third ambiguity, noted by Legge, derives from definitions of personnel management, such as that provided by the IPM. Since the aims of the personnel function are stated in terms of both organizational efficiency and individual development and self-fulfilment, it cannot be 'automatically assumed that these two objectives are mutually compatible in organizations which, even if not profit-maximizing, are certainly cost-conscious.'[17] This reflects the fact, articulated by Thomason (1975), that mainstream personnel management has developed out of two diverse origins: 'the one paternalistically orientated towards the welfare of the employees and the other rationally derived from corporate needs to control.' In these origins, 'we have a foundation for understanding the ambivalence so often associated with the function.' In a few instances, the 'personnel' or welfare aspect of the role is emphasized. In most others, the 'management' or control aspect predominates. In the first case, personnel's accountability is to people; in the other it is more clearly managerial.[18]

This brings us to a fourth ambiguity in the personnel function. It derives from the observation that some see it as an 'organizationally dependent' role, whilst for others it is an 'independent professional' one. Where personnel is seen as being organizationally dependent, 'the emphasis will be upon personnel management as a process of helping to design and implement control procedures.' Where, on the other hand, personnel is seen as an independent professional role, 'the emphasis will fall more firmly upon the man-in-the-middle approach, with justice and fairness as animating criteria and reconciliation of conflict over ends and means being a more central concern.'[19] In the former instance, an executive function for personnel managers is implied, although this 'raises problems about role allocation between personnel and line management.' In the latter instance, 'the range of activities may be considerable, but they could become predominantly advisory rather than executive.'[20]

Critiques of personnel management

Given the personnel function's ambiguities, its conflicting ideological origins and its diffusion within the organizational setting amongst line managers and personnel specialists, it is not surprising that it is often criticized as being functionally inadequate. It was not until the 1930s, for example, that the creation of 'employment and welfare' departments began to interest a growing number of managements. But even then progress was relatively slow because the majority of employers were 'very reluctant to regard the labour problems of management as worthy of special study and attention.' Moxon (1951) puts this down to lack of legal regulation of the labour market, large scale unemployment and weakened trade unions.[21] Whilst the specialist personnel role has expanded and evolved since then, albeit not uniformly, it continues to have its critics.

Although the numbers of employed personnel specialists grew steadily throughout the 1940s and 1950s, in response to favourable economic and political circumstances, it was the 1960s and 1970s which saw the most rapid growth in their numbers, status and influence. Guest (1982) accounts for this by citing three factors: the growing complexity of organizational life; the growing body of knowledge and skills associated with personnel work; and the way the problems of industry were defined at both national and organizational levels.[22] Nevertheless, even in personnel's 'good years', the Donovan Commission questioned, given that companies had their own personnel specialists, why it was that they had not introduced effective personnel policies to control negotiation and pay structures within their firms? 'Many firms have no such policy and perhaps no conception of it.'[23] Several years later, after many firms had carried out Donovanite collective bargaining reforms, Batstone (1980) queried what, if anything, had personnel managers done for industrial relations? He concluded that if personnel managers fostered shop steward organizations and centralized personnel decisions, then they might well stimulate industrial action, not remove it.[24]

One of the most probing analyses of personnel management is provided by Legge (1978). In her research, two major themes emerge from the comments of British managers on the personnel function as they perceive it. One is line management's 'confused, hazy, and/or stereotyped perception' of the nature and scope of the personnel department. The other is middle and junior line management's view that 'personnel departments are "out of touch" with the kind of problems and constraints' facing them. Because personnel has difficulty in demonstrating success in either functional or organizational terms, Legge concludes that 'the authority of a personnel department and the specialists within it is constantly undermined.' Accordingly, she recommends a contingent rather than a prescriptive approach to the substantive issues of personnel management and the operating styles of personnel departments.[25]

Some of the most trenchant critiques of personnel management have been made during the 1980s. Manning (1983) argues, from a managerial viewpoint, that in many companies in the early 1980s personnel departments faced growing disenchantment and a steady decline in influence. 'Personnel as a function in management began the 1970s with great promise; at the beginning of the 1980s that promise remains unfulfilled.' He believes that personnel departments have failed to make the significant inroads into corporate affairs expected of them. 'Of all the major areas of management, personnel has the weakest conceptual base and the poorest technology.' In order to rectify the widespread apathy of line managers towards the personnel department, and to allay the fears of many managers that personnel seems too far removed from their operational problems, Manning recommends four key ways of developing the personnel role. But this requires the 'creative thinking that has been demonstrated so successfully in disciplines like marketing and finance.' The first is to challenge the principles underlying current thinking in the function. The second is to establish personnel in the strategic management of companies. The third is to create a body of coherent and credible technology to support that strategic role. 'And the final item is the effective use of computers to record and measure organizational performance.'[26]

Thurley's (1981) more academic analysis asks whether personnel management in the 1980s was sick and whether it might require 'urgent treatment'. He suggests that any claimed sickness rested on three allegations. First, it is asserted that personnel specialists are caught in a mismatch between abstract models of HRM and real-life activities which go unrecognized by other managers. Second, it is argued that personnel specialists cope by using their professionalism instrumentally but really conform with organizational norms. Third, personnel finds it difficult to develop overall strategies to break out of this situation, 'due to the constraints under which organizations have to work.' His conclusion is that personnel management is 'not particularly sick but is certainly suffering from stunted growth.' The reasons are, first, that personnel management has failed to generate an overall set of social, political and economic objectives acceptable to major decision makers. Second, there has been a failure to provide 'the R and D necessary to make social science research operationally useful.' Third, personnel managers have neglected to organize the personnel function effectively 'to facilitate innovation and higher performance' within enterprises.[27]

Looking back to the 1970s from a practitioner's perspective, Cowan (1980) concludes that the 1970s were wasted years for the personnel management profession. 'In fact we can look back on a decade that is the modern wasteland of personnel management.' Cowan identifies what did not happen: industrial democracy came and went; the social impact of Europe never materialized; new forms of work organization and work structuring proved illusory; harmonization of terms and conditions of employment was very limited; and equal opportunities did not make as much progress as expected. Above all, virtually no progress was made 'in finding a solution to Britain's industrial relations problems.' Cowan believes that what went wrong was a tendency to overestimate the rate of change in social affairs. 'So, although the strategies for the 1970s may well have been based on a social analysis of probable future developments, it was assumed that these would take place much more quickly than they did.'[28]

Writing several years later, Cowan (1988) adds that examining the growth of personnel management in the 1970s reveals a major paradox. During this period the personnel function gained considerable power and influence. These stemmed largely from increased union strength and new labour laws which highlighted the importance of industrial relations. Yet in hindsight, 'this greater power and influence did little, if anything, to improve the effectiveness of line management and, because of this, business overall.' With this experience in mind, Cowan argues that personnel management needs to increase its power and authority, and hence its contribution to business effectiveness, 'through the achievement of total management efficiency which means without blunting the thrust of line management.' It might then be possible 'to describe the years ahead as the "non-negotiating" nineties to reflect the environment that is likely to be experienced in that decade.'[29]

Criticism from a novel direction comes from Peter Armstrong (1987). His basic concern is that the personnel function is not responding sufficiently to the challenges posed to it by the business dominance of the management accountancy profession. According to Armstrong's analysis, the 'contracts manager' personnel role is being replaced by a polarized profession 'consisting of a mass of "clerks of works" . . . and a few elite "architects" of strategic human resources policy who continue to operate at the corporate headquarters level.' His diagnosis is that the current problems 'faced by the personnel profession have as much to do with the increasing dominance of management accounting systems in British companies as with the recession.'[30]

The conclusion which Armstrong comes to, on the basis of present evidence, is that the architect or business manager model of personnel management 'is relevant only to those companies which have expanded around a recognisable "core" of operational activities.' In those more typical highly diversified companies, 'there are no grounds whatsoever for supposing that the personnel function' is going to escape 'the general process of devolution and subordination to financial control which has been the fate of other managerial specialists.'[31] For Armstrong, the strategy of survival for the personnel profession in most large British companies lies in a 'modest and practical version of "deviant innovation".' As Legge and Exley (1975) indicate, this requires personnel managers acting proactively and skilfully and not as 'conformist innovators' by making their activities conform to the dominant values associated with organizational success. It involves them, rather, in attempting 'to change this means and ends relationship by gaining acceptance for a *different set of criteria* for the evaluation of organizational success and their contribution to it.'[32] This approach recognizes the fact of accounting controls within companies but 'seeks to exploit their problematic aspects as a means for promoting intervention by the personnel profession.'[33]

The HRM response

It would seem, then, for a variety of organizational reasons, as well as external factors deriving from technical change and competitive market pressures, that some organizations are developing an HRM response to personnel management. The trend is by no means universal and should not be exaggerated. But it has been commented upon by both students and practitioners of personnel management. Guest (1987), for example, in a seminal article on the topic identifies six underlying pressures behind the rising interest in HRM in Britain. They are: the search for competitive advantage; models of excellence in corporate enterprise; the 'failure' of personnel management to promote 'the potential benefits of effective management of people'; the decline in trade union pressure; changes in the workforce and the nature of work; and the availability of 'new models' of management involving a subtle blend 'of some of the "best" elements of scientific management and human relations.'[34]

Guest suggests that there are three ways in which the term HRM is being used. These are: a retitling of personnel management; a reconceptualizing and reorganizing of personnel roles, especially in the conceptual framework of the Harvard Business School; and a distinctively different and new approach to managing people. In analysing the nature of HRM as a philosophy of managing people, Guest sees it as only one approach amongst several, with others being 'equally legitimate and likely in certain contexts to be more successful.' Further, given the evidence that only some workers will seek out and respond to work environments providing 'challenge, autonomy, learning opportunities and self-control', Guest argues that HRM, being based on these assumptions, is only viable in those organizations employing workers with such orientations or where these workers can be recruited and selected. The limited evidence available 'suggests it would be unwise to assume that many blue-collar workers possess this orientation.' Indeed, drawing on a survey undertaken at the London School of

Economics on what respondents viewed as ideal models 'of good personnel management practice', Guest concludes that the HRM model 'was by no means the dominant one and it is interesting to note that the largest number of companies fell within the professional model.'[35]

One of the most interesting aspects of Guest's essay is his theoretical analysis of HRM. He sees HRM as having four policy goals: integration; employee commitment; flexibility; and quality. The goal of integration has four components. These concern: management strategy; 'vertical integration between strategic concerns, management concerns and operational concerns'; the attitudes and behaviour of line managers; and the view that all employees should be fully integrated into the business for which they work. Underlying these four elements of integration is the general proposition that if personnel management is integrated into strategic planning, 'if human resource policies adhere, if line managers have internalized the importance of human resources', and this is reflected in their behaviour, 'and if employees identify with the company, then the company's strategic plans are likely to be more successfully implemented.' As a result change is facilitated and resistance to it weakened.[36]

The goal of employee commitment seeks to develop feelings of involvement with the organization by individual employees. This makes them more satisfied, productive and adaptable workers. The theoretical proposition is that 'organizational commitment, combined with job-related behavioural commitment, will result in high employee satisfaction, high performance, longer tenure and a willingness to accept change.' In terms of the goal of flexibility, the theoretical proposition is that flexible organizational structures 'together with flexible job content and flexible employees will result in a capacity to respond swiftly and effectively to change', thus ensuring the high utilization of human and other resources within the enterprise.[37]

The final policy goal, quality, has a number of elements. These concern quality of staff, performance, management practice and public image, in particular the employer's human resources policies. To ensure high quality, considerable attention is normally given in HRM to recruitment and selection, training, appraisal, goal setting and job design. In these ways, human resources are fully utilized 'by providing high quality challenging jobs for high calibre staff.' Here, the theoretical proposition is that the pursuit of policies designed 'to ensure the recruitment and retention of high quality staff to undertake demanding jobs, supported by competent management, will result in high performance levels.' Having identified these goals, however, Guest warns that many British companies, for very sound reasons, may not want to practise HRM. The opportunity of change 'seems most likely to arise when a new chief executive is appointed, when a major crisis arises which creates opportunities for change or at a greenfield site.'[38]

A series of 20 case studies conducted by researchers at the University of Warwick's Centre for Corporate Strategy and Change indicate that companies undertaking developments in HRM have done so under strong competitive pressures. According to these findings, HRM in such firms has not developed in a vacuum. In practice 'a complex set of business environment changes have led to a series of generic strategic responses', with seven 'interdependent' responses driving developments in HRM. These are: competitive restructuring; decentralization of decision making; internationalization of markets; acquisitions and mergers; quality improvement; technological change; and new concepts of service and distribution management. Thus complexity of externally inspired change creates 'needs for new operating structures and systems, and new skills, knowledge and capability from staff at many organisational levels and in a variety of functions.' The origins of HRM issues, in other words, 'are manifestly connectable to the business and technical changes in the outer context of the firm.'[39]

The Warwick research team also identifies the main internal characteristics of firms where HRM changes are likely to take place. These include: changes in their top leadership; the implementation of major redundancy programmes; the creation of 'performance-orientated cultural change'; improvements in product quality and customer relations; attempts to create an overall 'culture for change'; the complementary development of strategic management and people management skills; and the 'decentralisation of responsibility for HRM activities' to line management. Such internal and external changes appear to have been managed by responses across the whole range of personnel activity. These include: skill supply; human resources development; selection and retention; rewards management; and employee relations.[40]

According to the Warwick team, there are a number of issues facing the personnel function where business performance gaps lead to strategic responses in managing change. One is the 'heightened sense of a skill performance gap in many firms', thus increasing awareness of a range of HRM activities. However, underlying 'good HRM practice' there appear to be 'three core issues' requiring the attention of the personnel function: 'their competences, credibility, and the need to develop themselves as developers.' The key competences involve broad training and experience across the full range of HRM activities, together with the capability of linking business and technical changes to HRM considerations. It also requires conceptual ability to think in business and HRM terms. There is also the necessity of developing internal process skills to facilitate change. HRM is therefore interpreted as 'the ability to take, and implement, a strategic view of the whole range of personnel practices in relation to business activity', thus linking business, technical and HRM skills.[41]

This research suggests that there is 'unfortunately a shortage of people with such skills and competences within firms.' Hence there is a trend in some companies towards putting line managers into senior positions to oversee the personnel function. This may 'represent a breakthrough in acceptance of HRM issues at the highest level, as well as . . . spreading the legitimacy of HRM issues into the line.'[42] The threat to established personnel specialists is, of course, implicit.

It is sometimes claimed that HRM thrives more in a non-union than in a unionized environment, if only because HRM is seen 'as unitarist and individualist in focus.'[43] Yet this need not be the case. Geoffrey Armstrong (1987), for example, in an address to the IPM National Conference argues that commitment through employee relations is the key to corporate success. In his view there are 'many dramatic examples' of companies that have made themselves successful 'through major shifts in their strategic direction.' This has been done by changing radically their approach to their employees, equipping and training them for change, and 'organizing and motivating them to contribute effectively to the competitiveness required.' To get the competitive edge, he argues, it is the quality of people, in particular the quality of a firm's managers, which makes the crucial difference. 'Increasingly, competition is between workforces, not just between products.'[44]

Armstrong identifies several organizational features of successful businesses in the 1980s. These include flatter structures, smaller corporate headquarters, multi-skilled managers, effective strategic planning and dynamic board leadership. It is the latter, above all, which creates 'the overall vision of where the organisation is going, what success looks like for the shareholders and other stakeholders . . . and develops and allocates management talent between businesses and functions.' Such enterprises also share, in Armstrong's view, common features in the ways they manage people. They create, for example, a sense of purpose and shared values, emphasize the primacy of customers, invest heavily in training and, most importantly, 'treat their employees as respected contributors to organisational success, not just as necessary costs of production.' Additionally they stress employment security based on employee flexibility, harmonization of conditions, 'encouragement of share ownership, "open-door" communications policies, opportunities for progression' and 'rewards for improving performance.'[45]

This is not to say that 'there isn't a role for Trade Unions, or for collective organisations of people at work, or for collective bargaining on matters affecting their interests.' Armstrong believes that there is: 'but it has to be based on a joint acceptance of the communal imperative that an organisation that fails to satisfy the needs of customers is dead in the water.' He has no time for adversarial industrial relations, where the right to bargain takes precedence over the needs of customers and the competitive needs of the business. In the 1960s and 1970s too many managers 'had lost sight of the business goals within which and in support of which our industrial relations [had] been working.' There is no looking back, Armstrong argues, and management will fail commercially in the increasingly turbulent and changing conditions of business, unless it gets better 'at convincing our people that we know what we're doing, where we're going and how we're going to get there.'[46]

No brief review of the HRM response to organizational, market and technological change would be complete without some reference to HRM developments in the United States. Indeed one of the major critiques of HRM as an approach to managing people is that the literature and practices are derived strongly from North American sources and experiences. In the papers published by the

Harvard Business School, after a colloquium on Human Resource Futures involving faculty members and senior executives in May 1984, Walton (1985) claims that American managers 'are in the midst of a pattern of profound change in the way we think about and manage human resources in business.' He proposes that the term 'high-commitment work system' is the essential ingredient in the future pattern of HRM: 'mutuality' is 'the most dominant theme of the future policies we envision.' He posits that senior managers '*in pace-setting firms* in a wide assortment of industries' [my italics] are revising their HRM policies to promote mutuality between managers and managed. It is manifest in all policy areas: employee voice; rewards; work organization; and human resource flows.[47]

In these papers, Lawrence traces the evolution of four earlier patterns of HRM, showing how each was rendered obsolete by changing economic, technical and social forces. He describes these as the 'craft', 'market', 'technical' and 'career' HRM systems. The craft system was dominant until about 1820; the market until 1914; and the technical until 1940. He believes that the career system is currently the dominant pattern, being based on long term employment which is career oriented, with promotion through the ranks. The balance of emphasis within the career system, he argues, is largely adversarial rather than being based on mutual interests. The emerging HRM system he describes is the 'commitment' system which draws heavily on American, British, European and Japanese models of HRM. In contrast to the four earlier systems, the commitment system provides near lifetime employment, slow promotion, lateral and vertical movement, and 'multi-level' consultations with employee representatives. It focuses on mutuality of interests between employers and employed rather than on adversarial relations. Nevertheless, history indicates that 'newer systems, even if they come to dominate the employment scene, do not totally displace earlier systems.'[48]

The main features of the commitment HRM system, according to Walton, are that jobs are defined more broadly, management is leaner and more flexible, and dynamic performance expectations replace minimum work standards. Compensation systems emphasize learning and collaboration, whilst employees exercise 'more voice' within their organizations. Lastly, union–management relations involve joint problem solving and planning, with employment assurance initiatives becoming a high priority policy issue. In Walton's view, the trend towards the commitment strategy is extensive but not yet dominant. It arises out of economic necessity which appears to be fuelling 'this transformation' and is shaped and paced by related factors. These include 'individual leadership in management and labour, philosophical choices, organizational competence in managing change and cumulative learning from change itself.'[49] The question remains – is HRM simply a management fad from the United States or is it a personnel strategy which British personnel managers will inevitably adopt?

New models for old?

Summing up the argument so far, it appears that new patterns of personnel management, HRM and its variants, are emerging in some organizations, in response to a series of endogenous and exogenous factors. Although the term HRM is North American in origin, in its British context the concept is increasingly associated with the development of proactive, business-centred personnel management policies. Within these, career management 'and the integration of stable core employees through their careful selection and intensive socialisation in key corporate values are highlighted as central personnel activities.'[50] Concepts of corporate 'excellence' and 'customer service' are stressed and, in contrast to the more traditional images of workplace conflict and adversarial industrial relations, team-based cultural values such as mutual trust, employee commitment and corporate integration are nurtured. The data which is available, in short, indicates that a perceptible qualitative shift is occurring in the personnel function in some organizations, away from the more traditional mediatory role of personnel managers.

The evidence for this is both anecdotal and research based. Hendry and Pettigrew (1987), for example, in outlining experiences of managing change in the Trustee Savings Bank, indicate how an HRM approach provided a way in which the personnel department was proactive both in relation to business needs and in influencing the pace of business development. It also played a key role in managing the evolution of corporate culture. Moreover, with its influence on recruitment, training, promotion and reward systems, as well as having the ear of staff in the workplace, 'the personnel function can play a crucial part in achieving an acceptable and appropriate synthesis of old and new goals and old and new staff.'[51]

Similarly, following business changes at Halfords, its personnel director claims that HRM 'has been and remains a strong thread running through the process we followed to reinvigorate the business and change its strategic direction.' He goes on to say that where a company is seeking to sort out its HRM, 'it may need to sort out its business first' and that HRM changes 'need to be closely linked to the business objectives and managerial process.'[52]

A number of case studies, examining changes in the way in which people are being managed were undertaken by Storey (1988) in a range of organizations. They comprised 15 major organizations and 25 medium sized ones. They covered both the public and private sectors, focusing on mainstream employers in the 'heartland territories of the British employment scene', not 'special cases' like IBM, Marks and Spencer and Nissan. Reporting on the situation in six of these organizations – Austin Rover, Ford, British Rail, Lucas, Eaton and the Health Service – Storey argues that some of the more significant changes bearing 'on the nature of the employment relationship' appear to be driven 'from organisational changes which, on the surface, are not always self-evidently industrial relations or personnel management initiatives'. These studies seem to highlight a 'degree of commonality in the kind of organisational change processes' taking place in Britain today and indicate 'the way that the approach to "people management" is shifting in emphasis.'[53]

According to Storey's analysis, the cases reported illustrate two things. The first is that 'line managers at all levels seem familiar with a relatively common set of propositions and concepts.' These hinge 'on the desired outcome of competitive performance via a committed and competent workforce.' The aim of managing people no longer appears to be containment and compliance but competence and commitment. Competence is sought through more sophisticated techniques of 'flow management' and training and development. Commitment is seen as achievable 'through winning the hearts and minds of individuals rather than striking deals with collectives and their representatives.' Second, whilst the nature of the shift in emphasis in managing people seems to be significant, it is not, 'as yet, "transforming" in the full sense of that word.'

Nonetheless, there appears to be a philosophical underpinning to the kinds of initiatives identified. Moreover, the fact that managing people 'is now widely perceived as primarily the responsibility of line managers, business managers, and manufacturing systems engineers' possibly reflects the amount of organizational change that has taken place in Britain during the 1980s.[54]

Recent shifts of emphasis within the personnel function, however, should not be overstated. Obviously, for a variety of reasons, some organizations have experienced far greater change than others. Yet even where top management has introduced job flexibility, performance related pay and direct communications with the workforce, all does not change overnight because of such initiatives. Indeed, a favoured approach of employee relations managers in the unionized environments reported by Storey is 'broadly to continue with maintaining the procedures in good order.'[55] Also, as Torrington and his colleagues (1985) point out, in examining the time distributed by personnel specialists amongst different areas of personnel work, 'the pre-eminence of employee relations is clear: greatest discretion, most time, most important and growing in importance.' The trend they perceive in personnel management 'is a gradual increase in emphasis on manpower control at the same time as a high commitment to employee relations, but the two are not necessarily found in the same place at the same time.'[56] Where change has occurred in the personnel function, it seems that it is generally incremental and evolutionary in nature, not a major paradigmatic shift.

In short, what is being observed, as research extends and broadens our knowledge and understanding of the personnel function, is the overwhelmingly contingent nature of personnel management philosophies and practices. Personnel management styles and activities, in other words, strongly reflect the cultural and contextual circumstances of the organizations in which they originate. HRM, which is itself heterogeneous and diverse in its emphases, is best described as a business-oriented approach to managing people at work, within which the personnel function adapts. And HRM arises from specific organizational circumstances. These include pressures for change, deriving often from product market competition and sometimes technological imperatives and corporate needs for success. HRM developments also require top managerial initiatives aimed at integrating corporate resources, including the company's 'human resources', to enable them to work together with a sense of common purpose and collective identity. But HRM is not appropriate to all organizations. The danger is to view HRM as a managerial panacea and a *universal* set of strategic prescriptions for all personnel management situations, at all times.

What seems to be emerging, then, is a 'new model' of the personnel function, and its variants, in some organizations, the HRM model. According to Gowler and Legge, this 'derives from a model of employees as actors capable of exercising choice and initiative . . . and whose commitment has therefore to be won, as overt control of performance is likely to prove counterproductive.' This perspective of 'personnel management in the future' provides an optimistic image of the function. It highlights 'the tasks of developing and rewarding a resourceful, elite core of administrative, professional, technical and clerical employees, integrated by client/customer centred values.' It has a 'social action' perspective and is the most favoured one in the 'consensus model of personnel management in the future.'[57]

In contrast, there is a second functionalist or 'systems' perspective of personnel management which 'presents a deterministic image of employees – as reactive rather than proactive, as human resources rather than resourceful human beings.' In this case, cost effectiveness rather than cost minimization is perceived to be 'a guiding theme, with emphasis on value for money, rather than the cheapness of the human resource'.[58] It is an approach which is strongly rooted in the traditional, professional role of personnel management.

To conclude, it is clear from reviewing recent literature that a variety of 'models', 'traditions', 'perspectives' and 'theories' of the personnel function have been proposed. Of these, the term 'model' is probably the most useful concept on which to build, since it seeks to provide images of the structure, form and content of modern personnel management. In using the word in this sense, one can identify, in effect, three dominant models of the modern personnel function. These are the 'paternalist welfare model', the 'professional personnel model' and the 'HRM model'. Although variants of each of these could be developed, and other models proposed, these three 'ideal types', and their selected characteristics, can provide a tentative framework for analysing and classifying contemporary personnel management. This can be seen in Figure 25.

Figure 25
Dominant models of the personnel function

Selected characteristics	Paternalist welfare model	Professional personnel model	HRM model
Personnel characteristics			
orientation	welfare	occupational	managerial
ethic	moral	service	market
philosophy	humanist	manpower control	employee integration
emphasis	people	negotiation	development
ideology	paternalist	collectivist	individualist
role	person management	system management	resources management
strategy	none	conformist innovation	deviant innovation
culture	unitary	pluralist	neo-unitary soft pluralist
generic activity	staff relations	industrial relations	employee relations
Other characteristics			
status of workforce	staff	employees	professionals
contract with workforce	social	legal	psychological
role of unions	marginal	adversarial	collaborative
change	slow	moderate	continuous
market position	protected	stable	competitive
attitude to workforce	cost minimization	cost effectiveness	human investment

Source: FARNHAM D. *Sundridge Park Management Review.* Spring 1989

In its 'pure' form, the paternalist welfare model of the personnel function is, in outline, welfare oriented, humanist in philosophy and unitary in culture. Its generic activity focuses on 'staff relations', where the role of the unions is marginal and where social and moral expectations provide the basis for contractual relations between employers and their staff. As a model of the personnel function, paternalist welfarism draws heavily on theories of social psychology and individual behaviour. It is a model, relatively speaking, which appears to be declining in importance.

The professional personnel model, in contrast, has an occupational orientation, a manpower control philosophy and a pluralist culture. Its generic activity is normally industrial relations and, consequently, it provides an adversarial role for the trade unions. Other features of the 'pure type' professional personnel model include a cost effective attitude towards the workforce, an emphasis upon negotiation, a collectivist ideology and a service personnel ethic. Conformist innovation is the typical strategy for 'professional' personnel specialists, whilst contractual relations between employers and employees are predominantly legalistic in nature.

The 'pure type' HRM model of the personnel function is managerial in orientation and individualist in ideology. It has a market ethic which is supported by a personnel philosophy of mutuality, allied with employee commitment and employee involvement. As 'professionals', employees are expected to have a strong psychological compact with their employer which overrides the basic legal obligations between them. Although considered to be professional workers, employees within this model are not necessarily deflected from joining appropriate trade unions where these are recognized. In managing their 'employee relations', however, some employers utilizing the HRM model prefer a non-union environment. Others, where they negotiate with trade unions, are more likely to seek 'collaborative' single union or 'new style' deals involving job flexibility, 'no strike' arrangements, employee participation, harmonization of terms and conditions and 'pendulum' arbitration. Personnel strategies are normally of the deviant innovation type and HRM cultures are typically neo-unitary or soft pluralist in nature. As such, they draw substantially on elements of Anglo-American, European and Far Eastern human resource concepts.

In practice, of course, few 'pure' models of the personnel function exist. Although in some organizations either the paternalist or the professional or the HRM model predominates, in others the personnel function is 'mixed' and comprises elements of two or more of the models or their variants, thus reinforcing the ambiguities inherent within personnel management. Of these three 'dominant models', the paternalist and the professional are rooted firmly in the culture and practices of traditional personnel management in Britain, which started with the appointment of factory welfare officers at the beginning of the century. The HRM model, which is transcultural, is growing in importance but by no means universally practised, is seen by some to be the 'emergent "consensus" functionalist image of personnel management in the 1990s.'

Although challenging this 'emerging monolithic image of "personnel management in the future",' Gowler and Legge explain 'the dominance of what we might now term the "proactive" functionalist view of personnel management.'[59]

In their view, this image of the personnel function has achieved 'its consensus status' because it justifies personnel's power base. Its earlier power bases of the 1970s 'have been undermined by declining traditional union power, changed legislative direction and a reserve army to perform new firm specific tasks.' Thus in becoming centrally involved 'in the management of the organization's symbolic order "in search of excellence",' this new model of the personnel function lays claim to 'an expandable area of activity.' And it is 'one associated with images of leadership rather than the threatened downgraded position associated with recession.'[60]

The modern personnel function, in other words, appears to be infinitely adaptable to specific organizational, cultural and market circumstances. What the research evidence indicates, therefore, is that a new model of personnel management, the 'human resources manager', does appear to be slowly gaining ground in a relatively small group of successful private businesses, dominated by volatility and change. In most other cases, however, the professional 'personnel manager' continues to operate, providing a more traditional base for personnel work. This means, in practice, that both the 'new' and the 'old' models of personnel management appear to coexist – normally in different organizations. But the HRM model must not be exaggerated. As Storey and Sisson (1989) conclude, despite the powerful advocacy of the 'excellence' literature, 'there is little evidence of a strategic approach to human resource management being adopted in most organizations.'[61]

References and footnotes

1 GUEST D. 'Has the recession really hit personnel management?' *Personnel Management.* October 1982. p37.
2 STOREY J. (ed) *New Perspectives on Human Resource Management.* (London, Routledge, 1989). p3.

3   *ibid.*
4   TORRINGTON D. *and* MACKAY L. *The Changing Face of Personnel Management* (London, IPM, 1986). p177f
5   WATSON T. *Towards a General Theory of Personnel Management and Industrial Relations.* (Nottingham, Trent Business School, 1985). p34f.
6   TORRINGTON *and* MACKAY. *opcit.* p178f.
7   TYSON S. 'The management of the personnel function'. *Journal of Management Studies.* 24(5), 1987. p22.
8   TYSON S. 'Is this the very model of a modern personnel manager?' *Personnel Management.* May 1985. p22.
9   TYSON (1987) *opcit.* p526.
10 TYSON S. *and* FELL A. *Evaluating the Personnel Function.* (London, Hutchinson, 1986). p135f.
11 FOWLER A. 'When chief executives discover HRM.' *Personnel Management.* January 1987. p3.
12 *ibid.*
13 ARMSTRONG M. 'HRM: a case of the emperor's new clothes?' *Personnel Management.* August 1987. p31f.
14 IPM. 'Statement on personnel management and personnel policies.' *Personnel Management.* March 1963.
15 LEGGE K. *Power, Innovation and Problem Solving in Personnel Management.* (London, McGraw-Hill, 1978). pp19 and 23.
16 *ibid.* p22.
17 *ibid.* p23.
18 THOMASON G. *A Textbook of Personnel Management.* (London, IPM, 1975). p26.
19 *ibid.* p39.
20 GUEST D *and* HORWOOD R. *The Role and Effectiveness of Personnel Managers: a Preliminary Report.* (London, LSE, 1980). p11.
21 MOXON G R. *Functions of a Personnel Department.* (London, IPM, 1951). p7.
22 GUEST (1982). *opcit.* p37.
23 ROYAL COMMISSION ON TRADE UNIONS AND EMPLOYERS' ASSOCIATIONS. *Report.* (London, HMSO, 1968). para. 95.
24 BATSTONE E. 'What have personnel managers done for industrial relations?' *Personnel Management.* June 1980. p39.
25 LEGGE. *opcit.* pp52, 66 and 136. See also chapter 4 above pp92–4 and 105–9 and chapter 5, pp129–33.
26 MANNING K. 'The rise and fall of personnel.' *Management Today.* March 1983. p73f.
27 THURLEY K. 'Personnel management in the UK: a case for urgent treatment?' *Personnel Management.* August 1981. pp24–9.
28 COWAN N. 'Personnel management in the eighties: will we waste another decade?' *Personnel Management.* January 1980. p23.
29 COWAN N. 'Change and the personnel profession.' *Personnel Management.* January 1988. p36.

30 ARMSTRONG P. 'The personnel profession in the age of management accountancy.' *Working Paper: Industrial Relations Research Unit*. University of Warwick, 1987. See also his contribution in STOREY J (ed) (1989). *opcit.*, 'Limits and possibilities for HRM in an age of management accountancy'.

31 *ibid*. p17.

32 LEGGE K *and* EXLEY M. 'Authority, ambiguity and adaptations: the personnel specialist's dilemma.' *Industrial Relations Journal*. Vol. 6, No 3, 1975. p59f.

33 ARMSTRONG (1987). *opcit*. p18.

34 GUEST D. 'Human resource management and industrial relations.' *Journal of Management Studies*. 24(5), 1987. p504f.

35 *ibid*. pp506, 509 and 511.

36 *ibid*. p511f.

37 *ibid*. p513f.

38 *ibid*. pp515 and 517.

39 PETTIGREW A, SPARROW P *and* HENDRY C. 'Competitiveness, strategic change and human resource management.' *Personnel Management*. November 1988.

40 *ibid*.

41 *ibid*.

42 *ibid*.

43 GUEST (1982). *opcit*. p518.

44 ARMSTRONG G. 'Commitment through employee relations.' Paper presented to the IPM National Conference, 22 October 1987.

45 *ibid*.

46 *ibid*.

47 WALTON R. 'The future of HRM: an overview' in WALTON R. *and* LAWRENCE P R (eds). *HRM Trends and Challenges*. Boston, Mass., Harvard Business School, 1985. p3f.

48 LAWRENCE P R. 'The history of HRM in American industry' in *ibid*. pp15–34.

49 *ibid*. pp5 and 35–65.

50 GOWLER D. *and* LEGGE K. 'Personnel and paradigms: four perspectives on the future.' *Industrial Relations Journal*. September 1986. p232.

51 HENDRY C. *and* PETTIGREW A. 'Banking on HRM to respond to change.' *Personnel Management*. November 1987. p31f.

52 RICHARDS L. 'Strategic HRM'. Paper presented to the IPM National Conference, 20 October 1988.

53 STOREY J. 'The people-management dimension in current programmes of organisational change.' *Employee Relations*. 10(6), 1988. p17ff.

54 *ibid*. p25.

55 *ibid*.

56 TORRINGTON D, MACKAY L *and* HALL L. 'The changing nature of personnel management.' *Employee Relations*. 7(5), 1985, p15.

57 GOWLER *and* LEGGE, *opcit.* p212ff.
58 *ibid.* p232f.
59 *ibid.* pp225 and 233.
60 *ibid.* p233.
61 STOREY J *and* SISSON K. 'Looking to the future' in STOREY J (ed). *opcit.* p172.

Bibliography

ACKOFF R L. *A Concept of Corporate Planning.* NY, Wiley, 1970.

ACTON SOCIETY TRUST. *Management Succession.* London, Acton Society Trust, 1956.

ADVISORY CONCILIATION AND ARBITRATION SERVICE. *Code of Practice 1. Disciplinary Practice and Procedures in Employment.* London, HMSO, 1977a.

ADVISORY CONCILIATION AND ARBITRATION SERVICE. *Code of Practice 2. Disclosure of Information for Collective Bargaining.* London, HMSO, 1977b.

ADVISORY CONCILIATION AND ARBITRATION SERVICE. *Code of Practice 3. Time off for Trade Union Duties and Activities.* London, HMSO, 1978.

ADVISORY CONCILIATION AND ARBITRATION SERVICE. *Industrial Relations Handbook.* London, HMSO, 1980a.

ADVISORY CONCILIATION AND ARBITRATION SERVICE. *Advisory Booklet No. 1. Job Evaluation.* London, ACAS, 1980b.

ADVISORY CONCILIATION AND ARBITRATION SERVICE. *Annual Report 1981.* London, HMSO, 1982.

ADVISORY CONCILIATION AND ARBITRATION SERVICE. *Annual Report 1985.* London, HMSO, 1986.

ADVISORY COUNCIL FOR APPLIED RESEARCH AND DEVELOPMENT. *The Applications of Semi-Conductor Technology.* London, HMSO, 1978.

ALLEN M (ed). *The Times 1000 1982–1983.* London, Times Books, 1982.

ALLEN M (ed). *The Times 1000 1989–1990.* London, Times Books, 1989.

ANTHONY P D. *The Ideology of Work.* London, Tavistock, 1976.

ANTHONY P D. *The Conduct of Industrial Relations.* London, IPM, 1977.

ANTHONY P *and* CRICHTON A. *Industrial Relations and the Personnel Specialists.* London, Batsford, 1969.

APPLEBY R C. *Modern Business Administration.* 3rd ed. London, Pitman, 1981.

ARMSTRONG G. 'Commitment through employee relations'. Paper presented to the IPM National Conference, 22 October 1987.

ARMSTRONG M. *A Handbook of Personnel Management Practice.* 2nd ed. London, Kogan Page, 1983.

ARMSTRONG M. 'HRM: a case of the new emperor's clothes'. *Personnel Management*, August 1987.
ARMSTRONG P. 'The personnel profession in the age of management accountancy'. *Working Paper: Industrial Relations Research Unit*, University of Warwick, 1987.
ARON R. *18 Lectures on Industrial Society*. London, Weidenfeld and Nicolson, 1961.
ASHLEY W J. *The Economic Organization of England*. London, Longman, 1914.
ASSOCIATION OF SCIENTIFIC TECHNICAL AND MANAGERIAL STAFFS. *Technological Change and Collective Bargaining*. London, ASTMS, 1979.
BAINS M A. *The New Local Authorities: Management and Structure*. London, HMSO, 1972.
BALL A R. *British Political Parties* 2nd ed. London, Macmillan, 1987.
BALL A R. *Modern Politics and Government*. 4th ed. London, Macmillan, 1988.
BARBER D. *The Practice of Personnel Management*. 2nd ed. London, IPM, 1979.
BARNARD C I. *The Functions of the Executive*. Cambridge, Mass., Harvard University Press, 1968.
BARRETT B *and others*. *Industrial Relations and Wider Society*. London, Collier Macmillan, 1975.
BATSTONE E. 'What have personnel managers done for industrial relations?'. *Personnel Management*. Vol. 12, No. 6, June 1980.
BELL D. *The Coming of Post Industrial Society*. London, Heinemann, 1974.
BENDIX R. *Work and Authority in Industry*. Berkeley, University of California Press, 1974.
BENNETT R. *Managing Personnel and Performance*. London, Business Books, 1981.
BERLE A A *and* MEANS G C. *The Modern Corporation and Private Property*. 4th ed. NY, Harcourt, Brace and World, 1968.
BEVERIDGE W H. *Full Employment in a Free Society*. London, Allen and Unwin, 1944.
BEYNON H. *Working for Ford*. Harmondsworth, Penguin, 1973.
BLACK J. *The Economics of Modern Britain*. Oxford, Martin Robertson, 1979.
BLAU P *and* SCOTT W R. *Formal Organizations*. London, Routledge and Kegan Paul, 1963.
BLAUNER R. *Alienation and Freedom*. Chicago, Chicago University Press, 1964.
BOURNE J. *Management in Central and Local Government*. London, Pitman, 1979.
BRECH E F L (ed). *The Principles and Practice of Management*. 3rd ed. London, Longman, 1975.
BRIDGE J. *Economics and Personnel Management*. London, IPM, 1978.
BRITISH INSTITUTE OF MANAGEMENT. *Summary Recommen-*

dations of the Constitution and Structure Working Party. London, BIM, 1983a.

BRITISH INSTITUTE OF MANAGEMENT. *Annual Reports 1985 and 1989*. London, BIM, 1985 and 1989.

BROWN D *and* HARRISON M J. *A Sociology of Industrialization: an Introduction*. London, Macmillan, 1978.

BURNHAM J. *The Managerial Revolution*. London, Greenwood Press, 1962.

BUTLER D *and* SLOMAN A. *British Political Facts 1900–1978*. 5th ed. London, Macmillan, 1980.

CAMBRIDGE ECONOMIC POLICY GROUP. *Cambridge Economic Policy Review*. Cambridge, Gower, 1982.

CANNON J. *Cost Effective Personnel Decisions*. London, IPM, 1979.

CARLSON S. *Executive behaviour*. Stockholm, Strombergs, 1951.

CARTER G M *and* HERZ J H. *Government and Politics in the Twentieth Century*. London, Thames and Hudson, 1969.

CARTWRIGHT D (ed). *Studies in Social Power*. Ann Arbor, University of Michigan, 1959.

CENTRAL POLICY REVIEW STAFF. *Social and Economic Implications of Microelectronics*. London, CPRS, 1978.

CENTRAL STATISTICAL OFFICE. *Social Trends No 6 1975*. London, HMSO, 1975.

CENTRAL STATISTICAL OFFICE. *Annual Abstract of Statistics 1982*. London, HMSO, 1982.

CENTRAL STATISTICAL OFFICE. *Social Trends No 13*. London, HMSO, 1983.

CENTRAL STATISTICAL OFFICE. *Economic Trends: Annual Supplement 1985 Edition*. London, HMSO, 1985.

CENTRAL STATISTICAL OFFICE. *United Kingdom National Accounts*. London, HMSO, 1989.

CENTRAL STATISTICAL OFFICE. *Social Trends No 20 1990 Edition*. London, HMSO, 1990.

CENTRE FOR EDUCATIONAL RESEARCH AND INNOVATION. *Education and Work: the Views of the Young*. Paris, OECD, 1983.

CERTIFICATION OFFICE FOR TRADE UNIONS AND EMPLOYERS' ASSOCIATIONS. *Annual report of the Certification Officer 1988*. London, HMSO, 1989.

CHAMBERLAIN N W. *The Union Challenge to Management Control*. NY, Harper, 1948.

CHANDLER A D *and* DAEMS H (eds). *Managerial Hierarchies*. London, Harvard University Press, 1980.

CHECKLAND S G. *The Rise of Industrial Society in England 1815–1885*. London, Longman, 1964.

CHILD J. *British Management Thought*. London, Allen and Unwin, 1969a.

CHILD J. *The Business Enterprise in Modern Industrial Society*. London, Collier Macmillan, 1969b.

CHILD J (ed). *Man and Organization*. London, Allen and Unwin, 1973.
CHILD J. *Organization: a Guide to Problems and Practice*. London, Harper and Row, 1977.
CLARK D G. *The Industrial Manager: his Background and Career Pattern*. London, Business Publications, 1966.
CLEGG H A. 'Pluralism in industrial relations'. *British Journal of Industrial Relations*. Vol. XIII, No. 3, 1975.
CLEGG H A. *The Changing System of Industrial Relations in Britain*. Oxford, Blackwell, 1979.
CLEMENTS R V. *Managers: a Study of their Careers in Industry*. London, Allen and Unwin, 1958.
COMMISSION FOR RACIAL EQUALITY. *Fact Paper 1: The Basic Figures*. London, CRE, 1978a.
COMMISSION FOR RACIAL EQUALITY. *Fact Paper 2: Immigration – Numbers and Dispersal*. London, CRE, 1978b.
COMMISSION FOR RACIAL EQUALITY. *Annual Report 1982*. London, CRE, 1983a.
COMMISSION FOR RACIAL EQUALITY. *Code of Practice: Race Relations*. London, CRE, 1983b.
COMMISSION FOR RACIAL EQUALITY. *Equal Opportunity in Employment: a Guide for Employers*. London, CRE, 1983c.
COMMISSION OF THE EUROPEAN COMMUNITIES. *A European Community – Why?* Brussels, EEC, 1979.
COMMISSION ON INDUSTRIAL RELATIONS. *Report No 34. The Role of Management in Industrial Relations*. London, HMSO, 1973.
CONSERVATIVE PARTY. *The Conservative Manifesto 1983*. London, Conservative Central Office, 1983.
COSER L A. *The Functions of Social Conflict*. 2nd impression. London, Routledge and Kegan Paul, 1965.
COWAN N. 'Personnel management in the eighties: will we waste another decade?' *Personnel Management*. Vol. 12, No. 1, January 1980.
COWAN N. 'Change and the personnel profession'. *Personnel Management*. January 1988.
CRICHTON A. 'The Institute of Personnel Management in 1950 and 1960'. *Personnel Management*. Vol. XLIII, No. 38, December 1961.
CRICHTON A. *Personnel Management in Context*. London, Batsford, 1968.
CRICK B. *In Defence of Politics*. 2nd ed. Harmondsworth, Penguin, 1964.
CROSLAND C A R. *The Conservative Enemy*. London, Cape, 1962.
CURWEN P J *and* FOWLER A H. *Economic Policy*. London, Macmillan, 1979.
CUTHBERTSON K. *Macroeconomic Policy*. London, Macmillan, 1979.
DAHRENDORF R. *Class and Class Conflict in Industrial Society*. London, Routledge and Kegan Paul, 1959.
DAHRENDORF R. *The New Liberty*. London, Routledge and Kegan Paul, 1975.
DAHRENDORF R. *On Britain*. London, BBC, 1982.

DANIEL W. 'Who handles personnel issues in British industry?' *Personnel Management*. Vol. 15, No. 12, December 1983.

DANIEL W W *and* STILGOE E. *The Impact of Employment Protection Laws*. London, Policy Studies Institute, 1978.

DEPARTMENT OF EDUCATION AND SCIENCE. *Higher Education in the 1990s: a Discussion Document*. London, HMSO, 1978.

DEPARTMENT OF EDUCATION AND SCIENCE. *Statistics of Education 1979. Schools Vol. 1*. London, HMSO, 1981a.

DEPARTMENT OF EDUCATION AND SCIENCE. *Statistics of Education 1979. Vol. 2. School Leavers CSE and GCE*. London, HMSO, 1981b.

DEPARTMENT OF EDUCATION AND SCIENCE. *Statistics of Education 1979. Vol. 3. Further Education*. London, HMSO, 1982a.

DEPARTMENT OF EDUCATION AND SCIENCE. *Statistics of Education 1979. Vol. 6. Universities*. London, HMSO, 1982b.

DEPARTMENT OF EMPLOYMENT. *Industrial Relations Draft Code of Practice*. London, HMSO, 1972a.

DEPARTMENT OF EMPLOYMENT. *Training for the Management of Human Resources*. London, HMSO, 1972b.

DEPARTMENT OF EMPLOYMENT. *Industrial Relations Draft Code of Practice*. London, HMSO, 1972c.

DEPARTMENT OF EMPLOYMENT. *Manpower Paper No. 11. Women and Work: a Review*. London, HMSO, 1975.

DEPARTMENT OF EMPLOYMENT. *The Changing Structure of the Labour Force*. London, Department of Employment, 1976.

DEPARTMENT OF EMPLOYMENT. *Code of Practice. Closed Shop Agreements and Arrangements*. London, HMSO, 1980a.

DEPARTMENT OF EMPLOYMENT. *Code of Practice. Picketing*. London, HMSO, 1980b.

DEPARTMENT OF EMPLOYMENT. *Trade Union Immunities*. London, HMSO, 1981.

DEPARTMENT OF EMPLOYMENT. *Employment Acts 1980 and 1982*. London, HMSO, 1982.

DEPARTMENT OF EMPLOYMENT. 'Unfair dismissal cases in 1981'. *Employment Gazette*. Vol. 90, No. 11, December 1982.

DEPARTMENT OF EMPLOYMENT. *Code of Practice. Closed Shop Agreements and Arrangements*. London, HMSO, 1983a.

DEPARTMENT OF EMPLOYMENT. *Democracy in Trade Unions*. London, HMSO, 1983.

DEPARTMENT OF EMPLOYMENT. *Removing Barriers to Employment*. London, HMSO, 1989.

DEPARTMENT OF EMPLOYMENT AND PRODUCTIVITY. *In Place of Strife: a Policy for Industrial Relations*. London, HMSO, 1969.

DEPARTMENT OF INDUSTRY. *Microelectronics: the New Technology*. London, HMSO, 1978.

DEPARTMENT OF INDUSTRY. *Microelectronics: the Options*. London, HMSO, 1979.

DEPARTMENT OF TRADE. *Report of the Committee of Inquiry on*

Industrial Democracy. (Chairman, Lord Bullock). London, HMSO, 1977.
DEPARTMENT OF TRADE. *Companies in 1988 89*. London, HMSO, 1989.
DEPARTMENT OF TRADE AND INDUSTRY. *Business Monitor MA3*. London, HMSO, 1989.
DRUCKER P F. *Managing for Results*. London, Pan, 1964.
DRUCKER P F. *The Practice of Management*. London, Pan, 1968.
DRUCKER P F. 'New templates for today's organizations'. *Harvard Business Review*. January–February 1974.
DRUCKER P F. *Management*. London, Pan, 1977.
EASTON D. *A Framework for Political Analysis*. NJ, Prentice-Hall, 1965a.
EASTON D. *A Systems Analysis of Political Life*. NY, Wiley, 1965b.
EATWELL J. *Whatever Happened to Britain?* London, BBC, 1982.
EDMONDS J. 'Time to rethink: a role [for unions] for the 1990s'. *Financial Times*. 21 December 1983.
ELDRIDGE J E T *and* CROMBIE A D. *A Sociology of Organizations*. London, Allen and Unwin, 1974.
EQUAL OPPORTUNITIES COMMISSION. *Equality Between the Sexes in Industry: How Far have we Come?* Manchester, EOC, 1978.
EQUAL OPPORTUNITIES COMMISSION. *Code of Practice: Equal Opportunity Policies, Procedures and Practices in Employment*. London, EOC, 1982a.
EQUAL OPPORTUNITIES COMMISSION. *Sixth Annual Report 1981*. Manchester, EOC, 1982b.
EQUAL OPPORTUNITIES COMMISSION. *A Model Equal Opportunity Policy*. London, EOC, 1983a.
EQUAL OPPORTUNITIES COMMISSION. *Job Evaluation Schemes Free of Sex Bias*. London, EOC, 1983b.
EQUAL OPPORTUNITIES COMMISSION. *The Fact about Women is* . . . Manchester, EOC, 1986.
ETZIONI A. *A Comparative Analysis of Complex Organizations*. NY, Free Press, 1961.
EVANS A. *What Next at Work?* London, IPM, 1979.
EZRA D. 'How I see the personnel function'. *Personnel Management*. Vol. 14, No. 7, July 1982.
FALK R. *The Business of Management*. 3rd ed. Harmondsworth, Penguin, 1963.
FARNHAM D. *The Corporate Environment*. London, IPM, 1990.
FARNHAM D *and* McVICAR M. *Public Administration in the United Kingdom*. London, Cassell, 1982.
FARNHAM D *and* PIMLOTT J. *Understanding Industrial Relations*. 4th ed. London, Cassell, 1990.
FAYOL H. *Industrial and General Administration*. Trans. G. Storrs. London, Pitman, 1949.
FAZEY I H. 'A growing confidence'. *Financial Times*. 4 January 1984.
FIELDER F E *and* CHEMMERS M M. *Leadership and Effective Management*. Glenview, Scott Foresman, 1974.

FLANDERS A. *Management and Unions*. London, Faber, 1975.
FORTE R. 'How I see the personnel function'. *Personnel Management*. Vol. 14, No. 8, August 1982.
FOWLER A. *Personnel Management in Local Government*. 2nd ed. London, IPM, 1980.
FOWLER A. 'Proving the personnel department earns its salt'. *Personnel Management*. Vol. 15, No. 5, May 1983.
FOWLER A. 'When chief executives discover HRM'. *Personnel Management*. January 1987.
FOX A. *Royal Commission on Trade Unions and Employers' Associations Research Papers: 3 Industrial Sociology and Industrial Relations*. London, HMSO, 1966.
FOX A. *A Sociology of Work in Industry*. London, Collier Macmillan, 1971.
FOX A. 'Industrial relations: a social critique of pluralist ideology' in CHILD J. (ed). *Man and Organization*. 2nd ed. London, Allen and Unwin, 1985.
FOX A. *Man Mismanagement*. London, Hutchinson, 1974.
FRASER R (ed). *Keesing's Contemporary Archives*. Vol. XXIX (1983). London, Longman, 1983.
FRENCH J R P *and* RAVEN B. 'The social bases of power' in CARTWRIGHT D (ed). *Studies in Social Power*. Ann Arbor, University of Michigan, 1959.
FRIEDRICHS G *and* SCHAFF A. *Microelectronics and Society*. Oxford, Pergamon, 1982.
FRIEDSON E. 'Professions and the occupational principle' in FRIEDSON E. (ed). *The Professions and their Prospects*. London, Sage, 1973.
FRIEDSON E (ed). *The Professions and their Prospects*. London, Sage, 1973.
GAITSKELL H. 'Public ownership and equality'. *Socialist Commentary*. June 1958.
GALBRAITH J K. *The New Industrial State*. Harmondsworth, Pelican, 1969.
GALBRAITH J K. *Economics and the Public Purpose*. London, Deutsch, 1974.
GAMBLE A. *The Free Economy and the Strong State*. Basingstoke, Macmillan, 1988.
GENNARD J *and others*. 'The content of British closed shop agreements'. *Department of Employment Gazette*. Vol. 87, No. 11, November 1979.
GENNARD J *and others*. 'The content of British closed shop arrangements in British industry'. *Employment Gazette*. Vol. 88, No. 1, January 1980.
GERSHUNY J. *Social Innovation and the Division of Labour*. Oxford, OUP, 1983.
GOFFMAN E. *Asylums*. Harmondsworth, Penguin, 1968.
GOLDTHORPE J *and others*. *The Affluent Worker: Industrial Attitudes and Behaviour*. Cambridge, CUP, 1968.

GOWLER D *and* LEGGE K. 'Personnel and paradigms: four perspectives on the future.' *Industrial Relations Journal.* September 1986.
GRANT J V *and* SMITH G. *Personnel Administration and Industrial Relations.* London, Longman, 1977.
GROSSMAN G. *Economic systems.* NJ, Prentice-Hall, 1967.
GRUNFELD C. 'Donovan – the legal aspects'. *British Journal of Industrial Relations.* Vol. VI, No. 3, 1968.
GUEST D. 'Has the recession really hit personnel management?'. *Personnel Management.* Vol. 14, No. 10, October 1982.
GUEST D. 'Human resource management and industrial relations'. *The Journal of Management Studies.* 24(5), 1987.
GUEST D *and* HORWOOD R. *The Role and Effectiveness of Personnel Managers: a Preliminary Report.* London, LSE, 1980.
GUEST D *and* HORWOOD R. 'Characteristics of the successful personnel manager'. *Personnel Management.* Vol. 13, No. 5, May 1981.
GUEST D *and* HORWOOD R. *Success and Satisfaction in Personnel Management.* London, LSE, 1982.
HALSEY A H. *Change in British Society.* Oxford, OUP, 1986.
HANDY C B. *Understanding Organizations.* Harmondsworth, Penguin, 1976.
HARBISON F *and* MYERS C A. *Management in the Industrial World.* NY, McGraw-Hill, 1959.
HARBURY C. *Descriptive Economics.* 6th ed. London, Pitman, 1981.
HARVEY-JONES J. 'How I see the personnel function'. *Personnel Management* Vol. 14, No. 9, September 1982.
HASKEY J. 'The ethnic minority populations of Great Britain'. *Population Trends 54*, Winter 1988.
HAWKINS K. 'The decline of voluntarism'. *Industrial Relations Journal.* Vol. 1, No. 2, 1971.
HEATER D. *Contemporary Political Ideas.* London, Longman, 1974.
HENDRY C *and* PETTIGREW A. 'Banking on HRM to respond to change'. *Personnel Management.* November 1987.
HENDRY D *and* ERICSSON N. Quoted in note of a meeting of the Bank's panel of academic consultants. *Bank of England Quarterly Bulletin.* Vol. 23, No. 4, December 1983.
HOWELLS R *and* BARRETT B. *The Health and Safety at Work Act: a Guide for Managers.* London, IPM, 1975.
HUNT J. *Managing People at Work.* London, Pan, 1981.
HUNT J. 'The shifting focus of the personnel function'. *Personnel Management.* Vol. 15, No. 2, February 1984.
HUNTER L C *and* MULVEY C. *Economics of Wages and Labour.* 2nd ed. London, Macmillan, 1981.
HUNTER L C *and* ROBERTSON D J. *Economics of Wages and Labour.* London, Macmillan, 1969.
HYMAN R. *Industrial Relations: a Marxist Introduction.* London, Macmillan, 1975.

INSTITUTE OF DIRECTORS. *Institute of Directors.* London, IOD, 1983.

INSTITUTE OF PERSONNEL MANAGEMENT. 'Statement on personnel management and personnel policies'. *Personnel Management.* Vol. XLV, No. 363, March 1963.

INSTITUTE OF PERSONNEL MANAGEMENT. *The Institute of Personnel Management.* London, IPM, 1980.

INSTITUTE OF PERSONNEL MANAGEMENT. *IPM Digest.* No. 216, July 1983.

INSTITUTE OF PERSONNEL MANAGEMENT. *Index of IPM Policy Statements No. 4.* London, IPM, 1984.

INSTITUTE OF PERSONNEL MANAGEMENT. *IPM Annual Reports* from 1957–58 until 1988–89. London, IPM.

INTERNATIONAL LABOUR OFFICE. *Introduction to Work Study.* Geneva, ILO, 1965.

JARRETT A. 'How I see the personnel function'. *Personnel Management* Vol. 15, No. 1, July 1982.

JENKINS C. 'Is personnel still underpowered?'. *Personnel Management.* Vol. 5, No. 6, June 1973.

JENKINS C *and* SHERMAN B. *The Collapse of Work.* London, Eyre Methuen, 1979.

JOHNSON T J. *Professions and Power.* London, Macmillan, 1972.

KAHN-FREUND O. *Labour and the Law.* 2nd ed. London, Stevens, 1977.

KATZ D *and* KAHN R L. *The Social Psychology of Organizations.* NY, Wiley, 1966.

KEMPNER T *and others. Business and Society.* London, Allen Lane, 1974.

KENNEY J *and others. Manpower Training and Development.* 2nd ed. London, IPM, 1979.

KERR C *and others. Industrialism and Industrial Man.* 2nd ed. Harmondsworth, Penguin, 1973.

LABOUR PARTY. *Democratic Socialist Aims and Values.* London, Labour Party, 1988.

LABOUR PARTY. *Meet the Challenge: Make the Change.* London, Labour Party, 1989.

LANDES D S. *The Unbound Prometheus.* Cambridge, CUP, 1969.

LAWRENCE P R. 'The history of HRM in American industry' in WALTON R *and* LAWRENCE P R (eds). *HRM Trends and Challenges.* Boston, Mass., Harvard Business School, 1985.

LEGGE K. *Power, Innovation and Problem Solving in Personnel Management.* London, McGraw-Hill, 1978.

LEGGE K *and* EXLEY M. 'Authority, ambiguity and adaptation: the personnel specialist's dilemma'. *Industrial Relations Journal.* Vol. 6, No. 3, 1975.

LEWIS D. *Essentials of Employment Law.* London, IPM, 1983.

LEWIS R. 'The historical development of labour law'. *British Journal of Industrial Relations.* Vol. XIV, No. 1, 1976.

LEWIS R. 'Kahn-Freund and labour law: an outline critique'. *Industrial Law Journal.* Vol. 8, No. 4, 1979.
LIKERT R. *New Patterns of Management.* NY, McGraw-Hill, 1961.
LINDLEY R M *and others. Britain's Medium-Term Economic Prospects.* Warwick, University of Warwick Manpower Research Group, 1978.
LINDLEY R M (ed). *Economic Change and Employment Policy.* London, Macmillan, 1980.
LITTLEJOHN J. *Social Stratification.* London, Allen and Unwin, 1972.
LOCKYER K. *Production Management.* 4th ed. London, Pitman, 1983.
LOW PAY UNIT. *Minimum Wages for Women.* London, LPU, 1980.
LUPTON T. *Industrial Behaviour and Personnel Management.* London, IPM, 1978.
LYONS T P. *The Personnel Function in a Changing Environment.* London, Pitman, 1971.
McCARTHY M. 'Personnel management in the health service'. *Personnel Management.* Vol. 15, No. 9, September 1983.
McCARTHY W E J. *The Closed Shop in Britain.* Oxford, Blackwell, 1964.
MACINNES J. *Thatcherism at Work.* Milton Keynes, Open University Press, 1987.
MACKINTOSH J P. *The Government and Politics of Britain.* 4th ed. London, Hutchinson, 1977.
MAHONEY T A *and others.* 'The job(s) of management'. *Industrial Relations.* Vol. 4, No. 2, 1965.
MANNING K. 'The rise and fall of personnel'. *Management Today.* March 1983.
MANPOWER SERVICES COMMISSION. *Cohort Study of the Unemployed.* London, MSC, 1981a.
MANPOWER SERVICES COMMISSION. *A New Training Initiative.* London, MSC, 1981b.
MANPOWER SERVICES COMMISSION. *Manpower Review 1982.* London, HMSO, 1982.
MANPOWER SERVICES COMMISSION. *Corporate Plan 1983–1987.* Sheffield, MSC, 1983b.
MANPOWER SERVICES COMMISSION. *Technical and Vocational Education Initiative.* London, MSC, 1983c.
MANPOWER SERVICES COMMISSION. *Towards an Adult Training Strategy.* Sheffield, MSC, 1983d.
MANPOWER SERVICES COMMISSION. *Annual Report 84/85.* Sheffield, MSC, 1985.
MANSFIELD R *and others. The British Manager in Profile.* London, BIM, 1981.
MANT A. *The Rise and Fall of the British Manager.* London, Macmillan, 1977.
MARGERISON C J. 'What do we mean by industrial relations? A behavioural approach'. *British Journal of Industrial Relations.* Vol. VII, No. 2, 1969.
MARKS W. *Politics and Personnel Management.* London, IPM, 1978.

MARSHALL T H. *Citizenship and Social Class*. Cambridge, CUP, 1950.

MARWICK A. *British Society Since 1945*. Harmondsworth, Penguin, 1982.

MELROSE-WOODMAN J. *Profile of the British Manager*. London, BIM, 1978.

METCALF D *and* RICHARDSON R. 'Labour' in PREST A R *and* COPPOCK D J. *The UK Economy*. 9th ed. London, Weidenfeld and Nicolson, 1982.

MIDGLEY M. 'Why the feminists cannot succeed if they try to go it alone'. *The Guardian*. 4 January 1984.

MILIBAND R. *The State in Capitalist Society*. London, Quartet Books, 1973.

MILLS C W. *The Power Elite*. NY, OUP, 1959.

MINER J B *and* MINER M G. *Personnel and Industrial Relations*. 3rd ed. NY, Macmillan, 1977.

MINTZBERG H. *The Nature of Managerial Work*. NJ, Prentice-Hall, 1973.

MINTZBERG H. 'The manager's job: folklore and fact'. *Harvard Business Review*. Vol. 53, No. 4, July–August 1975.

MITCHELL B R *and* DEANE P. *Abstract of British Historical Statistics*. Cambridge, CUP, 1971.

MORRIS D (ed). *The Economic System in the UK*. 2nd ed. Oxford, OUP, 1979.

MORRISON H, 'Employment in the public and private sectors 1976 to 1982' in CENTRAL STATISTICAL OFFICE. *Economic Trends*. No. 352. February 1983.

MOXON G R. *Functions of a Personnel Department*. London, IPM, 1946.

NATIONAL ECONOMIC DEVELOPMENT COUNCIL SECTOR WORKING PARTY. *Report on the Micro-Electronics Industry*. London, HMSO, 1978.

NATIONAL ECONOMIC DEVELOPMENT OFFICE. *A Study of UK Nationalized Industries*. London, NEDO, 1976.

NICHOLS T. *Ownership, Control and Ideology*. London, Allen and Unwin, 1969.

NICHOLS T *and* BEYNON H. *Living with Capitalism*. London, Routledge and Kegan Paul, 1977.

NICKELL S J. 'The determinants of equilibrium unemployment in Britain'. *The Economic Journal*. Vol. 92, No. 3, September 1982.

NIVEN M N. *Personnel Management 1913–63*. London, IPM, 1967.

OFFICE OF POPULATION CENSUSES AND SURVEYS. *Census 1981. National Report. Great Britain. Part 1*. London, HMSO, 1983a.

OFFICE OF POPULATION CENSUSES AND SURVEYS. *Census 1981. National Report. Great Britain. Part 2*. London, HMSO, 1983b.

OFFICE OF POPULATION CENSUSES AND SURVEYS. *Population Trends*. Vol. 57, Autumn 1989a.

OFFICE OF POPULATION CENSUSES AND SURVEYS. *Population Trends*. Vol. 58, Winter 1989b.

OFFICE OF POPULATION CENSUSES AND SURVEYS. *Population Trends* Vol. 59, Spring 1990.

O'HIGGINS P. *Workers' Rights.* London, Arrow Books, 1976.

OLIVER G. *Marketing Today.* London, Prentice-Hall, 1990.

ORGANIZATION FOR ECONOMIC COOPERATION AND DEVELOPMENT. *Work in a Changing Industrial Society.* Paris, OECD, 1975.

O'SHAUGHNESSY J. *Business Organization.* London, Allen and Unwin, 1968.

OWEN D. *Face the Future.* Oxford, OUP, 1981.

PAHL J M *and* PAHL R E. *Managers and their Wives.* Harmondsworth, Penguin, 1972.

PARKER P. 'How I see the personnel function'. *Personnel Management.* Vol. 15, No. 1, January 1983.

PARKER S R *and others. The Sociology of Industry.* 4th ed. London, Allen and Unwin, 1981.

PATTERSON T T. *Job Evaluation.* London, Business Books, 1972.

PETTIGREW A *et al.* 'Competitiveness, strategic change and human resource management'. *Personnel Management.* November 1988.

POLLARD S. *The Genesis of Modern Management.* Harmondsworth, Penguin, 1968.

POOLE M. 'A back seat for personnel'. *Personnel Management.* Vol. 5, No. 5, May 1973.

POOLE M. 'A power analysis of workplace labour relations'. *Industrial Relations Journal.* Vol. 7, No. 3, Autumn 1976.

PORTER L W *and* LAWLER E E. *Managerial Attitudes and Performance.* Homewood, Irwin, 1968.

PORTER L W *and others. Behavior in Organizations.* NY, McGraw-Hill, 1975.

POST OFFICE ENGINEERING UNION. *The Modernization of Telecommunications.* London, POEU, 1979.

PREST A R *and* COPPOCK D J (eds). *The UK Economy.* 9th ed. London, Weidenfeld and Nicolson, 1982.

PRICE R *and* BAIN G S. 'Union growth revisited: 1948–1974 in perspective'. *British Journal of Industrial Relations.* Vol. XIV, No. 3, 1976.

REDDISH H. 'Written memorandum of evidence to the Royal Commission on trade unions and employers' associations' in BARRETT B. *and others. Industrial Relations and the Wider Society.* London, Collier Macmillan, 1975.

RICHARDS L. 'Strategic HRM'. Paper presented to the IPM National Conference, 20 October 1988.

ROBINSON D. 'Government pay policy' in MORRIS D (ed). *The Economic System in the UK.* 2nd ed. Oxford, OUP, 1979.

ROSE R. *Politics in England.* 5th ed. London, Faber, 1989.

ROYAL COMMISSION ON THE NATIONAL HEALTH SERVICE. (Chairman: A Merrison). *Report.* London, HMSO, 1979.

ROYAL COMMISSION ON TRADE UNIONS AND EMPLOYERS' ASSOCIATIONS 1965–1969. (Chairman: the Right Hon. Lord Donovan). *Report*. London, HMSO, 1968.

RUSH R *and* ALTHOFF P. *An Introduction to Political Sociology*. London, Nelson, 1971.

SAYLES L R. *Managerial Behavior*. NY, McGraw-Hill, 1964.

SILVERMAN D. *The Theory of Organization*. London, Heinemann, 1970.

SMITH D J. *The Facts of Racial Disadvantage*. London, Political and Economic Planning, 1976.

STATISTICAL OFFICE OF THE EUROPEAN COMMUNITIES. *Employment and Unemployment 1974–1980*. Luxembourg, Office for Official Publications of the European Communities, 1982.

STATUTES

Trade Union Act 1871 (34 and 35 Vict., c102).

Conspiracy and Protection of Property Act 1875 (38 and 39 Vict., c86).

Trade Disputes Act 1906 (6 Edw. 7, c47).

Contracts of Employment Act 1963 (c49).

Industrial Training Act 1964 (c16).

Trade Disputes Act 1965 (c48).

Redundancy Payments Act 1965 (c62).

Equal Pay Act 1970 (c41).

Industrial Relations Act 1971 (c72).

Employment and Training Act 1973 (c50).

Health and Safety at Work etc Act 1974 (c37).

Trade Union and Labour Relations Act 1974 (c52).

Sex Discrimination Act 1975 (c65).

Employment Protection Act 1975 (c71).

Trade Union and Labour Relations (Amendment) Act 1976 (c7).

Race Relations Act 1976 (c74).

Employment Protection (Consolidation) Act 1978 (c44).

Employment Act 1980 (c42).

Employment Act 1982 (c46).

Trade Union Act 1984.

STEWART R. *Managers and Their Jobs*. London, Macmillan, 1967.

STEWART R. *Contrasts in Management*. London, McGraw-Hill, 1976.

STEWART R. *The Reality of Management*. Revised edition. London, Pan, 1979.

STEWART R. *Choices for the Manager*. London, McGraw-Hill, 1982.

STOCK EXCHANGE. *The Stock Exchange Survey of Share Ownership*. London, 1982.

STOREY J. 'The people-management dimension in current programmes of organisational change'. *Employee Relations*. 10(6), 1988.

STOREY J (ed). *New Perspectives on Human Resource Management*. London, Routledge, 1989.

STOREY J *and* SISSON K. 'Looking to the future' in *ibid*.

SURREY M J C. 'The domestic economy' in MORRIS R (ed). *The Economic System in the UK*. 2nd ed. Oxford, OUP, 1979.

THAKUR M. *OD: the Search for Identity*. London, IPM, 1974.
THOMAS R F. *Business policy*. Oxford, Philip Allan, 1977.
THOMASON G. *A Textbook of Personnel Management*. 1st ed. London, IPM, 1975.
THOMASON G. *A Textbook of Personnel Management*. 4th ed. London, IPM, 1981.
THOMASON G. *A Textbook of Human Resource Management*. London, IPM, 1988.
THOMPSON J D. *Organizations in Action*. NY, McGraw-Hill, 1967.
THURLEY K. 'Personnel management in the UK: a case for urgent treatment?'. *Personnel Management*. Vol. 13, No. 8, August 1981.
THURLEY K and WOOD S (eds). *Industrial Relations and Management Strategy*. Cambridge, CUP, 1983.
TORRINGTON D and CHAPMAN J. *Personnel Management*. 2nd ed. London, Prentice-Hall, 1983.
TORRINGTON D and HALL L. *Personnel Management: a New Approach*. London, Prentice-Hall, 1987.
TORRINGTON D and MACKAY L. *The Changing Nature of Personnel Management*. London, IPM, 1986.
TORRINGTON D et al. 'The changing nature of personnel management.' *Employee Relations*. 7(5), 1985.
TORRINGTON D and WEIGHTMAN J. 'Technical atrophy in middle management'. *Journal of General Management*. Vol. 7, number 4, Summer 1982.
TOURAINE A. *The Post Industrial Society*. NY, Random House, 1971.
TOWERS B. *British Incomes Policy*. Nottingham, IPM, 1978.
TRADES UNION CONGRESS. *Trade Unionism*. London, TUC, 1966.
TRADES UNION CONGRESS. *Good Industrial Relations: a Guide for Negotiators*. London, TUC, 1971.
TRADES UNION CONGRESS. *Employment and Technology*. London, TUC, 1979.
TRIST E L and others. *Organizational Choice*. London, Tavistock, 1963.
TURNBULL G. 'How I see the personnel function'. *Personnel Management*. Vol. 14, No. 5, May 1982.
TURNER B A. *Industrialism*. Harlow, Longman, 1975.
TYSON S. Specialists in ambiguity: personnel management as an occupation. Unpublished PhD thesis. University of London, 1979.
TYSON S. 'Is this the very model of a modern personnel manager?' *Personnel Management*. May 1985.
TYSON S. 'The management of the personnel function'. *Journal of Management Studies*. 24(5), 1987.
TYSON S and FELL A. *Evaluating the Personnel Function*. London, Hutchinson, 1986.
UNIVERSITY OF WARWICK INSTITUTE FOR EMPLOYMENT RESEARCH. *Review of the Economy and Employment*. Spring 1982.
UNIVERSITY OF WARWICK INSTITUTE FOR EMPLOYMENT RESEARCH. *Review of the Economy and Employment*. Autumn supplement 1982.

URWICK L. *The Elements of Administration*. London, Pitman, 1947.
URWICK GROUP. *Employee Relations Survey 1982/83*. London, Urwick, 1982.
VICKERS G. *Freedom in a Rocking Boat*. Harmondsworth, Allen Lane, 1970.
VROOM V H *and* YETTON P W. *Leadership and Decision Making*. Pittsburgh, University of Pittsburgh Press, 1973.
WALTON R. 'The future of HRM: an overview' in WALTON R *and* LAWRENCE P R (eds). *HRM Trends and Challenges*. Boston, Mass., Harvard Business School, 1985.
WALTON R *and* LAWRENCE P R (eds). *HRM Trends and Challenges*. Boston, Mass., Harvard Business School, 1985.
WATSON T J. *The Personnel Managers*. London, Routledge and Kegan Paul, 1977.
WATSON T. *Towards a General Theory of Personnel Management and Industrial Relations*. Nottingham, Trent Business School, 1985.
WEDDERBURN K W. *The Worker and the Law*. 3rd ed. Harmondsworth, Penguin, 1986.
WEEKES B. 'Law and the practice of the closed shop'. *Industrial Law Journal*. Vol. 5, No. 4, 1976.
WHINCUP M. *Modern Employment Law*. 4th ed. London, Heinemann, 1983.
WILSON E. 'The heel of capitalism on the neck of feminism'. *The Guardian*. 3 January 1984.
WOODWARD J. *Industrial Organization: Theory and Practice*. London, OUP, 1965.
WOODWARD J (ed). *Industrial Organization: Behaviour and Control*. London, OUP, 1970.
WRIGHT J F. *Britain in the Age of Economic Management,* Oxford, OUP, 1979.

Index